BEYOND THE UPRISING

BEYOND THE UPRISING

A Polish Girl's Journey

CYNTHIA GRANT BOWMAN

To order additional copies of this book, contact:
Xlibris Corporation
1-888-795-4274
www.Xlibris.com
Orders@Xlibris.com
42319

CONTENTS

PROLOGUE

Warsaw, occupied Poland, early 1940s

Two Polish girls walk quickly down a street in dense fog, hoping to get home without meeting any German soldiers. The girls are nervous, and for good reason. One has lost her "Kennkarte." Without this identity Poles can be arrested by the Nazis and possibly deported to a labor or concentration camp. The other girl, a pretty dark-haired girl named Maria, is a member of the Polish resistance. In her school briefcase she is carrying forbidden documents and codes, for delivery to a unit of the AK, or underground Home Army.

Suddenly two German soldiers appear in front of them, out of the fog, as if out of nowhere. "Halten sie! [Stop!]", they shout. One soldier begins to inspect the first girl's knitting bag. Maria gives her identity card to the other soldier. After looking at it, he asks for her friend's card. His comrade's eyes move to Maria's briefcase. Maria realizes that their only hope is to create a distraction, and fast. She cries, in fluent German, "She has lost her card. What are we to do? We don't know how to get another." She speaks loudly, in an impassioned tone. Poles do not speak to Germans this way. Astonished, the soldier reaching for Maria's case turns to see what his patrol leader will do. Will he arrest them? Shoot them on the spot? Plaques mark many places in Warsaw where this was the outcome.

Instead the patrol leader responds to the appeal. Somehow this pretty young girl's distress reaches across the gulf between the Nazi occupiers and their unwilling subjects. He tells the girls how to get a replacement for the lost card. "You must go immediately to a police station," he says, "and petition the commander for a new one." They thank him profusely and promise to do so right away. The briefcase forgotten, the Germans move on. After they have gone, Maria has to wait several minutes before she stops shaking. Then she continues to the assigned spot, where she delivers her contraband material.

Chicago, Illinois, early 1990s

I first noticed Maria Chudzinski in the halls of the law school where I taught. I saw a woman in her late sixties or early seventies, about five feet tall, who walked with a determined gait. Her hair was pale gold and always perfectly coiffed. She was always very stylishly dressed. I felt a rare sense of life and of delight about her. For some reason, she intrigued me. I discovered that she worked in a small office in the international section of the law library, surrounded by dusty old tomes.

Each year the law school had a big Christmas party for all of its staff—a sit-down, turkey, stuffing, and pumpkin pie sort of affair. This was one of the few occasions when faculty and staff mingled socially. I seized an opportunity to sit down next to Maria one December. She knew me as a relatively new professor and immediately began to talk to me.

Maria was full of rapid-fire conversation on all kinds of topics. Although accented and occasionally ungrammatical, her English was fluent and her face expressive. She began to tell me about the elaborate Christmas celebrations in the Polish community—all the traditional dishes for the Christmas Eve dinner and how much preparation she would need to do in the next few days. It was obvious that she relished this activity.

One day in the summer of 1994, I picked up the daily newspaper—and there was a picture of Maria. She was part of a small group photographed with Vice President Al Gore. The caption explained that the delegation was going to Warsaw to commemorate the 50th anniversary of the Warsaw Uprising, the armed insurrection of Poles who attempted to liberate the city from Nazi occupation as the Soviet armies advanced in the summer of 1944. The *Chicago Tribune* described Maria as having been "a young soldier, so petite that her gun was almost as big as she was." When asked by the reporter why she fought, Maria replied, "We wanted to get free. You didn't even think twice. You did it."

I've always been fascinated by the conflagration that engulfed Europe just before my birth, reading histories of the era as a girl and seeking out courses about the period in college and graduate school. Perhaps I was motivated by a desire to understand the terrible events that had so affected my parents' generation. So when Maria returned from the anniversary events in Poland, I went to her small office in the law library. "Tell me about it," I said. From then on, tales from Maria's past were added to our conversations about Polonia (as the Polish diaspora is called), our families, and our travels.

In 2000, I had just returned to school from spring break when I learned that Maria's husband Bruno had died. I ran into her in the hall. She told me Bruno had been sick for a long while with Parkinson's disease and that she had left him with a home health care aide while she went on a visit to Poland. He had had a stroke while she was there and by the time she reached Chicago, he was on life support. She looked pale and grieved. In her late seventies herself, she confessed that she was having a hard time learning to live alone, and that she missed having someone to take care of. It was quite a while before the sparkle returned to Maria's eyes.

Some time later, I was struck with an astonishing thought: "Why not ask Maria Chase if you could write the story of her life?" I turned this idea over in my mind. It would be quite different from anything I had tried before, but it seemed so right that I couldn't resist. I could see Maria in my mind's eye, sitting in her tiny office surrounded by a library of heavy books. Many of the volumes in her section, the international section, were dusty from lack of use. "Maria is a living book," I thought, "an extraordinary story which must not be lost." As I thought about her life, I realized that, beyond the obvious drama of wartime, I wanted to understand Maria herself. I wanted to know how she had kept her tremendous vitality and made an utterly new life for herself in a strange culture and new language after losing home, family and country when she was barely out of her teens. How could anyone manage such losses and dislocations? How could Maria be so dynamic, so energizing after such struggles? I didn't know the half of it.

Maria was sitting in her small office when I arrived at the law school. "Would you let me write the story of your life?" I asked. "Oh, yes!" she replied immediately, happy and excited at the prospect. She did not seem to think it strange that someone would want to write her life story. Indeed, she confided, she had tried to write some of it down herself many years earlier. A day later, a sheaf of papers appeared in my faculty mailbox, containing some attempts she had made. Her written English was inadequate to the story. The next day, more papers appeared in my box. This time, it was an account of her experiences in the first days of World War II, but the descriptions had been rewritten by her son Andrew and were much better. I was fascinated by the accounts, and we made arrangements to begin.

The arrangement made perfect sense for both of us. Maria was now working only part-time and needed an outlet for her boundless energy. She was bored and lonely after Bruno's death. Retirement was looming, but she was reluctant to leave the daily structures of her work life and the people she knew in the library. Moreover, Maria *loved* to talk, and she wanted to tell the story of her life.

For me, the project provided a new focus. I hurried to acquire as many books as I could find on Polish history and culture, about which I knew almost nothing. Where I grew up in upstate New York in the 1950s, Poles were the butt of jokes. Late at night, so as not to interfere with my "day job," I began to learn the long, tragic and inspiring history of Poland, and to discover its music, art, and culture.

On the day of our first session, I followed Maria's directions to her house. It was at the end of a suburban-looking residential street on the northwest side of Chicago, a small two-story Georgian in yellow brick. Maria greeted me and showed me around. I was struck by the art on the walls. A large oil portrait hung over the piano, of a handsome dark haired woman in elegant clothing. "My mother," Maria explained.

———

For someone who survived the almost total destruction of Warsaw, Maria has an astonishing number of things from her past. In the small dining room hung another original art work, a water color of a Polish shepherd boy in boots and a wonderful hat, accompanied by a collie-like dog, against a background of fields and clouds. It was painted by a well-known painter about 1900, Maria explained. "My father bought it for almost $2000 before the war."

Over the couch hung a limited edition poster of a Spitfire airplane. Maria's husband Bruno had flown in the Polish Air Force as part of the campaign in Italy during the war. He loved the plane so much that his son Mark had bought the picture for him. On another wall was a large color photo-portrait of Maria herself, with short dark hair, dressed in a ball gown, hinting at the role she has played in the Polish community of Chicago over the last fifty years.

To start us off, Maria had brought downstairs a box of old photos and a number of picture books. There were pictures of Maria as a girl, of her parents and sister—Maria on a horse, on skis, at the beach; her father, a short dark-haired man looking very dapper, on some of his many travels throughout Europe; Maria and Bruno at their wedding; their two boys when they were little. Another was a photography book about the Warsaw Uprising, all of the text in Polish. Maria directed me to a page on which there was a picture of four girls sitting on what appeared to be a hillock, looking gay, as though at a picnic. One, in overalls, was a young Maria. In fact the girls were on a brief furlough shortly before the fiercest of the fighting in that section of Warsaw.

That day I asked Maria to give me a brief overview of her life, so that I would know where we were going and how to pace our interviews. It was frustrating to get the staccato description I had requested, and not to ply her with further questions at each turn, but eventually I had a chronological overview. We worked for about two hours. Then, much to my surprise, Maria began to bring beautifully prepared plates of food into the dining room. "I wanted you to try some Polish delicacies," she said, "and I don't like to eat alone." There were sausages and patés and cheeses and breads, pickled vegetables, and sweets—an over-abundance of food. Maria continued to talk animatedly while preparing, eating, and cleaning up—and I had put away my tape recorder and the computer I used for taking notes. But Maria loves to share food and conversation, so this ritual was incorporated into our interviews.

Thus began a journey that was to take me to Warsaw and Krakow, to abandoned RAF bases in England, and to insights about parts of Chicago that I thought I already knew. I discovered places I had never been, and worlds that no longer exist. I learned the incredible, little known story of the Polish Home Army, left to die by the cynical Realpolitik of the great powers. And I made a wonderful, inspiring friend.

Chapter 1

Origins

One look at the map of Europe explains much of Poland's history. For centuries, Poland has been the stage over which aggressive great powers have played out their struggles. Its precarious position between Germany and Russia has repeatedly posed a threat to the existence of Poland. The country ceased to exist as a separate political entity after it was partitioned by Germany, Russia, and Austria-Hungary in 1795. Poland re-emerged as a nation when those three empires disintegrated at the end of World War I. A sense of rebirth and vitality marked the interwar years, despite the many political, economic, and security problems faced by the new state.

The newly reconstituted nation was still an underdeveloped country. A slump in the rural economy in the 1880s had led to a vast wave of emigration from the countryside. Many peasants emigrated either to other countries or to the cities. Many of the lesser gentry left the land, moving to the cities, where they joined the professional classes and the intelligentsia. Yet the country was still overwhelmingly agrarian by the end of the Great War. The 1921 Census reported that 65% of the population were peasants, 27% manual workers, 5% intelligentsia and professionals, 2% entrepreneurs, and under 1% landowners.

The interwar period was one of intense nationalism and polarization. Ethnic tensions increased between the Poles and a variety of groups living within Poland's borders—Lithuanians, Ukrainians, Germans, Belarussians, and Jews. The 1921 Polish Constitution, like those in postwar France and Germany, gave a great deal of power to the parliament and very little to the president, and it provided for election by proportional representation.* As in other countries, proportional representation encouraged a multitude of small political parties.

---

*   Under proportional representation, representatives are not elected by districts in which the winner takes one seat. Instead the various political parties draw up lists of candidates, and each party is given a number of seats proportional to its percentage of the total vote. Formation of a government depends upon building a coalition

The divisions in Poland in the 1920s gave rise to peasant parties, socialist parties, Roman Catholic parties, conservative parties, parties of the extreme left and right, and variations upon these themes. The country was so split along ethnic and class lines that it was difficult to build parties that included more than one group or to build coalitions among the ones that existed. The result was that the government was extremely unstable, with regimes changing as soon as they failed to command a majority of the legislature—a total of fourteen times between November of 1918 and May of 1926.

On May 12, 1926, Marshal Józef Piłsudski, a renowned military leader whose political sentiments lay to the left, marched with his supporters across the Poniatowksi Bridge into the city and confronted the newly formed center-right government, demanding its resignation. Three days of fighting ensued in the center of the city before the government resigned and Piłsudski's group took over.

The new regime called itself "Sanacja." The word meant sanitation or cleansing, but it was used to signify the restoration of health to the nation in the face of instability, strikes and peasant uprisings. Although it never became a one-party state, the Sanacja government attacked the democratic opposition parties, arrested their leaders, and came down hard on rebellion in the countryside. In 1935, a new constitution was passed, giving the president more power over parliament; and proportional representation was subsequently abolished. Sanacja has been called "a secular authoritarian government of a non-fascist type"; much of civil society remained independent, including multiple parties, trade unions, and the church, unlike the totalitarian governments established in fascist Germany and Italy at this time.

The main opposition party was the National Democrats, a nationalist party established early in the century by Roman Dmowski. The party opposed Piłsudski's appeal for rapprochement with Russia; it also became increasingly anti-German, anti-minority, and anti-Semitic, portraying Jews as both an alien cultural entity and an economic threat.

At this time about three million Jews lived in Poland (almost 9% of the total population), a vibrant community going back to the thirteenth century. In 1931 Jews constituted one third of the population of Warsaw and were heavily represented in trading, the professions, and the intelligentsia. Forty-six percent of all lawyers and fifty percent of all doctors in Poland were Jewish. They were in direct competition with the developing middle class and gentry who had left the countryside. The conditions in which Polish Jews lived in the 1930s, however, became increasingly difficult as boycotts and quotas were directed against them.

---

among them. Proportional representation is said to foster the growth of many small parties in a country where many divisions exist because they can continue to sit in parliament without ever attempting to gain a majority.

The postwar governments of Poland faced severe economic crises. After World War I, the new country inherited four legal systems, six currencies, four railway systems, and three administrative and fiscal systems (from the Russians, Germans, and Austrians), and the Russians made every attempt to "deindustrialize" the country as they retreated. Severe economic distress prevailed in the rural areas, leading to new waves of migration. The population of Warsaw doubled between the wars.

Between June and December of 1923, the value of the Polish mark fell from 71,000 to one U.S. dollar to 4.3 million to a dollar. There were strikes and agrarian uprisings. Yet the new state initiated the most extensive social insurance legislation in Europe, as well as free public education that almost halved the high rate of illiteracy. But with threats from both east and west, almost one third of the budget went to the military. A brief period of economic improvement and prosperity intervened from 1926 to 1929, before the Great Depression brought it to an end.

While serious problems plagued the political and economic realms, the interwar period was one in which the arts—painting, poetry, drama, and music—flourished in Poland. The lively cultural scene was particularly evident in Warsaw, in literary coffee houses, satirical reviews, theaters, galleries, and concert halls. Yet many of the artists emphasized dark themes and impending catastrophe. In 1932, a 21-year-old Czeslaw Milosz wrote:

> *I'd like to live twice on this sad planet,*
> *In lonely cities, in starved villages,*
> *To look at all evil, at the decay of bodies,*
> *And probe the laws to which the time was subject,*
> *Time that howled above us like a wind.*

Maria Chmielinska was born in Warsaw in the summer of 1923. Like other young girls in Poland, she was called by the informal version of her name— Marysia (Ma-REE-sha), or Rysia by her family and friends. As a child growing up in the family of a prosperous Catholic lawyer in Warsaw, none of Poland's economic and political problems were visible to her, even the Great Depression. The politics of the time intruded upon the young Maria's consciousness only on a couple of occasions. One of her earliest memories (she was not yet three at the time) was of standing on the balcony of their apartment, which overlooked the street, when someone pulled her back inside, crying "You could be killed!" This occurred during Piłsudski's 1926 coup, in the three days of fighting in the city center, near where Maria lived. And in 1934, the Minister of the Interior was assassinated as he arrived for lunch at a club frequented by *Sanacja* government members at the end of her block. But Maria was largely shielded by her family from the violent events of the time. Perhaps her parents wanted to protect their children because of the many wars and revolutions they had seen in their own lifetimes.

Maria's father, Wacław Chmielinski, came from a family that belonged to the gentry. He grew up on a large estate north of Warsaw. Maria's paternal grandparents died before her parents were married, so that she knew of them only from stories. "My father's father was apparently a bon vivant," she tells me. "The story I heard is that they were at a ball in winter time; he got a chill, then pneumonia, and TB. He went to a place in the mountains for treatment, but died." His wife then lived with her parents, so Wacław was raised on his grandparents' estate. The only member of this family Maria knew was her father's sister Eugenia, who lived in Warsaw.

In the thirteenth century, noble families in Poland were awarded crests to acknowledge their military or administrative service. Maria still wears a ring with her father's crest on it, a symbol of her connection to the ancient, vanished world of feudal Europe. It seems a little strange in 21st-century America.

Maria's father, born in 1877, like many of his generation, was the first of his family to leave the land. He came to Warsaw to go to the university, studied law, and stayed on to practice it. In addition to his private practice, he became attorney for the city of Warsaw, a post he held through numerous changes of government.

Wacław was rather short, a dark-haired man with a pleasant face, elegantly attired in all his photos. He appears, like his own father, to have had a penchant for the good life. Although a hard worker, he liked to play, attending parties, theater and concerts, collecting art, skiing, and traveling throughout Europe. A photo shows him in Biarritz, sitting in a wicker chair in front of a palm tree, wearing light pants and a darker jacket, a dark bow tie and white shoes, handkerchief in his pocket, holding a walking stick, with a straw bowler hat on the table next to him—the image of the proper gentleman in casual attire. Wacław spoke Polish, French, German, and Russian and insisted that his daughters learn languages as well. Maria was an especially apt student, learning both French and German in addition to Polish as a child, a training that served her well.

Maria's mother, Jadwiga Lempcka, also came from the landed gentry. Born in 1890, she lived on her family's estate until her father died in 1900, when her mother moved to Warsaw. Jadwiga was educated, but studied home economics rather than going to the university. Like other upper- and middle-class women of that time, she did not work, and lived at home until she married Wacław in 1919. She was 29 and he was 42. Photos of her as a young woman show an intelligent face with wide-set eyes and dark hair. Later pictures show her body thickened by childbirth—one son, who lived only two days, and then two daughters. Maria describes both of her parents as very sociable, the life of any party they gave or attended. This is not hard to believe—Maria is like that herself.

Although Wacław and Jadwiga were city-dwellers, they maintained their connections with the countryside, visiting relatives and sending Maria and her sister Janina to stay on their estates. Thus Maria was well acquainted with life at the manor. A "coffee table" book in her Chicago home shows Polish manor houses, many photographed in misty conditions, as though to emphasize that the life of the manor is long dead, the land redistributed by the communist government after World War II. Most of the manor houses were long, low buildings made of wood, with sloping roofs covering the second story and many windows on the ground floor. The house was usually set at the end of a long drive, with gardens and woods surrounding it.

The estate where Maria's "aunt" and "uncle" lived (they were actually cousins of her parents, one of her father and one of her mother) was similar to the images in the coffee table book. "Outside the manor house was a formal garden," she tells me, "then park-like land, beyond which were buildings where workers lived with their families, often for generation after generation, then stables. My uncle had beautiful horses, Arabians and ones brought from England." Maria showed me photos of herself and her sister as young children on ponies, dressed in what my own mother would have called "Sunday-go-to-meeting" clothes. In another, a teenaged Maria sits comfortably on a large horse. "There were also barns for cows and pigs," she continues, "and a chicken house close to the kitchen, so the servants could take care of them."

Life on the manor was busy. Maria's uncle would go out into the fields each day in a small horse-drawn carriage to see how the seeding or harvest was going, although there was a supervisor who was constantly with the workers. Every evening all his supervisors would report to him in the house, and he would give them directives for the next day. His wife managed the life of the interior, although there were numerous servants—a cook, maids, and several girls as kitchen help; she was also in charge of the courtyard outside the kitchen where small animals were raised.

Maria remembers the manor house as always full of people. Members of the family who were not employed lived there, and other family and friends visited frequently. Five meals a day were served to them—breakfast, a second breakfast around 11, dinner at 1 or 2, a light meal or afternoon tea around 4 or 5, and supper between 7 and 8—all on a dining table set with linen tablecloth and china. In between meals, guests rode or read books, chatted, played games, or helped their hosts with the chores. Photos show that they spent a good deal of time on their dress and appearance as well.

Life in the country continued to play an important role for Maria's parents, the first generation to leave the land. They carried many aspects of the lifestyle with them into the city. In their 10-room apartment, meals were also formal, and served by a maid in black uniform and white cap. Maria's mother's job was to supervise the cook and maids, whom she would summon to the table by ringing a bell that hung down from the chandelier. Governesses cared for the children.

Maria's father always maintained some personal foothold in the country as well. He bought an alpine-looking country house in Skolimow, a few miles from Warsaw, and on the other side of the city, in Ozarow, he owned a "gentleman's farm," with orchards, berries, nurseries, and a special building for growing mushrooms. "My father did not believe in keeping everything in the stock market," Maria says, "so he bought real estate on the birth of each child, because the land would not lose its value." Most of the time the small farm was rented, but the property also contained a small coach house building that provided a refuge for Maria's family—then and later.

In Warsaw, the Chmielinski family lived in a huge apartment on Foksal Street, a short street that begins at Nowy Swiat, or "New World" Street, near the Church of the Holy Cross (famous as the place where Chopin's heart is enshrined). Warsaw was a city of boulevards, palaces and gardens, with a lively cultural scene and elegant shops along Nowy Swiat. At the other end of Foksal stood a palace owned by the aristocratic Zamoyski family, surrounded by a park. The street was lined with large stone apartment buildings. Their facades were ornate, some adorned with statues. Like other buildings on that street, Foksal 13 was constructed around a large courtyard, with entrances to the apartments spread out around it. The marble staircase up to Maria's home was decorated with statuary, with windows open onto the courtyard at each landing. The family lived on the third floor—"the second floor, if you are European," Maria clarifies.

The apartment's large entrance hall had modern furnishings, but the rest of the rooms were filled with antiques. The sitting room, with its three windows onto the street, held eighteenth-century furniture and "looked like a museum." Maria took piano lessons there. But the dining room appears to have been the center of community life. Most of Maria's memories are set in it. Its ceilings were high and inlaid with mahogany, and the thick wooden doors were carved in a decorative fashion, with Maria's father's crest providing part of the design. The furniture—a dining room table that could seat thirty, a large side table/buffet, and the chairs—were all made of heavy dark wood. A grandfather clock bore the coat-of-arms of Maria's mother.

The master bedroom overlooked the street and had both a window and a balcony. Each of the girls had her own room, and Maria's opened off the dining room. "I spent my time mostly in my room or in the dining room, where I did my schoolwork," she says. There was also a long hall leading to the large kitchen, but all of the doors were kept closed because her father did not like kitchen smells drifting into the apartment. Off the kitchen were rooms for the servants.

By the front hall there was another small sitting room where Wacław carried on a small private law practice and met his clients in the evening. There was an office on the side for his secretary, a typewriter, and storage of his legal papers.

Between 6 and 8 p.m., before the family had supper, a maid would sit in the front hall and usher in clients to consult him.

Maria was born four years after her parents' marriage, an infant boy having died before her birth. Janina ("Nina" or "Ninka") was born four years later. Maria and her mother, accompanied by two servants, were at their country house in Skolimow when her mother left quickly for Warsaw for the premature birth of her sister. "My mother brought her back in a baby carriage," Maria remembers. "I wondered what happened that people were not looking at me now but at the baby instead."

Like other girls of her social class in Warsaw at that time, Maria was educated by a private teacher up to sixth grade. "A group of six to eight girls and the teacher would meet in someone's home," she says. "We took Polish, history, geography, math, and science. At the end of each year both a written and an oral exam would be given at the school each girl wanted eventually to attend." At sixth grade Maria entered a private school located opposite the Polish parliament. "It was run by two old maids who were killed by the Germans during the Uprising," she says. The curriculum, which extended for four years, and then an additional two years of "lycée," included Latin, more advanced math, chemistry, history, geography, Polish literature, and foreign languages. Maria studied French, having begun speaking it with a French governess when she was very young. Her father engaged a German speaker to tutor the girls as well.

Although Maria's school was secular (there were no parochial schools), religion was taught twice a week, and a priest came in to instruct in catechism. Maria remembers: "He wore long robes with tiny buttons up the front, and his big stomach stuck out. When we were bored, we counted all the buttons on his body."

The academic program was supplemented by instruction in singing, drawing and painting, as well as sports, including playing palant (a game similar to baseball) on the sports field nearby. After school, Maria had piano lessons at home and took a variety of other classes, such as musical gymnastics, tennis and swimming.

When school was not in session, the family spent long stretches of time out of town, at their own country houses, at the beach near Gdansk, in the mountains, or at spas. Even if Jadwiga were with them, a nanny would come along to look after the children. Mountain air was considered particularly good for their health, so spas in the mountains were a frequent locale. When she was older, Maria would also go skiing in the mountains with her father. She remembers how she particularly loved to be pulled along on skis behind a sleigh.

Both girls were quite thin, and so were subjected to courses of treatment to make them gain weight. At one spa, they were made to stay outside on a verandah for a one to two hour rest each day, inside a sleeping bag made of sheepskin, and given various tonic oils to make them strong. The girls hated this regimen. "I would try to get a lounge chair at the edge of the porch," Maria says, "so I could pour the tonic out as soon as the attendant left."

Holidays, especially Christmas, were elaborate occasions at the Chmielinskis' apartment on Foksal. The family would buy a huge freshly-cut tree either in the town square by the royal castle or in front of the church of Saint Alexander. When erected in the sitting room, it would reach to the top of the tall ceiling. Maria glowed as she described how it smelled of the forest. "We decorated it just before Christmas Eve," she says. "We were one of the few families to have electric lights for the tree, ones made like candles, instead of real candles, because once the tree caught fire. We also hung little fireworks on the tree, which we lighted, and would make special decorations, some from eggshells and some from colored paper." On Christmas Eve, a family member disguised as Saint Nicholas (one year Maria peeked and discovered her cousin in this role) would make a grand entrance and give out presents under the tree.

Dinner on Christmas Eve was elegant, with the men in tuxedos and the women in evening gowns. Close family and friends would swell the group to about twenty. The dinner was highly ritualized. The celebration could not begin until the first star appeared. Before sitting down, an opłatek—a special wafer symbolizing the Christ child—was broken and shared, while family members, starting with the father and mother, would exchange good wishes for the new year. Family members would sometimes send a piece of their opłatek to ones who were far away, as a symbol that they were breaking the wafer together even though separated by war or a repressive political system. (The opłatek ritual persists among Poles in Chicago, where the wafers are sold in Polish stores.)

The dinner was elaborate, though meatless, because Christmas Eve was a fast day. "You had to have certain courses," Maria describes. "The starter was herring and salads. Then there was beet soup with little dumplings stuffed with dried mushrooms, and aspics. The main course was fried or baked fish, usually carp, prepared with raisin sauce and served with poppyseed noodles. At the end there were fancy cakes, tortes, mixed nuts, dates, and dried figs." Over the years, Maria has replicated this dinner in Chicago, though with a smaller group. On Christmas Day, the Chmielinski family attended church and then, their fast over, shared a turkey dinner.

The woman who presided over this household, Jadwiga Chmielinska, had few of what we think of as the duties of a "housewife"; those were performed by the nanny, governess, maid and cook. "Life was so different; it seems outrageous now," says Maria. "Peasant women worked hard, but upper-class women were weaklings; they didn't do anything." The children had no household duties at all. "I never had to make my own bed," says Maria. "I wasn't allowed even to peel a potato; my parents would say, 'Go study.' I didn't learn to cook until after the war."

When Maria was young, her mother would pick her up at the end of the school day at the private home in which her classes were held. Then, along with the other mothers on the same errand, they might go to a nice café. If the café was close to a park or ice skating area, the children would play and the women would sit and chat over their coffee and pastries. A favorite café of Maria's when she was young was the Café Blikle, which still stands (or more likely was reconstructed after the war) near the intersection of Foksal and Nowy Swiat. It looks as if it were straight out of late-nineteenth-century Vienna—and the awning over the outdoor tables boasts that the establishment has been there since 1869.

Apart from her general supervision of the children and servants, Maria's mother did occasional work for charities, such as a group that looked after the children of prison inmates. Otherwise she spent her time reading, playing bridge, meeting or "calling on" people, and arranging parties. Jadwiga was very outgoing, and the couple entertained frequently, so this took up a good deal of her energies. She would accompany the children on trips out of the city, even though she did not physically care for their needs herself.

In short, the child Maria and her family enjoyed a level of wealth and comfort which few people enjoy today anywhere.

Chapter 2

Growing Up

In May of 1932, when Maria was not quite nine years old, the Chmielinskis decided to move to a larger apartment. They found one in the same building, which meant that Wacław would not have to change the address for his private law practice. They planned the move over the three-day Whitsunday holiday weekend, so they would have more time to settle in to the new quarters.

That Friday evening Jadwiga was sitting in the dining room, sorting her jewelry in preparation for the move. A maid was helping her. "Mother sent me to the master bedroom," Maria recalls, "to bring some piece of jewelry that was on the big dresser there. When I couldn't find it, she called out to me in the words of a Polish proverb, 'To send you to get something is like sending you to get death.'" Suddenly, from the other room Maria heard an odd noise, like someone gargling. She immediately had a sense that something was terribly wrong. She ran back and found her mother still sitting in the chair, but her head had fallen back against it.

Maria ran to the kitchen, where she called through the open window for the cook, who was in the new apartment preparing it for the move. Then she ran, crying, to her sister's bedroom, where five-year-old Ninka was with the governess. "My mother has died!" Maria cried out. The governess said, "Don't cry, people often faint and they don't die." But eight-year-old Maria was right. At age 42, Jadwiga Chmielinska had died of a blood clot.

Maria's father, who was seeing clients in another part of the apartment, was summoned to the dining room; he asked the governess to keep the girls in the room with her. Later, Maria pretended to be asleep when her father came into the room. She heard him tell the governess that Jadwiga was dead.

Wacław consulted Maria's aunts about whether she should be allowed to see her mother's body. They advised against it. "I've always been glad for this," she says, "because my only memories of my mother are of a person full of life."

Wacław decided to send the children away for the long holiday weekend, to the estate of one of his cousins not far from Warsaw. They stayed there until the funeral. A photo of Maria and Janina taken during that weekend is especially moving. They lie together in a hammock, with Maria turned toward her sister, her arms protectively cradling the younger girl. Both girls' eyes are swollen, and dark circles underline them. Ninka's face is a picture of tragedy, a jarring sight on the face of a five-year-old child. Her mouth is downturned, but Maria's lips curve ever so slightly upward, as though she knows that she is supposed to smile for a camera, no matter how she feels. Or perhaps to convey that she is in charge, and will take care of her sister through this, their first ordeal.

The funeral took place at the Church of the Holy Cross, where Maria's parents had been married and where the family attended Sunday Mass. The exterior of the church is dominated by a large statue of Christ, bowed down under the cross he carries. The interior is Baroque, with a spacious pillared central aisle and side chapels filled with colorful paintings. To a small child, it must have looked enormous.

Large white announcements of the death, bordered in black, were displayed on the exterior wall of the church and on the outside of the house where the Chiemelinskis lived. The family, dressed in black, walked behind the horse-drawn carriage that bore Jadwiga's body from the church to Powazki Cemetery. "I remember walking behind the casket with my father," Maria says. "That is all I remember about the funeral and the burial." In accordance with custom, for a year and six weeks after their mother's death the girls wore black bands around their hats and on their left arms.

It took Maria a long time to recover from the death of her mother. "I was very close to my mother and stuck to her like glue, even though I had a governess. When she wanted to go out on her own, she would say she was going to the dentist. I hated the dentist." After her mother's death, Maria would go with her governess to play in the park at the end of the street by the Zamoyski palace and would see other children with their mothers. Sometimes one of them would ask, "What is your mother doing? Is she coming to pick you up?" "I couldn't even say that my mother had died," she recalls, "I was so upset." The sadness remained for many years.

Wacław Chmielinski grew into the role of single parent, even though he was a busy man. He was very interested in his daughters' education and encouraged them to study, to go to the theater and concerts, and in other intellectual pursuits. He advised them, wisely, that "The main thing in life is to be healthy and to have a good education. Wealth you can lose. Poland is in a vulnerable position with two enemies on its borders. You can lose everything, but not that." He assumed that both girls would go to the university and hoped that one might follow him into the law. "My father wanted me to be a lawyer and take over his practice," Maria says. "But I wanted to be in the diplomatic corps. I loved travel, could learn languages, and liked to do and see different things." Maria would have made a wonderful diplomat.

When the girls were older, Wacław would take them with him to shows and for weekend trips. People liked him, and he found it easy to attract both clients and social friends. When Maria complained, as a teen, that he didn't know how to handle the family properly, he responded, "But all my clients come to me with their problems!"

Looking back, Maria thinks that Wacław was a very good father. "The French governess would argue with the Polish governess; he would take time from his practice to handle the dispute." It must have been tempting to send the motherless girls away to boarding school, especially when they were teenagers, and he did suggest it. But when Maria said she did not want to go, Wacław did not force the issue. "Once when we were in Rabka, he took me to a convent school, but I wouldn't even go in and said 'I will run away if you put me here,' so he didn't."

As the photograph taken the day after their mother's death foretold, Maria stepped into more of a role in the care of Ninka—sometimes reluctantly. When they were a bit older, her father would take them to a resort and leave them with a nanny. When Maria wanted to go off alone with her friends, the nanny would not let her leave her sister. At these times, she resented Ninka.

The two girls spent a great deal of time together on vacations away from Warsaw, and Janina often created problems for her sister. When Maria was fifteen and Janina eleven, they were left for a week at a ski resort, with Maria in charge. One day, they went together up a mountain on a railway with their skis. "I told Ninka," she recalls, 'I will ski down and you will ski down after me.' I had to go down in zig-zags. When I got to the bottom, I looked up and Ninka was standing at the top, screaming to come get her." Angrily, Maria made her way back up the mountain.

On another occasion, the two girls were in Vienna and went to the Prater amusement park to ride the huge ferris wheel. Ninka wanted to see the "ghost palace," an attraction featuring little two-person cars that traversed dark corridors and was intended to scare the riders. "There were mirrors that made it seem like a train was about to hit you," Maria describes, "but it's your train and at the last moment it turns away. We got to a small bridge, which was shaking, rather like at Disneyland today. Ninka said she would not go, that she wanted to get out, and screamed, 'No! I won't go!' So I got out and walked with her against the traffic all the way back to the entrance." "I will never take you anywhere again!," Maria said as they emerged. But of course she did.

My favorite picture of Maria from this general period shows a girl of twelve, with dark hair parted in the middle and worn in long braids over her ears with white bows at the end of each braid. In those days, Polish girls did not cut their hair until they were much older. Her eyes are far apart and seem to twinkle; her mouth curves upward in a smile, but not an open-mouthed grin. The impression is of a girl who is intelligent and knows what she is about, who is self-possessed. She would need all her intelligence and fortitude to survive the years that were ahead.

Women liked Wacław, and several pursued the wealthy widower. "One Easter vacation, he told us, at a party at a cousin's estate he had to hide behind one of those big ceramic furnaces* from one very tall woman who was after him." He would bring home potential candidates to see how they related to the girls. They liked one of his girlfriends a lot, but he decided not to marry her because she was too young, too close to the age of his daughters; Wacław was nearing sixty. He took his daughters to visit another candidate, and Ninka told Maria that they would have a hard time if he married her.

Ultimately Wacław did decide to remarry. Maria's explanation is that "We were growing up, and we needed someone to introduce us to the 'world,' that is, to chaperone us to parties and to present us to other families if we wanted to get married." Wacław's choice was Stefania Witkowska, 45 years old and never married, who was the administrative assistant to Stefan Starzynski, mayor of Warsaw. Stefania had been visiting the family for years, but Wacław asked 13-year-old Maria for her approval before they wed.

The wedding took place on February 27, 1937, five years after the death of Jadwiga, in a fashionable small church near City Hall. Maria remembers that the church was packed, even though the couple had decided to get married just two weeks earlier and had not sent out invitations. The reception was an elegant dinner at home for twenty. Maria remembers, "Our apartment was full of flowers people had sent, like a garden, with no room to put more flowers. One man sent a Norfolk pine in a big basket with one hundred (Ninka and I counted them) long-stemmed roses around it, though it was February."

To give the newly-wed couple some time alone, the two girls were sent away for the summer to a camp for well-to-do Polish children. The camp was on an island, an hour by boat from Split, in Yugoslavia. Maria and Janina didn't want to go, but Wacław insisted. Angry at their father, the girls left by train with a group of forty children from Warsaw. At a time when anti-Semitism was spreading through Europe, their group included both Christian and Jewish girls; and Maria recalls that no one thought of any one of them as different from the rest.

And so Maria and Janina spent the summer of 1937, while Hitler was preparing his aggressive attacks upon Europe, swimming, reading, playing and

---

* Upper-class Polish homes were typically heated by very large, often beautifully decorated, ceramic stoves.

boating on an island in the Adriatic. Cows and goats wandered about the island. Grapes grew on arbors, but bees made picking them a risky venture. Janina was stung, and her mouth remained swollen for three days. Maria got into water over her head one day, and had to be rescued. However, told that she must learn to swim if she were to go kayaking, she quickly did so. Her first trip to Venice, a city she still loves, was an excursion from that camp.

Predictably, there were tensions between the girls and their new stepmother. Some were of the usual sort, with the girls pointing out to Stefania how she did things differently from their mother, provoking her anger. And Stefania, who had no experience with children, was different from their mother in many ways. While their mother had come from the landed gentry, the new stepmother was from a lower social class and had always worked. She also appears to have been rather jealous, especially of Janina, because Wacław doted on the girl. "When Ninka was born prematurely, my father was on vacation in France," Maria says. "Maybe he felt guilty about this. Anyway he was very fond of Ninka." As a result, Stefania "would pick on Ninka; there was always some struggle between them."

Looking at it from Stefania's point of view, she was required to move into an ongoing family, to live in an apartment that had been decorated by her new husband's first wife, and to rely on servants who had been chosen by that wife and been close to her. She was always arguing with the servants, and they hated her. She must have felt an outsider in many ways. She worked late, for example, and the family often had dinner in the middle of the day without her. When the cook left for the day, she would leave food out for the maid to serve to the family for supper and to Stefania whenever she returned.

But Stefania was also a moody and difficult person. One day, for example, the family had tongue for dinner. Stefania always maintained that she could not eat tongue, that it made her sick. She had supper late that day, by herself, and unknowingly ate pierogi dumplings made from the leftover tongue, with no ill effects. In the morning, the maid learned that the pierogis were made out of the leftover tongue. As she served breakfast, she said, gleefully, "Madam, you complain that you can't eat tongue because it makes you sick, but you ate it last night and you feel fine." Stefania, who was indeed fine, immediately proclaimed that she was sick, that she had been poisoned, and went to bed in a darkened room for several days. "I asked if we should call a doctor," Maria says, "but she said 'Oh, no.' She gave us two or three days of hell. Poor woman, she was venerated in her office, but she didn't know how to live."

Occasionally tensions between Maria and Stefania would boil over. "Once during the war," Maria says, "I had an argument with my stepmother that made me so mad that I used a bad expression; girls back then wouldn't dare do that. I immediately realized how bad it was, and jumped up to say 'I'm leaving.'" Wacław's sister Eugenia, who lived in Warsaw and often visited the family, was there and said, "Where will you go?" Maria replied, "I don't care. I can't stay with my stepmother." So Eugenia slipped Maria a key, saying "Go to my apartment" and then remained herself to try to smooth things over at dinner. Maria stayed at Eugenia's apartment several days before returning home.

Despite the tensions in the Chmielinski household after the death of Maria's mother and her father's remarriage, and the increasingly threatening political situation in Europe, Maria's life as a teenager continued to be one of privilege. Two stories, both about hair, give a flavor of the period.

Maria remembers her Aunt Eugenia with affection, as a good-hearted person who would play old tunes for them on the piano from memory. But Eugenia had her eccentricities. She had curly hair, which she would set by winding it on paper rollers. Eugenia was so concerned about looking nice that she would keep these rollers on under her hat (no respectable woman went out without a hat in those days) until she reached the second floor landing at their apartment building, where she would pause to pull out the rollers, so that her curls would be perfect when she arrived.

One Saturday, Eugenia came over for dinner with the family. Maria, who was then about 15, said she wanted to go to the theater. Her father, who often had free passes to shows, said "Take one and go." Maria called several of her friends, but none could accompany her. A girl her age could not be allowed to go alone, of course. So Aunt Eugenia piped up to say, "I'll go with you." She retired to prepare herself and emerged with her hat on once again.

Maria and Eugenia went to a big theater near the opera house, where they had tickets in the front row. As they were going in, an attendant approached Aunt Eugenia and said there was a new regulation that prohibited wearing a hat in the theater. She breezily replied, "All right." The two went in to their seats in the middle of the front row, and Maria began to look around to see if any of her friends were there.

A few minutes later, the attendant appeared again and said, "Madam, I told you to take off your hat." Thinking that she was helping, Maria reached up, grabbed her aunt's hat, and took it off. To her amazement, Eugenia's head was totally covered in white curling papers. She wanted to laugh but at the same time was embarrassed as only a teenager can be, because she had spotted friends in the audience. Her aunt quickly jumped up and rushed to the washroom to remove the papers from her head; she returned with a beautiful head of curly hair. But when she passed the attendant at intermission, it was quite clear that she was furious.

The second story is about Maria's own hair. Polish girls at that time wore their hair long and in braids. As Maria grew older, she would pin her braids onto the back of her head or wind them into a crown on top. But she grew tired of the braids and wanted to be more stylish. They bothered her when it was hot and flopped around when she played tennis. "I kept telling my parents, 'I want to cut my hair short, I want to cut my hair short.'"

But the braids were very important to her father. One day, when Maria was at least 16, he came to her room after he had finished seeing clients in the evening and said, "You see, you wanted to cut your hair short. A client came in today and said 'My son is getting married to a girl who is in our social class and who sticks to her principles. She has long hair.'" Long hair was somehow associated with living a socially correct and principled life.

One afternoon Wacław was about to take a short nap before seeing clients, when Maria came in and started her refrain "I want to cut my hair short, I want to cut my hair short." Her father was tired and said, curtly, "Do whatever you want." He didn't really mean it, but Maria ran quickly to a beauty parlor and had her hair cut to the top of her shoulders, returning home with the two braids.

After seeing his clients, her father came into her room. "What have you done?," he exploded. Later, he admitted that she looked good with short hair. But Maria kept the two braids in her drawer until her last days in Warsaw, long after Hitler had brought her privileged existence to an end.

Maria's father, Waclaw Chmielinski

Maria's mother, Jadwiga Lempicka Chmielinski

Maria and her sister a few days after their mother's death

Maria and Janina riding ponies

Maria as a young girl

Maria, Janina and their father skiing

CHAPTER 3

The Coming of the War

On September 1, 1939, Nazi Germany invaded Poland, the first Blitzkrieg in history. Hitler threw a vast army against the country: 2,600 tanks (the Poles had 180), more than 2,000 airplanes (the Poles had 420), and some 1.8 million troops. The Poles, relying heavily upon cavalry and infantry, fought back valiantly, inflicting heavy casualties upon the Germans. The French and British failed to come to Poland's aid. When the Soviet Union invaded on September 17, pursuant to its late-August secret pact with Hitler, Poland was doomed.

Warsaw was heavily bombed from the start of the hostilities. The national government fled by the end of the first week of September, but the city fought on under the leadership of Mayor Stefan Starzynski. It was surrounded and besieged by September 14 but did not surrender until September 27. Portions of the army commanded by General Kleeberg continued to fight both German and Soviet troops until October 5, when Hitler held a victory parade in Warsaw. Large parts of the city had been severely damaged, and many ancient buildings were reduced to ruins.

After their decisive victory, Germany and the Soviet Union divided Poland into three parts. The western section was incorporated into Germany, the eastern section into the Soviet Union, and the central-southern section, including Warsaw and Krakow, was turned into a German colony, called the General Government. Within it, a regime based on terror was imposed; many Polish citizens were arrested and executed.

A Polish government in exile was established in Paris. It was forced to move to England when France fell to the Germans in the following year.

Maria remembers the late summer of 1939 as "hot, sunny and beautiful. The ash trees were in full bloom, filled with what seemed like thousands of little red fruit. Birds were chirping and insects rattling. The air smelled of late summer. Nature was alive, and gloriously so. Into such beauty and life came tragedy and destruction." She was sixteen.

The Chmielinski family was spending the end of their annual summer vacation in the far northeastern corner of Poland, close to the Russian and Lithhuanian borders, near Lake Narocz. Maria had spent the first half of August at her aunt and uncle's estate, but the family always went on vacation together during the second half of August. "Everyone went on vacation then," she says. The Polish Secretary of State was negotiating with the Germans, and rumors of war were in the air; but the international situation was confusing. "My father was always an optimist and did not behave as if expecting the worst, so we went on vacation that year too. In fact, he had wanted to go to France, but decided to stay in the country because of the rumors." Near the end of the month, they were still trying to enjoy the beautiful weather despite reports of international tension on the radio.

When the radio reported military encounters at the Polish-German border it became clear that war was imminent, and panic spread. Tourists rushed to leave the peaceful surroundings and return to their homes. But Maria's father said, "Don't panic; we still have time." However, because he was counsel for the city of Warsaw and Maria's stepmother was assistant to Mayor Starzynski, both were called back to Warsaw. "The rush to leave began on Thursday," Maria remembers, "and we left on Sunday, among the last to leave." En route, they saw signs of the impending conflict. When they changed trains, they were ushered into a waiting room by a soldier in full battle gear, holding a rifle with a bayonet on it.

Arriving in Warsaw, they found a city caught up in tension and hard at work. People were digging trenches in the heart of the city for use as air raid shelters. Everyone, young and old, lent a hand. Maria and her sister, who was twelve years old, worked in the trenches, digging as hard as they could. Fearing for their safety, their parents decided to send them to stay with relatives in the country until the worst was over. They were still thinking that the war would proceed as World War I had, slowly. Like most people, they did not foresee the Blitzkrieg and quick defeat. Nor could they know Hitler's plans for the Poles or understand how bad it would be. So on August 31, 1939, Maria and Janina were dispatched by train to their aunt and uncle's estate east of Warsaw, where they had spent so many happy times during childhood.

The main Warsaw railway station was in chaos when they arrived. Travelers had to push and shove just to get through the crowds and board a train. Men were rushing to join their units in response to the rapid, if last minute, mobilization. Hundreds of people were embracing their loved ones and saying what was for many their last goodbyes. The compartments were filled with worried people trading stories of horrible things they had either heard about or (for those traveling away from the western borders) already seen. Soldiers carried gas masks for fear the Germans would use poison gas, as had happened in World War I.

The trip to Maria's uncle's estate was usually a two-hour ride. Because the transport of troops had to be given priority, their train, normally due at 5 p.m., arrived at 5 a.m. the next morning. The two girls and Emilka, the maid who had accompanied them, struggled to grab their belongings and push themselves off the crowded train. Luckily the horse-drawn carriage sent to meet them at the station had waited all night, and drove them the remaining two hours to the manor house. They arrived exhausted and barely awake. When they arose for breakfast, the girls' uncle told them that the war had started at 5 a.m. The Germans had already bombed Warsaw.

Anxiety was pervasive, even in the still peaceful countryside. News reports on the radio were discouraging. The Nazis were advancing rapidly through Poland. Inhabitants of Warsaw, they heard, were advised to evacuate if their work was not essential to vital services. Young people were urged to join the army units now scattered around the country.

Sometimes planes would be seen in the skies over the estate, although, situated as they were to the east of Warsaw, the fighting had not yet reached them. Polish officers requisitioned some of the estate's horses for use in the cavalry. Maria's uncle was not reluctant to surrender them for the emergency. In fact, he had trained many of the horses for this eventuality.

By the second week of the war, the roads bordering the estate were filled with refugees. They traveled on foot or by horse-drawn carriage; no gasoline was available. Many had left their homes with no more than the things they could carry on their backs. They came from all directions. Some were fleeing south from German columns advancing from Prussia. Some were escaping from the west toward the east, but before long, still others came from that direction as well, looking for refuge from the Soviet invasion. There were also soldiers who had been mobilized and were trying to find their units. Unless they could find provisions at farms along the way, the people on the road quickly exhausted their supplies of food.

The refugees were tired, hungry, and afraid. Part of the German Blitzkrieg strategy was to strike panic into civilians by bombing and strafing them from low-flying planes, thus disrupting troop movements on the roads. German planes would suddenly swoop down and shoot at the people passing by the estate, reminding Maria of wolves homing in on their prey. Many, soldiers and refugees alike, were killed by these attacks from the air.

The estate was quickly transformed into a way station for the refugees. Maria's relatives took in many of the weary travelers, the ones they knew, and set up an outdoor kitchen to feed the flood of people on the road. The cooks would make huge vats of soup, and Maria would help serve the people passing by, while watching the chaos. The family's dinner table expanded daily. An aunt with two sons who lived near the Prussian border fled her estate and took refuge at the manor house. Soon they were joined by relatives and friends fleeing from Soviet armies in eastern Poland.

When news arrived of the Soviet invasion on September 17, the Polish struggle against Germany appeared hopeless. Some of the family members who had taken refuge at the estate decided to stay for the duration. Reports circulated that the invading Russians were very hostile to the local Polish population, rounding up large numbers and sending them in cattle cars to Siberia. Although the relatives who had come from the west were eventually, after six years, able to return to their homes, those from the east never saw their estates again; the area was absorbed into the Soviet Union after the war.

On the estate news came either from the radio or via gossip from peasants. They learned about the Blitzkrieg and the September 27 surrender of Warsaw, although they didn't realize the amount of damage to the city. They heard that the government had run away soon after the war started and was now in France. Stories of the ill treatment of Poles by both the Germans and the Soviets caused a great deal of anxiety around the dinner table. Everyone wondered what would become of them. Many young people tried to escape through the Tatra Mountains to the south, to avoid conscription by the Germans, hoping to join the Polish army being formed in France.

Soon the bombs were falling closer and closer. Maria helped to dig air raid shelters in the beautiful park that surrounded the manor house. At the first sound of planes overhead, everyone would run to these makeshift shelters. From those times of group panic, Maria still remembers some incidents that amused her. "The head of the cooking staff was the oldest person at the estate. We used to laugh a lot about her, because she was the oldest, yet she was the most scared of us all. Despite her age, she was the first person to run into the shelter. And when she had entered the shelter she practically barricaded herself in, blocking others who were waiting to get in. It would take quite some time to get around this old woman who refused to budge from her perch at the door of the shelter. When she did finally move, after incessant pleas, the shelter would fill up rapidly. I also remember being chided by others in the shelter on a few occasions for wearing a white dress. The occupants of the shelter feared that the German planes would spot me very easily while I ran to the shelter, and thus would be able to bomb us without difficulty."

By late September, the end seemed imminent. The German and Soviet armies had taken over much of the country by the time the war arrived at the estate. One sunny afternoon, a Polish military unit arrived, sent to the area to place mines under the bridges. These soldiers, Maria remembers, "were all good looking men, who rode on very beautiful horses." As it turned out, they were the last of the Polish army, the unit commanded by General Kleeberg, the last to surrender. She recalls, "We prepared a hearty meal for them and waited impatiently to hear news from them from the front. To our surprise we learned from them that we were in the middle of a battle zone. According to the soldiers, there would be a great battle taking place on the following day near the estate. The conversation turned into a session on the precautions we should take in order to insure our safety. As the soldiers left the estate, their uniforms fading away down the tree-lined estate road, I felt danger in the air."

After a restless evening, those on the estate were awakened early in the morning by the sounds of shelling and gunfire. They could see shrapnel falling in the park and shells exploding in the distance. They were, indeed, in the middle of a battlefield. Artillery fire from both sides flew over the manor house. Its inhabitants rushed out of the house and into the shelter, panic-stricken.

The day wore on, and the sounds of battle continued. Maria says, "The day seemed to stretch out forever. Minutes seemed like hours, hours seemed like days." Since no one had paused for breakfast on their rush to the shelter, everyone was very hungry by afternoon. Maria volunteered to run into the house for food. Risking her life, she dashed into the empty house, crossed the large kitchen, and went in to the pantry, where she picked up a large container filled with milk. Walking back into the kitchen with the huge pot of milk in her arms, she heard footsteps nearby and froze. Almost immediately a German soldier in full gear approached, with his gun pointed at her. "I did not know what to do. For a second I contemplated escaping from the soldier. The chance never presented itself. I was helpless. I could not move for fear of being shot. I had met my first German soldier." Both were speechless.

The German soldier had been sent to investigate what was going on at the estate, which was suspected of harboring enemy soldiers. Maria's facility with languages saved her. Speaking German, she was able to convince the soldier that she was just getting food for relatives and friends hiding out in the makeshift shelter. After the house had been searched, Maria was allowed to return to the shelter and deliver the food.

The battle raged on until late in the afternoon, when the sounds of gunfire and shelling began to diminish. After securing the estate, the Germans set up their headquarters in the manor house. The residents, about twenty in number, were given two upstairs rooms, one for men and one for women. Maria was in a room with her sister, aunt, and other female relatives. One old aunt (really a cousin) was so scared that whenever she heard a bomb exploding she would start to pray loudly, saying, "Virgin Mary, let us live until tomorrow." Young Maria told her, "Please let us sleep. If we aren't going to live until tomorrow, just let us sleep."

Only the old, young, and female were left by the time the Germans arrived at the estate. Men who were of military age, like Maria's cousin Zbyszek, who had not had time to join his unit, had already run away lest they be conscripted by the Germans. Two cousins ran to the east, where their home had been, but were arrested by the Soviets and sent to Siberia.

The Germans issued blunt directives to the house's inhabitants. They were not to leave the house or get involved in anything that was happening on the estate. A curfew was imposed. Dressed in their gray uniforms and barking out orders, the German soldiers made Maria feel very uncomfortable. Worse still was to see the Polish officers brought in for interrogation. She found out from one of them that they were the last Polish units to capitulate. "As I glanced outside and saw the might of the German army encamped practically on our doorstep, I felt shivers run through my body."

After a few days, the Polish unit was finished. The Germans had apparently defeated the good-looking young soldiers who had gathered around the family's table the day before the battle. Maria comments, "Bravery could only go so far before it had to finally reckon with brute strength and force."

After the Polish defeat, the Germans moved out of the manor house, and life returned to some semblance of normal. It was difficult to know what was happening in other parts of the country because the Germans had confiscated their radios and warned the family that they would be severely punished if found listening to any radio broadcast. Radios had become illegal for the Polish population. The family surmised that the entire country was occupied by the Germans and the Russians. News arrived only with visitors. Friends who had tried to flee to the east returned to the estate with terrible stories about atrocities. People were being arrested and their property confiscated, and some were deported to Russia.

Now that the war appeared to be over, some of the people staying in the manor house left, but many remained. Some of the maids had run away for fear of the guns and artillery. Maria, who had no experience in a kitchen, helped the cook set table for the much-enlarged household and assisted her aunt with chores. After dinner, she returned to her habit of riding horseback. She liked to visit a forest that belonged to the estate but was four miles away. If she returned late, her aunt would worry and be convinced that she had been caught by the Germans.

As the weeks passed, signs of autumn replaced the summer landscape. To Maria, the change of season seemed like the only constant in a time of disruption and dramatic change. By the end of October, Poles had settled down as much as possible under the extraordinary circumstances. Maria's family at the estate was lucky. Many of her uncle's friends in the west of Poland, which was absorbed into the Third Reich, had lost their land or were deported to labor camps; other landowners in the west were arrested and shot.

Through all the fighting, the girls had been able to hear nothing from their parents in Warsaw—both mail and phone service had ceased. In early November, Emilka, their parents' maid, arrived to bring them back. Wacław and Stefania had been working closely with the mayor during the siege of Warsaw and could not leave the city. When Emilka arrived, she told them that the city had been severely damaged by bombing and that there was a tremendous shortage of food caused by a lack of deliveries from the countryside. They decided to carry back as much food as they could.

Unskilled at these matters, Maria set off into the countryside, bought a pig, and had the farmer kill it for her. Her aunt and uncle had gone away for a funeral (there must have been many in those days), so only the old cook was at home to tell her what to do. She nonetheless set about cutting up the pig. The cook smoked a ham for her, and Maria tried to make sausages. What came out of her work bore little resemblance to sausages, but it was edible.

Trains were running infrequently and were packed, and they could not have taken the food with them in a train. So they rented an uncovered, horse-drawn peasant wagon. They stashed all of the food at the bottom and sat on top of it.

Along the way, the carriage was stopped frequently by German troops who demanded to know who they were and where they were going. Each time, they searched the wagon for contraband. When the Germans asked what was in the bottom of the wagon, Maria said it was her clothes and other belongings. To her amazement, the Germans never found the meat and other food products, which would have been regarded as contraband.

The trip to Warsaw took almost three days, and they stayed overnight in a peasant home, sleeping on the floor. The country seemed to have been transformed in two short months from one of serenity and beauty into a land of poverty and destruction. "Before, it was very rustic and quiet, with peasants working on their little farms and displaying food for sale. Now we saw bombed houses in the small towns, even in small villages. We saw fields ruined by the refugees traveling through. Instead of displaying food for purchase, the farmers were now hiding their food."

When the carriage arrived in Warsaw, Maria was shocked at the destruction. The city was a shadow of its former self, "like a poor, ravaged soldier unable to hide her wounds and deep scars." As the horse-drawn carriage traveled slowly through the wounded city, the girls saw ruins everywhere. Hardly any house was unscathed. Some were gutted. Those that still stood were covered with dirt and dust; many were stained with smoke. Their windows were either boarded up or covered with white strips of tape to prevent damage when the house was shaken by explosions. Rubble lay everywhere, on the sidewalks and even in the streets, making it difficult to walk. Yet as Maria wrote fifty years later, the destruction was not just material. "The ruins all around struck me immediately, yet something else made an even bigger impact on my soul. The people I saw walking around were not the same ones that I had remembered [from] just a short while ago. They had changed. They walked around without a sense of conviction, as if someone had just told them that they had terminal cancer. Not a smile surfaced on any passing face. The once happy and proud residents of Warsaw had in two short months lost that magical zest that makes life enjoyable."

CHAPTER 4

Warsaw under Nazi Occupation

After the conquest of Poland, the Germans began to impose their race-based plan of domination. According to Nazi racial theories, non-Aryan peoples were considered sub-human: some were fit only to serve Aryans and others were destined for extermination. The secret German master plan called for extermination of the Jews and the ultimate extermination or enslavement of the remaining Poles. The western portions of Poland—and eventually the entire country—were to become part of an expanded German Lebensraum, or living space, and the Polish population was to be deported to work as unskilled labor for the master race.

The expulsion of Poles from areas incorporated into Germany began immediately, as did conscription of men and women for slave labor in the Reich. This intensified over the years, as workers were needed to replace Germans who had been drafted into the army. Jews were forced into ghettos, the largest of which was in Warsaw, and deported to the concentration camps at Treblinka and Auschwitz. Once Auschwitz-Birkenau was developed as a highly efficient extermination camp, the deportations speeded up. In April 1943, the Nazis' move to liquidate the remaining inhabitants of the Warsaw Ghetto was met with an armed uprising that lasted for three weeks. At the end of it, the ghetto was totally destroyed, and all of the surviving inhabitants sent to death camps.

Christian Poles were also subjected to conditions of terror and extreme deprivation. In 1940, some 10,000 Polish intellectuals and 3,500 political leaders were sent to concentration camps or executed. All persons in Poland were categorized according to race and issued identity cards, work permits, and ration books for calories that varied by racial classification. Any education above the primary level, except for a limited number of basic technical schools, was forbidden. All Poles aged sixteen and older were expected to work, and were subject to conscription for forced labor if they were not employed. Curfews were imposed. Any Pole found violating a curfew or selling on the black market or helping a Jew was to be summarily executed. These activities continued nonetheless.

31

One observer described life for the Poles in occupied Warsaw as follows:

> *The inhabitants of Warsaw were turned into hunted animals, who had to go outside to live, but who were constantly on edge, lest they were pounced on. One could go out to buy a bottle of milk and not return, then be found on the list of hostages . . . to be shot [as] 'enemies of German reconstruction'. One could be grabbed in a restaurant, in a shop, in a church, or in one's own home. Life became a daily game of chance with death.*

An underground resistance movement rapidly developed in Poland. At its height it included 400,000 people, the largest of any country in occupied Europe. It was called the Home Army, known by its Polish initials AK (Armia Krajowa), to denote that it was the part of the regular Polish army charged with fighting in the occupied homeland. The Communists having been almost obliterated by Stalin's earlier purges and the extermination of the Jews, the AK became the primary resistance group. An elaborate underground state was established, taking its orders from the government-in-exile in London. The AK carried out sabotage and intelligence operations both in the countryside and in the cities, derailing trains, damaging German transport, and assassinating Nazi officials. An underground press was published and distributed, to apprise the Poles of the news being kept from them after radios were prohibited and all news censored.

In response to the Poles' continuing acts of resistance, and especially after assassinations of German officials and sabotage of the German war efforts, large numbers of "hostages" were arbitrarily seized on the streets and publicly shot or hung. Lists of persons executed were posted to deter others from supporting the resistance.

Undeterred, the Polish underground state established ministries paralleling those of a government, to provide services to Poles living under the stringent terms imposed by the Nazis. One of the most substantial accomplishments of this underground state was to continue the operation of the forbidden educational institutions, on both the secondary and university levels. Secondary schools met secretly in students' homes. University classes, taught by former professors, continued disguised as trade schools, which were the only form of education the Germans permitted for Poles over the age of sixteen.

Food rationing reduced the average diet for Poles to starvation level. Between 1939 and 1945, the population of Poland was reduced by 22 per cent, or 6 million persons; 2.9 million of these were Jews. Only 10 per cent of the total deaths were from military operations. Ninety per cent died in prisons and death camps, from raids, summary executions, the annihilation of ghettos, epidemics, excessive work or starvation.

When Maria and her sister returned to Warsaw, food and other essentials were in short supply. Wacław told the girls apologetically that their life style would have to be different from what he could give them before the war and that their meals would be modest.

The ration cards issued to Poles allowed insufficient calories to sustain health, and the food that could be obtained with these ration cards was unpalatable. "The bread sold in stores was horrible," Maria tells me, "a gooey mess made of flour mixed with ground-up horse chestnuts." People brewed ersatz tea out of whatever was available. "My aunt was proud of a tea that she made from some kind of weed. It tasted good but you had to use the washroom every few minutes. It acted as a diuretic."

Maria's father was able to obtain some extras, like sugar and ersatz coffee, through his employment at City Hall; Maria would come to his office to help him carry it home. Like many others, however, they survived by buying additional food on the black market, despite the severe penalties for doing so. Their maid left to work in the black market, bringing produce to the city from the country; and the family bought butter, meat, and eggs from her, which were unavailable in the stores. Relatives would also bring food with them from the country.

The governess also left at the start of the war, to return to her native France. The departure of household staff changed the Chmielinskis' standard of living, but they did not dare to replace any of them because they feared that new employees might act as spies for the Germans. Eventually only the cook was left, and she had to have time off. The girls were required to learn new skills. One morning, Maria's father asked her to fix breakfast and suggested soft-boiled eggs. She told him she didn't know how to cook them. He replied, "Just say three Hail Marys, and they will be right." This was Maria's first cooking lesson.

Soon it was the winter of 1939-40, and heating fuel was hard to come by. The apartment on Foksal Street was heated by the traditional large ceramic stoves in each room. Before the war, the family had used about seven tons of coal to get through the winter, but now they could only get one or two tons, and even that was very expensive. It was obviously impossible to heat the entire apartment with what they could buy, so inventiveness was required. Instead of trying to use the huge floor-to-ceiling stoves, they made little metal stoves which they placed in the opening of the ceramic stoves, and hooked the small stoves up to the chimney. This method didn't use as much coal. Of course, it wasn't as warm either.

Electricity was available only intermittently. The Germans would cut off whole neighborhoods from the electric grid, sometimes for as long as six months. In the absence of power, the family used candles, but it was difficult to read in the winter when the days were very short. Kerosene was hard to get, so they reserved gas lamps for use in Wacław's office. He still had some clients who came to the home in the evening, and his legal work required a great deal of reading and writing.

After a year of this misery, Wacław had a bright idea. Directly below them lived a *Volksdeutsch* family, that is, Poles of German descent who had registered themselves as such (other Poles of German descent identified with Poland and refused to do so). The *Volksdeutsch*, unlike the Polish population, were supplied with power at all times. Maria's father bribed the janitor to hook up their lighting circuit to that of the German tenant, so that they could also have light after curfew. This arrangement worked quite well, and Maria could do her schoolwork.

One evening Maria was studying as usual, but as darkness fell the lights did not come on. Thinking that the janitor had forgotten to turn on the power, she left her books on the table and ran downstairs to find him. As she went down the outdoor staircase, which was now almost completely dark, she suddenly heard a loud German voice saying "Achtung! Halte! Hände auf! [Attention! Stop! Hands up!]" and saw the janitor walking up the stairs with three members of the Gestapo. The Germans were looking for a member of the Polish underground who they believed was in the building. Their suspicion immediately fell upon the girl running down the stairs after curfew. They surrounded Maria and began to pelt her with questions. "Who are you?" "Why are you here after curfew?" It seemed clear to them that she was a fugitive seeking refuge in the building.

The janitor came to Maria's aid. With passion, he told the Gestapo that Maria was certainly not a fugitive, that she was a long-term tenant in the building. After several more tense moments of questioning, the Gestapo told her to go downstairs and wait for them in the janitor's apartment, on the ground floor, next to the main entrance. When Maria arrived there, she could see more heavily armed German soldiers guarding the entrance to the building. From the looks on their faces, it was obvious that the situation was very serious.

Stranded with a number of others in the janitor's apartment, Maria was sick with worry. She was still unsure of her own fate. She knew that the Gestapo agents had gone upstairs and that, if they searched her apartment, they would find the forbidden schoolbooks she had been working on when she left. Unable to warn her parents, she waited nervously, not knowing what was going on above her head. Minutes passed, and then hours. After a while, she heard a scream, and shots rang out. There was no way to know if it had come from her family's apartment.

When the screams and shouts had subsided, the Gestapo returned to the janitor's apartment. Although they still seemed suspicious of Maria, they let her go. Apparently they had entered the apartment in which a member of the underground was hiding, but he escaped, by climbing a chimney onto the roof and jumping from there to the roof of an adjoining apartment complex. A woman in the apartment had let out the scream. She had also thrown illegal bulletins out of the window into the courtyard before the Gestapo entered the apartment. One of the building tenants had picked up the contraband materials; if he had not, the

Germans would have punished all the tenants of the building, perhaps shooting them then and there. When Maria finally entered her own apartment and closed the door behind her, it was with an enormous sense of relief. All of her schoolbooks were still in view, but the Germans had not searched their apartment.

Because so many buildings had been damaged in the bombing, German regulations required every residence to take in homeless people and set a minimum number of persons for each apartment, by size. Maria's cousin Zybszek's apartment had been bombed, and he came to live with them. His parents were frequently in residence as well, moving several trunks of their belongings from the country estate to the Chmielinskis' home in order to escape fighting between Germans and partisans in the countryside. If relatives had not moved in, the Nazis would have assigned complete strangers to live with the family. As it was, it became hard to find a place to study.

Later Maria's father took in others as well and managed to accommodate them in the apartment previously occupied by the family alone. A man who worked with Maria's father arranged for his daughter-in-law's family to move in with them after their own home was taken over by the Germans. The family had a daughter, Nola, who was a few years younger than Maria. The two girls spent a lot of time with each other because they could be together after curfew. "Nola's mother," Maria says, "was of Russian descent, and she was full of fun, unlike Poles, who tend to be very serious. Middle-class, educated Poles take everything to heart. They complain, debate, are always thinking of the future. They do not take life lightly. The Russians take life with a smile." I ask Maria if she has Russian blood. "No," she says, "I changed, because I spent most of my life in the West."

Despite the possibility that it could be raided at any time, it was definitely safer inside the apartment than on the street, where the Germans periodically rounded up random groups of Polish citizens and shot them on the spot, often in reprisal for actions by the underground. A school friend of Maria's was seized in a reprisal action and killed. Lists of people taken hostage were posted all over Warsaw. The Germans also stopped people to inspect the identity cards they were required to carry at all times. This presented a substantial problem for Maria, who was sixteen but not employed. She therefore did not have the work card that the new laws required. Anyone over sixteen on the street during the daytime was considered unemployed, and thus liable to be taken for forced labor. Maria carried a 500 złoty note in back of her ID card, in hopes that bribery would get her off.

A curfew required Poles to be off the streets by 7 p.m. in the winter, later in the summer. Anyone out after curfew could be summarily shot. Worst of all were the periodic "sweeps," in which German trucks filled with soldiers would suddenly close off a street. The soldiers would jump out and round up all the people around them before they could escape. "It was like the way dogcatchers pick up stray dogs," says Maria. The Germans would pack their prisoners into the trucks and take them to a police station to be "sorted." Some were then sent to forced labor in Germany, to work on farms or in munitions factories. Others were imprisoned and eventually executed, or sent to concentration camps, which amounted to the same thing.

One beautiful, sunny Sunday afternoon, Maria was returning to the apartment on Foksal Street, carrying illegal bulletins from the underground. Although Poles were forbidden to have radios, the AK monitored broadcasts from abroad and printed news bulletins in a hidden printing office. These bulletins, which Maria and many others distributed, reported not only what was going on in the world but also any information the AK was able to obtain about those who had been arrested in Warsaw and taken either to the dread Pawiak prison or to Gestapo headquarters.

As Maria approached the intersection of Foksal and Nowy Swiat with her cache of bulletins, she saw that Foksal was closed and that the German people-catching trucks were on the street. She quickly turned back, went to a friend's house, and kept checking until the Germans were gone. "I was very anxious. I didn't know what was going on or if my family and friends were being picked up. When I was finally able to return, I was overjoyed to see that they were still there."

The German reign of terror infected daily life in other ways as well. When Mayor Starzynski was arrested and ultimately executed for his valiant role in resisting the German conquest of Warsaw, Maria's stepmother Stefania, his assistant, went into hiding for a time, staying with friends or at the farm in Ozarow. Many professionals were fired and replaced by German administrators. Others, including attorneys like Maria's father, had to be licensed to practice. To obtain the license they were required to present documentation that the employee and his or her spouse did not have any Jewish members of the family for several generations. Maria's godfather, a well-known attorney, was unable to practice during the war years because his wife was of Jewish descent. Indeed, his wife went into hiding for long periods.

After forbidding Poles to have or listen to radios, the Germans set up loudspeakers on lamp poles to provide the news they wanted to be heard. They used the loudspeakers for all official announcements, including the coming of curfew each day, and to broadcast war news. When there was no news favorable to the Axis, they would make some up, in order to harm Polish morale.

The family became afraid to talk freely at the dinner table if any but their oldest and most-trusted servants were present, or on the telephone, for fear of wiretapping. But when only family were present, or with close friends, it was possible to speak relatively freely. There was no Polish Quisling* and relatively little informing. Maria lived and moved in a small and closed society, so she trusted the people with whom she interacted in social settings. So at parties or in public places such as parks, one could express political views, even though it was forbidden. But no one discussed the secret work most of them were doing for the underground.

Life was punctuated by Allied air raids on German targets in Warsaw, during which the authorities ordered all persons to seek shelter in basements, and periodically checked that they had done so. During much of the war, these raids came only at night. At these times, the Chmielinskis would rush to their basement with other residents of their building. The basement at Foksal 13 was unfinished and ordinarily used for the storage of coal. It was filthy, with nowhere to sit or lie down. So the building's residents would simply stand until they heard the "all-clear" siren.

One apartment in the building was occupied by Germans, who would come to the basement with the rest. The German women were particularly frightened by the bombs. Maria remembers seeing how scared they were in the basement—and that they wore fur coats but not hats, as "proper" women did. None of the Poles would speak to the Germans unless it was absolutely necessary. They particularly hated the *Volksdeutsch*.

Maria's Aunt Nina from the estate was also very frightened by the air raids. She and her husband had two rooms at the apartment, in which they kept their valuables. (No one trusted the Germans not to take materials from bank safe-deposit boxes.) Aunt Nina kept a bag with her jewelry in her bed. "When the air raid siren went off, she gave it to me to take care of. There was no elevator in our building, and my aunt couldn't walk very well. When she wanted to go out, a carriage would come and two men would carry her down the stairs on a chair. But when the bombs came, she'd give the jewels to me and then run down the narrow back staircase to the basement in five minutes!"

Despite the appalling stress of living under Nazi rule, life did go on. When Maria was much younger, she had heard her parents and relatives talk about past wars. "Their stories left me with a feeling that life ground to a halt during wartime, that the obsession with war permeated every action, every breath. During the war, I realized that this was not entirely true. Life moved on. Babies were born, people got married, and they died. They found ways to go on with daily life." So it was during World War II in Poland.

---

*   Vidkun Quisling was a Norwegian fascist who collaborated with the Nazis; his name has come to be a synonym for this type of traitor.

Social life changed its venue. Theaters were closed, and part of the price of a movie ticket went to the German army, so patriotic Poles boycotted performances. Anyone who did go was likely to end up with a sign pinned to his clothes, stating "Only pigs go to movie houses." So people would go to cafés to socialize, drinking ersatz coffee and eating scraps of bread instead of pastries. Famous Polish actors, singers, musicians, and composers were unemployed; they would work in the coffee houses as waiters and perform for the customers. Looking for a brief escape from tension, people would go to the cafés to see their favorite stars from prewar years.

Teenagers went through their typical developmental struggles during the occupation as well. Maria and Janina continued to fight with their stepmother. They occasionally stayed out after curfew, making their parents extremely anxious, with more justification than anxious parents in normal times. And Maria was determined to demonstrate her independence by showing her father that she could make her own money, even though he could support her and wanted her to spend full time on her studies.

She came up with the idea of making gloves in her bedroom. She bought rabbit fur on the black market, pinned the skins on a wooden ironing board, and cut out the gloves. Other girls would come and make money by sewing them together. The business went well until the *Volksdeutsch* man whose bedroom was directly beneath Maria's "glove factory" complained to her father that he thought his daughter was making bombs over his head at night. Ever the persuasive advocate, Wacław convinced him that his daughter simply liked to study late. Maria remembers that the glove-making project "was fun, and it helped my girlfriends who were in bad financial shape." Under the circumstances, of course, it was also very dangerous.

One of the most dangerous activities during the German occupation of Poland was the simple act of going to school. Soon after the girls returned to Warsaw in November 1939, schools reopened and they went back to their respective grades. After a couple of weeks, however, the Germans closed all schools past the primary grades. Maria's sister continued in her old school but Maria herself could not. Under the new laws, she was supposed to go to work because she was sixteen.

Very quickly the Polish underground state established a system of secret schools for both secondary and university education. As in her earliest schooling, Maria went to small classes in private homes. For her last two years of high school, seven or eight girls would meet in an apartment, with one teacher coming in the morning and another in the afternoon. They continued to study their prewar curriculum from the now-forbidden prewar books. For Maria, this meant Polish literature, history, geography, math, chemistry, some physics, Latin and French.

The location of the classes changed frequently to evade German notice. The hardest part of each school day was getting to the home where school was scheduled to take place. The rule was to turn back if you saw anything suspicious near the school location, for example, Germans milling about. Many times Maria had to miss school because she sensed that something suspicious was going on close to the home selected for that day. In this way she developed a kind of sixth sense that served her well later, when she joined the resistance.

One day school was being held in Maria's own home. Eight girls were gathered around the big dining room table for the clandestine class. The first session of the day was over, and they were waiting for the next teacher to arrive when the door bell rang. When the maid (the cook now functioned in both roles) opened the front door, instead of the next teacher, they could hear German voices. The maid returned to the room, white as a ghost, and asked Maria to go into the hallway to talk to the Germans. The other girls in the room quickly hid all the illegal schoolbooks.

When she got to the door, Maria found three German soldiers with her cousin Zybszek in tow. Because of her fluency in German, she was able to understand the soldiers' conversation. They were very suspicious. They searched first her cousin's room and then the whole apartment, while Zybszek stood helplessly by. The soldiers even stuck a sword into a large clothing hamper to be sure that no one was hiding inside. "They asked me why there were so many girls there, and I told them it was my birthday party."

While being interrogated by the German in charge of the group, Maria found out that her cousin had been picked up on the Poniatowski Bridge by a German patrol. He was riding in a carriage and had tried to conceal some contraband materials. He was in serious trouble. But the Germans had found nothing in their search of the apartment. Because they missed the textbooks and various illegal bulletins, they reluctantly accepted Maria's explanation of the girls' presence. They left, taking Zybszek, white-faced, with them. Maria asked where they were taking her cousin, but the soldiers told her "If you ask, we'll take you too."

Maria's parents were at work, and she could do nothing but wait for their return. When they came home, she told them what had happened. A sense of gloom fell upon the dinner table. Everyone was terribly worried but knew that there was nothing they could do. "We didn't know why he was arrested, what they had against him, how serious the offense. We speculated about why he had been taken and talked about possible horrors. We didn't expect to see him again soon, if ever. We couldn't just chat, as we normally did at dinner, so after a while no one spoke at all." Only a miracle would save Zybszek from a forced labor or concentration camp.

Suddenly the sound of the doorbell broke the silence. After some commotion in the hallway, Zybszek walked into the room. The family's gloom turned to amazement and joy. He explained that the Germans had taken him to be "tried," assigning a Polish policeman as a translator. When the translator heard Zybszek's last name, he asked if he had an uncle who was involved in equestrian competitions. Zybszek's uncle had, in fact, been very well known in the prewar international riding community. It seems that the translator was a big fan of Zybszek's uncle. As a result, he argued forcefully with the German judge that Zybszek was innocent and should be set free. Astonishingly, he succeeded, and Zybszek was allowed to return home. Such chances could be the difference between life and death for Poles under Nazi rule.

After two years of clandestine study, Maria completed the work for graduation from secondary school. She took exams in the late spring of 1941 and received a certificate called the "matura." The eight girls from her in-home school and eight boys from another gathered for a graduation party. It was not a very large group, for fear of attracting the attention of the Germans. The party took place during the day because of the curfew, in an open field near the house of friends in the suburbs. The guests shared some food and drink, talked, and made merry. Dancing was frowned upon during the occupation, though, as a sign of national mourning. As it turned out, the great entertainment of the day took place overhead. The partygoers began to see hordes of airplanes; they watched the planes, which were obviously German, flying toward the east. Clearly, something major was going on. It was June 22, 1941. Hitler had launched Operation Barbarossa, the invasion of his erstwhile ally, the Soviet Union.

After getting her matura, Maria was ready to enter university, but all of them had been closed. Higher education of any sort was prohibited for Poles. The underground state managed to reestablish the university system in secret, running programs in a variety of subjects, including medicine and commerce. Maria enrolled in the School of Commerce and Management. Her classes were held in a high school building under the pretense that they were vocational. Training Polish students in low-level clerical skills was still allowed. Because Maria was now over eighteen and not employed, fake papers (the underground became very skilled at producing these) had to be obtained for her to attend the school at all. The papers certified that the school offered, among other things, typewriting and shorthand, along with simple math, sales techniques, and the like.

The Germans made frequent surprise inspections of activities at the school. Whenever one appeared, the students would hide their prewar textbooks and the professor would quickly shift his lecture to simple math or shorthand. The German would sit down and listen and, after the professor was finished, question the students on what they had learned. They all became adept at lying and appearing to be simple-minded in their answers. Such cat and mouse games characterized Maria's wartime schooling.

Of course, studying itself was a challenge. The apartment on Foksal was overcrowded, without a corner where one could concentrate. The lights were sporadic, and air raids came often, especially during the evening hours when Maria was studying. It was hard to prepare for a final exam standing upright in an air raid shelter, or to take exams on the amount of sleep she was able to catch between raids. Yet no excuses were accepted by the professors in the underground schools.

Maria also had to find time for another after-school activity—training for the underground army, the AK.

CHAPTER 5

The Home Army

At age 17, in the winter of 1940-41, without telling her family, Maria joined the Home Army, or AK. Oddly, given the risks attached to joining a resistance group in a totalitarian state, she doesn't remember exactly how she made her first contact with the AK. It appears to have been "in the air." Most of her classmates and friends joined up. Probably a friend asked Maria to join her unit. A large number of those in the Home Army were quite young. So many in Maria's unit were students that it was called the "Academic." For security reasons, the members met only in groups of six to eight; the whole unit never met at one time.

What motivated a schoolgirl to join the resistance? All Maria can say on this point is that Germany had treated Poland very badly, that she felt she had a duty to her country, and wanted to help in any way she could. She doesn't remember being afraid, though she was aware of the risks. With the confidence of youth, she simply thought that everything would turn out all right. "I guess when you are younger, you accept dangerous challenges without questioning them," she says now.

After joining, Maria was given a false name and assigned to a unit. Her new name was Iwonka Komięga. The surname refers to a kind of boat,* denoting that Maria's unit was from the section of Warsaw with a water port; people with names referring to water or ships belonged to that unit. Her unit was charged with delivery of illegal materials of a variety of types from one part of the city to another or from one person to another. Messengers would report to a designated location and were given assignments after recitation of a password; the password system worked by giving a specified answer to a specific question. The messengers would then deliver what they were given to a specified place, to a person identified only

---

* According to the Unabridged Polish-English Dictionary, a komięga is a river barge for grain transport.

by his or her *nom de guerre* and recitation of the password. Passwords, rendezvous points, times of day, and days of the week were changed frequently. Maria's work was done, by and large, in the hours after school, the period when she had taken piano lessons and other classes prior to the war.

Maria's first assignments involved distribution of the underground press, but these duties soon expanded to delivery of messages, arms, and ammunition. Whenever possible, she would carry the items on her person rather than in a bag that would be inspected by the Germans patrolling the streets. In winter, she carried them in her muff. Sometimes Maria was stopped by friends in the street, perhaps ones she hadn't seen for a long time, while she was carrying illegal materials. She would pretend to be calm but was in fact extremely nervous, lest the group attract the attention of a German patrol. If the Germans searched her and found what she was carrying, she knew that everyone in the group was likely to share her fate.

The episode set out in the Prologue to this book took place during this period. The two girls confronted by the German soldiers were Maria, carrying contraband documents in her school briefcase, and Krystyna, her best friend. "It was so foggy that they appeared as if out of nowhere," she tells me. Krystyna, who had lost her Kennkarte, looked to Maria to get her out of the situation. Maria's quick decision to distract the soldiers from her own bag by making a commotion about Krystyna's lost card demonstrated both the bravado and the skills at deception she had developed after several years of Nazi occupation. Yet the Germans might well have reacted quite differently to her vehement argument; they might even have shot the two girls on the spot. Maria puts down the success of her ploy to luck. "Luck was often the only reason you survived," she tells me. But it is clear that Maria's charm, quick wits, and resourcefulness played an important role in the girls' luck. The incident also shows the toll the constant danger was taking on her. As soon as the patrol moved on, all her carefully controlled emotions emerged. "I began to shake all over." She realized how close they had come to being just another statistic in the war. Yet, after taking several minutes to pull herself together, she forced herself to repress the fear and complete her assignment to deliver the papers to the underground. "You get used to it," she tells me. "You have to."

Later Maria was assigned to a second unit to be trained for the armed uprising everyone knew was being planned. The soldiers-to-be were given drills and learned how to march. They were trained to drop to the ground in the face of enemy fire. They studied how to handle guns—how to load and unload them, how to clean them, and how to shoot, though they had to practice without actually firing ammunition. Possession of guns and ammunition was prohibited for Poles, except for limited hunting purposes, so the military training had to be done surreptitiously, in small groups. The AK also had to preserve its limited stores of ammunition.

Maria and her sister Janina were close during the war years, and Janina repeatedly told Maria that she wanted her to help her enlist in the underground. Maria told her that she was not old enough yet but that she'd help her join a medical unit later. She thought that would be safer. However, one evening, when Ninka was about 15, she came to Maria and told her that she had joined up on her own. She wanted to be on the front lines, she said, and had joined a unit that promised to train her to fight with partisans in the forests. Maria tried to dissuade her as best she could without saying anything that would lead her sister to stop sharing confidences with her.

The very next day, Maria's stepmother came home from her latest place of hiding. When curfew hour arrived, Ninka had not come home. Hours went by as the family became increasingly worried, and Wacław said he was going to call the police. Maria said "No! Don't do that!" She still had not told her family that she had joined the underground, although she had been a member for a long time. Now it was necessary. She also told them what Ninka had confided to her and that she was convinced she must have gone to join her new unit. Maria promised to use her own underground connections to track Ninka down and bring her back. Expecting the Gestapo at any minute, the family began to hide anything that could incriminate them, shredding some of Maria's AK messages and hiding others. They pushed their gold coins underneath the wallpaper in the dining room.

At 6 a.m., when curfew was over, Maria went out into the city to look for her sister. Her own connections in the underground were very good by now, and she quickly found out that the unit Ninka had joined was directed by Communists. Someone in the AK had in fact spotted her sister and reported that she was seen going to a certain street. "I spent a whole week lurking in the doorways of big buildings on that street trying to catch a glimpse of Ninka. I found out later that Ninka had in fact passed by during that time, but her hair had been cut and bleached blond as a disguise, so I didn't recognize her."

After a short time, the unit Ninka had joined realized that she was far too young and inexperienced to fight with partisans in the forests of Poland, and they sent her to support herself by working as a maid for a lawyer's family not too far from where she grew up. Ninka quickly tired of this assignment. She didn't know the first thing about housekeeping and feared that she would be recognized by other attorneys who might come to call. But she was afraid to go home after disappearing without permission.

After Ninka had been away almost ten days, she went to her favorite teacher at school and asked her what she should do. The teacher offered to mediate with Ninka's family, and went to Wacław, who promised not to ask any questions if she simply returned. Ninka came back immediately—and her stepmother rushed her to the hairdresser to return the brown color to her hair. When she was a year older, Ninka did in fact join the underground, but in an AK unit that specialized in nursing.

After tension-filled assignments, Maria and other friends involved in underground work would meet at cafés in the evening. Many people they knew had been killed. They drank to distract themselves and to dull the losses they were absorbing. One of Maria's cousins and the father of a close friend were killed in the 1940 massacre at Katyn Forest, which only came to light in 1943.* Another friend was involved in a resistance group charged with carrying out political assassinations, and lost his life when the group killed General Franz Kutschera, SS commandant and chief of police for the Warsaw district on February 1, 1944. A school friend was taken hostage by the Germans and shot. And when the Germans burned the Ghetto, all they could do was watch the smoke.

Amid the terrors and deprivation attendant upon the occupation of her country, Maria was entering the period of life when she normally would have been meeting men suitable for marriage. Not even Nazi oppression could entirely bring such matters to a halt. Although there was no pressure to marry from her parents, Aunt Eugenia, a widow, acted as a matchmaker from time to time. When young men came to call and Maria did not like them, Eugenia would say, "Don't be too choosy; instead of a canary you'll get a sparrow."

The accepted way to meet candidates for marriage at that time was through introduction by family or friends. Maria met her first boyfriends in the early 1940s. During the war, her father still tried to get the girls out of Warsaw for the summer months; and in 1942 he rented a small cottage in the countryside south of Warsaw, where they had several friends. "It was on the outskirts of a village," she says, "several little cottages that had been owned by persons the Germans had deported. They were primitive, and weren't winterized." Maria and her sister stayed there all summer, and Wacław would come on the weekends, relying on friends to supervise his daughters when he was not there.

The people running the cottage community had a son a little older than Maria, with whom she would go boating on the river. "He became very fond of me." There was also a boy named Kazimierz on a nearby estate with whom she spent time. He was later killed in a concentration camp. "I remember especially

---

*   4,231 Polish officers, almost all professionals who had been reservists called up to serve when the Germans invaded in 1939, were killed at Katyn, near Smolensk, in 1940. The mass grave was discovered in 1943, revealing the victims, their identification still intact, with their hands tied behind their backs. Each had been killed by a bullet at the base of the skull. The Germans trumpeted the news to the Poles as proof of Soviet barbarism. The Soviets argued that the officers were killed during the German invasion of their country, but ultimately admitted responsibility for the massacre in 1990.

one thing that he said to me. At that time, I used to put a bunch of the tiny red berries from the mountain ash tree in my hair for decoration. Kazimierz told me 'When you get old and have gray hair, still wear that, Maria. I will always remember you that way.'" An odd conversation for teenagers, but not perhaps in a time when death and destruction were all around.

There, in the country, Maria met her first serious love. His name was Bogdan. Bogdan's parents had been displaced from their estate in Pomerania when the Germans incorporated that section of Poland into the Third Reich. His father had then taken over the administration of a large estate not far from the cottage where Maria and her sister were staying. Bogdan worked for him, supervising the workers at the estate. He was very good-looking, tall and blond, and about four years older than Maria. "One day I was in the country with some other young people, and a group came from a bit farther away. He was among them. We were right away attracted to each other, and he started courting me. He was very attractive, always cheerful, and concerned about me. He was very popular, and all the girls had an eye on him since he was so good-looking and full of life. I was impressed to be the one chosen by him."

Photos from that time show that Bogdan was about a foot taller than Maria and very nice-looking indeed. He has a thoughtful look about him and an engaging smile. He wears his pants tucked into tall boots and a short, double-breasted jacket—the clothes of a country gentleman. He carries a hunting rifle and binoculars and wears an ammunition belt. (Bogdan obviously had obtained the special permission from the Germans required for Poles to have guns or ammunition of any sort; it was usually given only to persons in the country who needed it to hunt.)

Maria looks very alive and happy in the photos with Bogdan. The broad smile I know so well lights up her whole face. In some pictures, her hair is long and dark, though pulled back from her face; in others, she wears it piled on top of her head. One photo in particular conveys the nature of their relationship. Maria and Bogdan are sitting very close together on a brick wall somewhere in the countryside or in a city park; their bodies touch. Their faces are inches apart, as Bogdan leans in protectively. They are smiling as they gaze into one another's eyes.

"He would describe the estate they owned in northern Pomerania and how eventually we would be there together. He gave me a ring, and I gave him a ruby ring that had belonged to my mother, although we were not formally engaged." On long walks together, they discussed the underground, in which they were both involved. "I would get some ammunition for his unit, bullets. He would tell me where to go, and I would deliver it to him either in the country or keep it until he came to get it himself. In his letters, he would ask 'Did you get the toys for my son?' This meant, 'Did you get the new delivery of bullets for my gun?'" At age 19, Maria had fallen in love.

Bogdan's older sister was an attorney in Warsaw, and Bogdan would come in to the city to see her and visit Maria. He visited her family, and there were "uncomfortable dinners with my parents," she says. "At least, he felt uneasy the first time, because he knew he was being judged, whether he was a proper match for me. And I felt uneasy, because I wanted him to like my family as well. Sometimes he would pick me up from school and we would walk along Nowy Swiat or go to a café to a performance by a popular singer. Sometimes he would come with other young people from the estate."

On one such occasion, in the fall of 1943, when Maria was 20, they hosted a party at the apartment on Foksal. There were four boys, Maria, her best friend Krystyna, Ninka, and some others. It was Sunday, and Maria was supposed to go to a birthday party with her parents but asked to be excused. Her parents agreed, on condition that the young people behave themselves during their absence. They were not to dance because the country was in mourning. Maria said they would play bridge, and her parents left.

The boys had brought alcohol with them. Everyone drank some, even 16-year-old Ninka. Preparing to set the table, Maria asked Ninka to go to the dining room and get silverware from the huge chest that contained her mother's trousseau, including the monogrammed silver. This was during a period when the Germans had turned off all the electricity to the neighborhood, so Ninka took a candle in a holder. Suddenly Maria heard screams from her sister. When she and Bogdan ran into the dining room, they saw flames; the heavy drapes by the glass door to the balcony were on fire. Bogdan grabbed the huge, heavy drapes and put out the fire, but they were already half destroyed.

The most unfortunate part of this incident was that the drapes were the only household furnishing that belonged not to Maria's mother but to Stefania, her stepmother, and it was Ninka who had set them on fire. After all the guests had departed, Ninka got drunk. She started to dance with an umbrella, saying "Andrew and George love me, and they will bring flowers when I die." The cook/maid was laughing at her. Maria took Ninka to the bathroom and poured cold water over her head, hoping she would act sober when their parents returned.

When Wacław and Stefania came back, Maria met them at the door, saying, "Please, Daddy, don't get excited." They were shocked when they saw the dining room, and it was clear that her stepmother was very angry about the drapes. It was hard to find a place in wartime Warsaw that could repair such a luxury item. They searched the city for some time but ultimately found a place that could do so. The incident did not improve the relationship between Ninka and her stepmother.

Shortly after Christmas 1943, Bogdan's older sister came to Maria's parents and formally invited Maria, in the name of their parents, to visit them on the estate. Maria's father agreed, and she set off, accompanied by the sister. The train was packed; people were squashed into the corridors. A group was singing, accompanied by an accordion. Maria was worried because she didn't have the right documents—she still had no employment card. When they reached the station, soldiers entered the train. The whole station was surrounded. The Germans were checking documents, arresting some people and taking them away. Maria thought to herself, "It looks like it's the end of me."

Quick thinking again saved the day, this time on the part of Bogdan's sister. There were Germans stationed in the manor house at the estate where Bogdan's father was living and working. His sister spotted one of the soldiers who lived there and quickly went to talk to him. He agreed to smuggle Maria out of the station, and promptly did so. Maria had escaped yet another time.

Maria stayed at the estate for two weeks. The guestroom in which she was staying was off the living room. Next to that were the Germans' quarters. They also came into the living room from time to time. One day Bogdan was in Maria's room, where they were cleaning and loading a rifle, when a German came in. Unusually, he knocked before opening the door. "We managed to hide the gun under the bedspread. I jumped on Bogdan's knee to pretend we were making love so that he would not check the room." The soldier was embarrassed and withdrew quickly. On another occasion, Bogdan and Maria hid guns they were working on in the water jug the maid brought to the room each day (there was no indoor plumbing). It was, of course, strictly prohibited for them to have these weapons, which were by no means covered by Bogdan's hunting exemption.

Maria and Bogdan remained close from 1942 until they were separated by the Warsaw Uprising in 1944. She took his picture with her into exile when the city fell in October. Bogdan survived the war, but Maria never saw or talked to him again. She did learn from his sister that he got married and became an administrator at one of the old estates in the north of Poland after it had been turned into a collective farm by the Communists.

CHAPTER 6

Interlude

It took more than ten hours of interviews at Maria's house, over a period of three months, for me to learn about her early life and the wartime period before the Uprising. By May 2002, we were ready to begin talking about her experiences during the Warsaw Uprising. I was keen to do so, because I had made arrangements to stop over in Warsaw in July, on my way home from work in Africa. I planned to visit the places where Maria had lived and fought, to get a lively visual experience of what might be left of her past. But in the last week of May, I learned that Maria was in the hospital, so sick that she could not have visitors.

After several days, I finally was able to speak to Maria by phone. She was obviously very weak and not ready for visitors. She had been diagnosed with pneumonia of uncertain origin; her doctors were trying a variety of antibiotics but had so far failed to knock out the infection. I stopped by the hospital a few days later, on a Thursday evening. She was in the elegant pavilion Northwestern had recently built. All rooms are private, and have views of Lake Michigan and ample space for visitors, even overnight. Maria's room was filled with flowers from her many friends.

Despite the luxurious surroundings, I found Maria alone and miserable. She kept moaning repeatedly, "Just kill me; I can't take it." She had trouble breathing and was wracked by pain when coughing. I decided to stay with her until her family arrived for their evening visit. Nurses came in and asked her to drink several glasses of barium in preparation for a test that would take place that evening. To my surprise, Maria refused, in a grumpy and tired but determined manner. After some discussion I helped to negotiate with the nurse that she would take the test without barium. I promised to accompany her. I waited just inside the radiology unit, while I pondered the change in Maria. It was understandable that she was without energy, given that she was so sick. But I was astonished by her depression. I had never seen her when she was not full of life and hope. I had never seen her be ungracious to anyone. My heroine of the resistance seemed afraid.

When we got back from the test, Maria's son Andrew and his wife had arrived, so I quickly left. When I called a day or two later to talk, Maria was very apologetic about having been so grumpy and ungracious—as though she had failed in her social duty. I reassured her that I was not offended. In fact, I was quite worried about her. It crossed my mind that the whole project would need to be abandoned, but that didn't concern me so much as the idea that I might lose my new friend.

The following Monday, I visited Maria in the hospital and found her in much better shape. We chatted, and she was obviously delighted to have a visitor. She apologized about how she looked, which I took as a good sign. On Wednesday she was released, but told that she must convalesce for some time. Her older son, Mark, took her to his house in Park Ridge, a suburb, where I visited her a week later. In the meantime we talked on the phone several times. Sometimes she sounded weak and sad, and at other times her bubbly self. I was a little concerned about whether I would be able to get the information I needed before leaving for Africa at the end of June, less than three weeks away.

Before my departure I went to see Maria at Mark's home in Park Ridge. His wife gave me a lemonade and an air conditioned place to sit with Maria—it was a 90-degree day. Taping the interview proved to be impossible because the dog was barking and children were playing in the background. But both of us felt a sense of urgency, so we leaned over a map of Warsaw in my guidebook, and began to talk about those days in August 1944.

CHAPTER 7

The Uprising

By the summer of 1944 the tide seemed to be turning against the Germans. The Allied invasion of France began in June, and by late July the Soviet army entered Polish territory. On July 23, the Germans began to evacuate civilians and administrators from Warsaw, and on July 28, Soviet forces started shelling Praga, a suburb across the Vistula River. Moscow Radio broadcast an appeal to the citizens of Warsaw to rise up against the Germans.

On July 31, 1944, the commander of the AK in Warsaw, General Bor-Komorovski, gave the order that the long-awaited uprising would begin the next day at 5 p.m. The Home Army only had enough arms and ammunition to last for about three days. They expected that the Soviet Army would quickly break through, but wanted to liberate the city before the Soviet troops arrived, thus presenting Stalin with a nationalist government in place.

In fact, Bor-Komorovski's intelligence was faulty, and only one isolated unit of the Soviet army was near the city. A German counterattack soon tied up the Soviets and their guns fell silent. Most historians believe that Stalin never intended to cooperate with the AK, but rather to allow the Germans to destroy the nationalist resistance prior to Soviet entry into Warsaw, clearing the way for the establishment of a Communist puppet state. The Allies, dependent upon the Soviet forces moving from the east for victory over Hitler, did not want to risk alienating Stalin. Thus the Uprising was doomed from the start. As so many times in their history, Poles were the losers in the Realpolitik of the Great Powers.

Nonetheless, on August 1, 1944, the Home Army in Warsaw quickly mobilized. At 5 p.m., attacks on the Nazi occupiers began, with the enthusiastic support of much of the civilian population. In the first few days, the AK took control of large parts of the city, as well as the gas, electric and waterworks. They failed to take the bridges, the airport or the main train station. About 30,000 inadequately armed soldiers faced the Germans. Although British and Polish pilots attempted air drops to supply the city with arms and food, Stalin denied them landing rights in Soviet territory, forcing the planes to travel round trip from Italy, resulting in heavy losses.

The Germans soon regrouped and counterattacked the insurgents, with Luftwaffe air raids, incendiary bombs, and long-range artillery from the opposite bank of the Vistula. Because the regular German army, the Wehrmacht, was tied up fighting the Soviet army to the east, the attack was carried out largely by police and SS units, several of them composed of hardened criminals who were given permission to carry out large-scale attacks on the civilian population. The counter-attack on two districts—Wola and Ochota—in early August forced the AK to withdraw from those areas and was followed by the execution of almost 50,000 Polish civilians there.

After the first week of fighting, the command group of the Home Army moved to Old Town, the beautiful ancient city on the banks of the Vistula, with its winding medieval streets, city walls and castle. From August 19 to September 2, the Germans attacked Old Town, destroying and burning most of its historic buildings. Miraculously, during the nights of August 31 and September 1-2, some 1,500 soldiers and 500 civilians escaped through the sewers to the center of the city, which was still in Polish hands. Old Town fell on September 2, and the Germans turned their attention to the Powisle district to the south, which fell on September 6. Not long after, Bor-Komorovski began talks to negotiate a surrender.

"A week before the Uprising, in late August, I went to a meeting of my unit to be assigned places to stay when it started," Maria says. "The Germans were in disarray and shock after their defeat by the Russians, crossing the Vistula in chaos, but then they reorganized and began calling for 100,000 young people to dig fortifications throughout the city." The Poles of Warsaw did not respond to the German call.

Maria herself was already doubtful about the timing of the Uprising and its chance of success, given the German reorganization and superior force. Nonetheless, the leader of her unit proclaimed, "The Uprising will take place even if it is the wrong time, to cover the pages of history with our blood." Despite her personal misgivings, Maria did as she was told and spent the last week of July in a building on Marshallkowska Street, assigned to an office on the top floor; there were only desks and chairs and no place to hide. As it happened, Renia, a friend of hers, lived one floor below. "My friend's father was in charge of that office and came up; I tried to hide but he found me there," she says. "What are you doing here?" he demanded. "I said that I had to be there." "Then," he said, "you must stay with us." And so Maria spent the last week of August with her friend's family, waiting for the signal that the Uprising was to begin. When Maria did not return at night, her parents knew it was because of her involvement in the AK. When Ninka left for her unit, their father was surprised, however, and said, "Rysia [Maria's nickname] I understand, but you?"

Tuesday, August 1, 1944 was cloudy and humid. Maria's friend Renia was getting married at 11 a.m. in the chapel of a convent not far from the Chmielinskis' home. Early that day, Renia's brother told Maria that the Uprising would begin at 5 p.m. but asked her not to tell his sister lest the knowledge spoil her wedding. So Maria went home from the building on Marshallkowska Street to dress for the wedding. "I changed into a new suit that had been made for me; it had square shoulders, was quite short, above the knee, and had a long, loose jacket." After changing, she went to the wedding.

"At 11," she reports, "during the ceremony, the factory siren went off, as it usually did when a raid was coming, but it was the sign for the underground that the Uprising was to start that day. Just after the service ended, a fellow in an AK communications unit approached me and my close friend Krystyna and said the action was about to start." They skipped the wedding reception and went to their respective homes to pack and change.

When Maria arrived home, her parents were at work and her sister had already gone to her medical unit. It was too dangerous to leave a note, so she told the maid to tell her parents that she had gone. "I changed into sports clothes and ski boots, which helped walking in the debris; my knapsack was all ready." As she walked down the stairs of the apartment building, the caretaker—who the family had always suspected was a Communist or an informer—revealed his support for the AK by asking, "Going so late? My son left two days ago."

Many who were there have described the bustling city on the afternoon of August 1, as people rushed to get to their units, some of them carrying bulky packages with equipment, a feeling of anticipation in the air. As Maria joined these crowds, she stopped at the home of a girlfriend to say goodbye. Then she reported to a building at Mazowiecka No. 4, a large courtyard building with a restaurant on the first floor, in the center of the city, not far from her home.

The unit of 70 girls, including Maria and her best friend Krystyna, gathered on the top floor of this building and awaited further instructions. They did not know what would happen next. If action started, they were trained for a variety of tasks—some as messengers; some even had training as nurses. Maria knew that she was to be in a guard unit, for which she had received training in military procedure and how to handle a gun.

> At five o'clock, as arranged, the main German strongpoints were rushed, infiltrated, or bombarded by groups of dashing young men wearing red-and-white armbands . . . . Soon, the red-and-white banner was waving atop the Prudential Building, the city's tallest. A major German arsenal and storehouse was captured. So, too, were the main post office, the power

station, the railway office in Praga, and wide swathes of the city. The cost was 2,500 lives—80 per cent of them from the Home Army. It was a similar total to that of Allied losses on the Normandy beaches on D-Day.

The girls in Maria's unit could hear the action start at the main Post Office nearby. All night long, German and Polish soldiers fought for possession of the building in which the girls were hiding. It changed hands several times, and the girls could hear German voices on the stairs. They remained quiet to avoid discovery. "Commandant Teresa," Maria tells, "crawled between rooms taking our identity papers and destroying them lest the Uprising fail and the Germans retaliate against our families." In this way Maria lost the papers that established her educational history (a transcript of her courses, exams passed, and professors' signatures). As a result she was unable later in life to get recognition of the fact that she had completed several years of university study.

By morning, the building was in Polish hands. It was raining. The girls went downstairs to look for breakfast, only to discover that the café across the street was in ruins. They were taken by their unit leader to a small square nearby, the Plac Dabrowskiego, and instructed to run, one by one, from the northeast corner of the square, to Szkolna, a street that opens off the southwest corner of the square, to reach the district headquarters of the AK. The Germans shot at each girl as she ran, but miraculously no one was hit. The youngest, Maria recalls, were the most courageous. Maria herself does not remember feeling afraid.

When she reached Szkolna, Maria was assigned to work as a security guard outside the building. She stood four-hour watches, four on, four off, four on and four off, grabbing sleep whenever and wherever she could, generally on the floor. She never slept a whole night through during the 63 days of the Uprising, and never on anything resembling a bed.

At night, big German tanks rolled down Swietokrzyska Street, a boulevard intersecting with Szkolna. It took the Germans some time to discover that tanks were useless in fighting an insurrection in a city with narrow streets. There was simply no room for them to maneuver. Maria's unit threw homemade grenades (bottles with gasoline) at the tanks from their third-floor window. "I don't remember that we destroyed any, though," she reports.

During her four-hour breaks from guard duty, Maria was busy with other tasks. Some days she would go to other parts of Warsaw to get bread or supplies, including arms and ammunition. When she picked up grenades from the "factory" where they were made and carried them back in her knapsack, she was aware that "If a sniper got me, I would really be gone." After the first days of the Uprising, the AK and civilians dug passages that led from the basement of one house to another, so that it was possible to walk underground throughout Warsaw. Trenches were dug in the streets, to afford some protection from snipers. Many civilians moved to the basements of buildings, and many were afraid to come out.

> *After the first week . . . when neither side had gained a decisive advantage, Warsaw became the scene of long, relentless battles of attrition. Every day, usually at dawn, the Germans would return to their chosen sectors like workmen returning to a building site. Unable to dislodge their adversary by standard infantry tactics, they would call up the bombers and the heavy guns, pound the insurgent positions into mounds of rubble, demolish a few barricades, and gain a few yards or a couple of streets. Next morning they would find that half the barricades had been rebuilt during the night and booby-trapped, and that the shattered buildings provided perfect cover for unseen snipers and grenade throwers. In this way, practically every building and cellar had to be fought over time and time again before the Germans could secure a disputed sector.*

Soon after Maria's unit arrived at Szkolna, there was an air raid. Maria was assigned to get everyone out of the building into the basement shelter. She brought up the rear and was only half way down when a bomb hit the building. The blast somehow propelled her into the basement. "I can't explain how I got there, I was just suddenly there. People in the shelter were hysterical—some crying, some praying—because the entrance was covered with rubble, trapping them in." It took more than an hour to dig a way out.

During this period, the center of the city, where Maria was stationed, was largely in the hands of the Poles, though German snipers preyed upon them. Despite all the dangers, "There was a terrific spirit," she remembers. "Catholic services were held in the courtyards. We felt free. We could sing Polish anthems and patriotic songs once again. We didn't know what the future would bring but there were moments of real joy. You could walk around and there were no Germans. The atmosphere was fantastic, after five years of occupation and terror."

Maria, a lifelong practicing Catholic, remembers going to Mass during the Uprising. "I did not attend Mass in church; I attended Mass usually on location, where I was stationed. Priests celebrated Masses in the open air, in courtyards, in the ruins of bombed-out buildings. We didn't have time to go to church. Most of the time you couldn't go far away from your unit; you had to be on the spot or nearby." The upsurge of religious practices and other types of support given to the insurgents and civilians by priests and nuns—food, nursing, sanctuary— undoubtedly contributed to morale.

After the bombing of the building on Szkolna, Maria moved to a seven-story building with a restaurant and night club, the Adria, which stood opposite the Philharmonic Hall. Before the Uprising, it had been used exclusively by Germans.

Important AK units were headquartered there; and Maria's platoon was assigned to stand guard in front. She stood holding a large Russian-made machine gun, checking IDs and demanding a password. During her breaks, she took turns guarding German prisoners in the basement of a nearby building and helped to take care of the wounded POWs.

After a while, water became scarce, and wells were dug here and there. Sometimes Maria would be assigned ten German POWs with buckets to take to the wells and bring back water for the soldiers. She would walk behind them—all five feet of her—with a big French rifle from World War I that had to be reloaded after each shot. "I must've looked very comical," she muses. "I prayed that there would be no raids during this time, because they could easily attack me. People took pictures of me during the Uprising because I looked so funny—so small and such a big gun."

While Maria was working at the Adria, the mother of Renia, the friend who was married on August 1, came by one day to ask for help; she and a friend needed to go somewhere but didn't have the proper identification. "When I got off work, I took them. We were walking toward the Plac Napoleon [an immense open square southeast of the Adria] when the German heavy artillery started to attack. It came from a train that was outside Warsaw. It was called the 'cow' because it made a noise like a cow before it would go off. There were two kinds, one burning everything; the other would explode into small pieces. I was walking with these two ladies near the Plac Napoleon and could hear it. I said 'We need to turn back.' At that moment it started to fall on us, the kind that burns things; people burned by it would be purple. I got in between the two ladies, took their arms and started to run. The street was uneven, there was so much debris. We could feel the heat coming. The mother of my girlfriend said 'Leave us. We will not make it.' But I said 'no' and pulled them and we got out. I saw my friend's mother years later and she remembered that I saved her life."

By late August, the parts of Warsaw controlled by the AK began to contract substantially.

> *The decision to evacuate the Old Town had been taken during the night of 25/26 August after seven days of constant bombardments and massed attacks. The armed defenders had been reduced from 8,000 to 1,500. The first stage was to bring out the AK Command and Government authorities through a previously unused sewer, which started only 200 metres (650 feet) from the German positions and passed directly underneath them. The second stage was to mount a flurry of local counter-attacks to divert the Germans and to cover the exodus of the Home Army's main detachments. The third stage was to extract the rearguard Parasol Battalion. Each stage was executed on successive nights from 31 August to 2 September.*

Old Town fell to the Germans while Maria was stationed at the Adria, and people escaped through the sewers to the city center, where Maria was. Maria remembers, "A friend of mine, Janusz, who had been in the school of commerce and economics with me, came to the Adria where we were stationed. He said 'I came through the sewers. I want to get home to tell them I survived Old Town.' His family was in a different part of the city, on the other side of Jerozolimskie [Jerusalem Boulevard]. 'They wouldn't let me through, told me to try at night after dark but in the meantime I sent notices through girl messengers to my family.' He spent the day with us, then when it was getting darker he walked out. I was on duty, standing in front of the Adria. Half an hour after he left, our sanitary patrol arrived with stretchers. Janusz had been hit by a sniper while crossing Marshallkowska and had been killed on the spot." He survived the siege of Old Town only to die trying to show his family that he was safe.

Most of the time she was a guard at the Adria, Maria slept there as well, on two chairs pushed together or on the floor of an unused room. The building was older and very sturdy, so that if one portion caught fire another area might still be safe. At the end of August or in early September, however, the building was hit by a shell larger than Maria (at another point she describes it as larger than her coffee table). The Germans were apparently aiming at the Philharmonic building across the street. "I was in the cafeteria in the basement. It went across the building at a slant and didn't explode so few were killed, but the electricity and thus the lights went off and the air was full of dust and the smell of ammonia. We had to move in case more hit. They took the whole garrison of us to a small courtyard. There was heavy action, trying to hit the Philharmonia. We were standing there for an hour, next door to the Philharmonia, where the bombs were coming down, waiting to see what would happen. If one bomb hit us, the unexploded bomb would go off, and all of us would go up in the air."

After the raid, the AK brought in German POWs from a technical unit to defuse the unexploded shell. "They were afraid to touch it, and it took them quite a few days to disarm it. Then we took the insides out and used it for our homemade ammunition," Maria says. A short while after the Adria was damaged, Maria moved to quarters on Szpitalna, to the south of the Plac Napoleon, but continued her guard duty at the Adria.

As more and more buildings were bombed, the face of the city changed. Maria recalls, "During the Uprising, there were more and more ruins. The city was falling down gradually. The Germans were destroying it in a logical way, place by place, area by area. It became very hard to walk. When I was walking with Renia's mother and her friend, we had to walk up and down on debris." People who had been in buildings that were bombed were covered with ash, gray ghosts.

For one entire week, Maria was assigned to lie down all day in the Plac Napoleon with a large arrow made of a Polish flag. At that time, the square was a large open space surrounded by late 19th century buildings, along with Warsaw's one skyscraper, the Prudential building. From where Maria lay, she could see that the Prudential building was heavily damaged by bombs. Her task was to move the large arrow whenever the wind changed to show any Allied planes seeking to drop supplies the direction of the wind at the ground. "Whenever I got up to change wind directions, the Germans would shoot at me. They were not far away, at the old Post Office [on the southeast corner of the square], and could see me." But no Allied planes ever came during the week Maria lay there.

On September 6, after six weeks with only one brief visit, Maria got a 24-hour pass to go the few blocks to her home. As more and more buildings in the city were destroyed by bombs, the refugees doubled up elsewhere. Many more persons were now staying in the apartment on Foksal. Maria's mattress and box-springs had been separated to accommodate them. When Maria and her friend Krystyna arrived at 2 a.m., Maria's father was upset by the lack of available beds and asked "How will you sleep?" But Maria was not troubled. She could no longer sleep on a bed; it was too soft for her after weeks of sleeping on the floor.

Nor was there much sleep that night, or the following day. There were constant air raids. The Powisle district lay directly to the east. "The whole day was bad," Maria says, "because that part of Warsaw was to be taken by the end of the day. There was a lot of activity, the battle was going on. So everyone in the house was going up and down to the basement shelter. It was up and down every two minutes. When it was dusk, we looked through the front window. The streets were full of people, five abreast, running away from the Germans, who were pushing them from the lower part of Warsaw."

In the midst of this activity, Maria's Aunt Nina was nonetheless making a big dinner, with food left over from what she had brought from the country. The table was stretched out with extra leaves, and many people were sitting around it when the maid brought in two steaming platters of pierogis (stuffed dumplings) with strawberry preserves inside. At that very moment, however, "a young attorney who had worked with my father at the city legal office came in and said 'I am commandant of the barricade going through Nowy Swiat [which was between Maria's home and her station]; we're not letting people through.' He said he would let us [Maria and Krystyna] through because we were soldiers going to our unit, but we must come right away. So I had to leave without even tasting the pierogi. Now I'd take some with me, but I was in such a hurry and so well brought up!"

As Maria rushed out, she stopped to hug and kiss her father. There was no time to say anything but good-bye. As they embraced, she had a feeling it was the last time. That part of Warsaw fell to the Germans the next day, and Maria had no way of knowing what had happened to her family. But as she left, all she could think about was the pierogi.

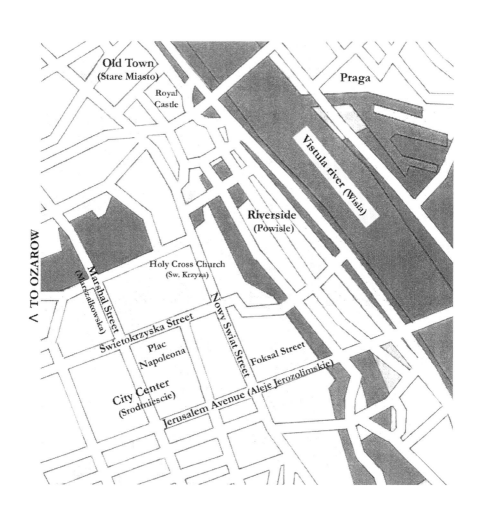

CHAPTER 8

The Surrender

After the AK began surrender negotiations in early September, the Soviet Union belatedly started to assist the beleaguered city. Polish and Soviet troops reached the Vistula by September 13. The Soviets also began air drops to the city and agreed to give landing rights to the Allied forces. A massive Allied air drop took place on September 18, but by that time so little of the city was still in Polish hands that most of the supplies landed in German zones. The Germans destroyed the bridges across the Vistula, and a valiant Polish-Soviet attempt to cross the river failed. But the attempts at assistance from outside breathed new life into the resistance fighters, who withdrew from the surrender negotiations and fought on for another two weeks. By the end of September, however, the areas in Polish hands were without electricity, water and gas, and both the soldiers and civilians were starving.

On September 30, General Bor-Komorovski ordered a surrender and arranged for a ceasefire to evacuate civilians from the city. Further negotiations resulted in an agreement that the AK would be treated as a regular army, as they had been by the Allies. This was a vital point, as it entitled AK fighters to the protections of the Geneva Convention. In early October 11,688 soldiers of the Home Army—all that remained of the initial 30,000—marched out of the city, surrendered their weapons, and became German prisoners of war. The remaining civilian population was evacuated from the city. Many were sent either to forced labor camps in Germany or to concentration camps in Poland.

In the two months of the Uprising, at least 200,000 residents of Warsaw died—an incredible 3,000 for each day of the fighting. Most of the city was destroyed. What was left was systematically dynamited, burned, and bulldozed by Hitler's specific order. The Soviet Army entered the ruined and deserted city on January 17, 1945.

In his history of World War II, Winston Churchill included this translation of the Homeland Council's final appeal:

> *. . . May God, Who is just, pass judgement on the terrible injustice suffered by the Polish nation, and may He punish accordingly all those who are guilty.*

Your heroes are the soldiers whose only weapons against tanks, planes, and guns were their revolvers and bottles filled with petrol . . . . Your heroes are the women who tended the wounded, cooked in bombed and ruined cellars to feed children and adults, and who soothed and comforted the dying. Your heroes are the children who went on quietly playing among the smouldering ruins. These are the people of Warsaw.

Immortal is the nation that can muster such universal heroism. For those who have died have conquered, and those who live on will fight on, will conquer and again bear witness that Poland lives when the Poles live.

By the time of Maria's last visit home, on September 6-7, the area controlled by the AK was rapidly constricting. Returning across Nowy Swiat, Maria and Krystyna were told to go immediately to the front line, which was then at Kredytowa Street, not far north. "We walked past two-story-high debris to get there; the ruins of houses were all around. People were being killed. As we reached the front, we were passing fellows on stretchers who had been wounded at the front. My heart was crying. I tried not to look at them."

Maria and Krystyna were assigned to cook for those on the front line, which was perhaps 50 yards away. "There were two brick stones with a small fire and huge vats, normally used to boil laundry, full of dry beans. I went to find wood in the debris for the fire. I didn't know how to cook, though Krystyna knew a little more. We did know that you usually soak dry beans overnight. But they weren't soaked, and the officers kept coming and screaming 'Why is dinner not ready? The boys are hungry!' We were guards, not cooks; they just presumed we'd know what to do."

At Kredytowa, Maria and Krystyna slept together in a basement on the uncovered springs of a bed. "They would get into your back," she remembers. "There were people around, one candle stuck into the wall, and one crazy cadet officer who was in shock after being wounded; he would constantly play the same song on an old gramophone, manually turning it. 'Tango Marina,' over and over." She describes all this with a smile, but it must have been like being trapped in some flickering absurdist nightmare.

With the area under AK control diminishing, travel around even the city center became treacherous. As another veteran describes:

The streets had become no-go areas . . . .

I could often only walk in a crouching position. But at the end of each block I had to emerge into the open, at times in plain view of German tanks. Bent in half, I had to run across the road making the best use of the flimsy protection offered by low barricades. Hence what in normal times would have been a thirty-minute walk along pleasant streets had become a perilous endeavour taking several hours.

The greatest hazard was crossing Marshal Street, the capital's main thoroughfare. It was some thirty metres wide, and intense German fire was repeatedly wrecking the two barricades erected across it. Constructed of paving stones, rubble, tram carriages, furniture, and anything to hand, the barricades were not strong enough to withstand the ceaseless cannonade. As I came out of a basement I took a deep breath, jack-knifed as low as I could, and dashed across.

After a few days, Maria and Krystyna were sent back to their unit, to transfer materials stored there to the south side of Jerozolimskie Street, because the area to the north was clearly going to fall into German hands soon. They were very thirsty, and when they discovered a bottle of red wine, they promptly drank it. They were to move the materials across the street after it became dark. "We then went to where we were to cross the large street under constant shelling. There was a ditch dug so you were a bit lower when you walked through so it was less likely snipers would get you, but we were sticking out. They were shooting from both sides, and it was quite dangerous. We were moving slowly since there were so many people and sniper activity. It was a beautiful warm night, like August; the sky was full of stars and moonshine. In the middle of the trip across, we had to stop a while because we were in the middle of a slow-moving crowd passing through. Perhaps there was too much shooting to let us out at the other end. I promptly fell asleep because of having drunk the wine on an empty stomach. Someone had to kick me to start again."

When the two reached the other side, their unit commander, Teresa, sent them to Mokotowska Street, about ten or twelve blocks south of the front. Space was scarce there because civilians from other parts of the city that had already fallen to the Germans fled to the city center, which was severely overcrowded. So Maria and Krystyna were told to stay with anyone they knew and to return at 8:30 the next morning. It was still comparatively peaceful in this section of Warsaw. Maria took Krystyna and her friend Nola, who had been with them since they crossed into the new district, to the small apartment of a newly married friend whose husband was out fighting. She was still living nicely and couldn't understand why they were so fearful. The four women slept crosswise together on a large divan bed.

The next day the Germans began to attack that part of Warsaw as well. Their hostess, who had mocked them the previous day for their fear, was in the shower when a bomb fell nearby. She was so shaken that she rushed out of the shower naked—into the arms of a major who was sharing the house with her!

"This was probably the last day they had water for showers," Maria says. "The water station was then bombed."

At Mokotowska, the members of the unit would report daily and be sent off on a variety of missions in different parts of town. The night after arriving, Maria was instructed to go back across Jerozolimskie to take messages into the area of heavy fighting. During the Uprising, Maria was generally very calm, never showing her feelings. This was an unusually difficult moment for her, however. After a very stressful period as a cook at the front line, she had reached an area of the city that was relatively peaceful and felt safe. "It was hard after relaxing for a day to return to hell. I forced myself to get up and go at 5 a.m., when it was daylight yet still comparatively calm, and did it really fast. Soon after it started to be bad in the other [southern] part of town as well."

Maria also went back to pick up her knapsack on Marshallkowska. Walking back in a ditch, she suddenly felt something warm on her neck. Just above the ditch, a man was urinating. Maria continued to walk, crying with rage; there was no way to wash. She remembers this incident, rather than the snipers, bombs, and deaths of friends, as one of the lowest points of the Uprising. It is as if she could only allow herself to feel what she could handle. All the deaths and the destruction of her native city were too much to process then, and maybe still.

> *Few historians have cared to describe the shocking state of affairs that prevailed in the Warsaw district in the last two weeks of September. In the centre of the city, on the perimeters of three shrinking enclaves still controlled by the Home Army, fierce fighting with German forces persisted day by day, as the lot of the surviving civilians went from very bad to terminal.*

As the days wore on, conditions became harder for both insurgents and civilians. There was no food. Maria tells of one three-day period during which she had nothing but ersatz coffee and sugar cubes. "Later," she says, "all the city was spitting because all we had was barley. But it was not properly cleaned so there was stuff covering it; it was so hard that when you ate it, you ended up with so much of this stuff you couldn't swallow that you had to go and spit. We also ate wheat with grains that were large and yellowish, but so hard to chew that after you ate half a meal, your jaw hurt."

"Towards the second part of the Uprising, people were getting stomach problems. Many had diarrhea, and I eventually got it too. How was I to function as a guard? I told a woman who was a unit commandant about my problem, and she said to go upstairs where there was vodka and blueberry syrup, to drink a glass made up of half and half. I did this, but the woman was wrong. It wasn't vodka; it was 100% pure alcohol. I took a mouthful and could barely breathe. It choked me; I saw a sky full of stars. But it did cure the diarrhea."

By now, of course, "civilized" hygiene was impossible. Maria wore an outfit like a gymsuit and, when she washed, had to pull the whole outfit off. "I prayed that no bomb would hit me while I was undressed. We had to go into the ruins to use the 'john'."

By September 12, the food situation was dire, and Maria's unit was sent to Czerniakow (southeast of the city center) to bring back any supplies that were left in storage there, as that area was already under fire. Maria left with the group at night. "Everything was on fire," she remembers, "but I knew my sister was in that part of Warsaw, so I got permission to separate after I got my load to carry back (a 20-pound can of tomatoes and a rifle). Krystyna and I would return by ourselves. I found my sister taking care of the wounded in an underground hospital and begged her to join my unit since the end was approaching. She promised she would come the next day but never did." That part of the city fell to the Germans soon after, and Maria had no way to know what had become of her sister.

On the way back that night, Maria and Krystyna walked slowly, so close to the German lines that they could hear the Germans speaking. A Polish cadet with his hand in a sling was with them. "He said to me, 'Little one, you are small, you go first.' So I did, walking quietly so the Germans would not hear, walking up and down, with debris all around. We had to practically crawl, with my load of canned tomatoes in one hand and in the other hand a World War I carbine. Suddenly we turned left, going through the ruins of a house where there was a huge storage space. We could hear someone moving. There were two men. Our cadet officer asked them the password for the day. They did not know it. The cadet said to take them as prisoners, which I did. On the way back we got into the basement of a movie house that was flooded and had to pull them out. When it was daylight, we went to headquarters and delivered the prisoners. We were sitting at the entrance when someone came and screamed at us 'Why did you take them as prisoners; they are officers!' We replied 'The cadet told us to.' 'He is a fake!' they yelled. We ran quickly away." Such confusion was not unusual during this period of the Uprising.

There was still one high point left: the Allied air drops on September 18.

> *On 18 September 1944, a huge fleet of Flying Fortresses of the US 8th Army Air Force flew from Britain to supply Warsaw . . . . When the Flying Fortresses passed over Warsaw around 2 p.m., they certainly created a grand spectacle. They were accompanied by sixty fighter escorts. The sky was a perfect blue. The planes were in wide-spaced formation, flying at a great height 'as if on parade'. The silver fuselages glinted in the sun. The engines left multistranded spirals of white vapour trails. A rhythmic roar shook the buildings far below, punctuated by the popping of AA guns. Suddenly, the*

sky was filled with a mass of multicoloured parachutes, slowly descending,
swaying in the breeze. On either side of the barricades, German troops and
insurgents watched in amazement.

Maria was among those amazed at the sight as several hundred planes came to drop food and ammunition for the insurgents. She recalls, "It was a beautiful sunny day. We went up on to the roof of a building near my girlfriend's house to watch. The whole sky was covered with parachutes, like umbrellas raining down on us. It was very pretty. But they didn't have the right information about the wind, and the Germans were all around, interspersed with us, so a lot went into German hands." Yet Poles who were in Warsaw on that day remember this event with joy, as a sign that they had not been forgotten by the rest of the world.

"Fifty years later, when I was with Vice President Gore's delegation, I met this little American guy who had been a war hero, a fighter pilot. We had our picture taken together, because he was up in the air that day and I was down. Later I went to a big surprise party for him at the Conrad Hilton [in Chicago]; the Polish consul came and decorated him with the cross of the Uprising. He had shot down eight Germans in one day, forty altogether."

The September 18th air drop was one of the last moments of hope for the insurgents. "We knew it was a lost cause," says Maria. "We had no food. The civilians were starving too. There was little ammunition. We listened to information from the west. Paris was liberated in a few days, but there was no end in sight for our fight. We realized the Allies could not reach us in time. We knew we couldn't hold on long after the Old City fell."

The deaths continued. One member of Maria's unit was killed toward the beginning of the Uprising, and Maria's unit commander Teresa was killed just before the end. "She was a nice woman," Maria remembers, "very aristocratic, a countess. Good-looking, slim, tall, very sporty-looking. Her son lost his leg during the Uprising; he was maybe 17 years old. Her husband and daughter got to Rome somehow. She was killed, and I was at her funeral just before the ceasefire. The funeral was held in the street. People would dig graves wherever there was loose ground. All over, on walls and streets, you would see plaques, wreaths, and votive candles." The resistance fighters took pains, even in the chaos of the Uprising, to honor their dead. With their long history of oppression, they must have understood, at some deep level, that such tribute was itself an act of resistance.

Bodies buried temporarily in the streets were eventually transferred from those spots after the war. Eva, a girlfriend and neighbor of Maria's who had just graduated from the school of medicine, was killed near the end of the Uprising. "She was one of the group eventually buried in the military part of Powazki Cemetery, the beautiful old cemetery that used to be on the outskirts of town [it is now surrounded by the city], in a separate section from where my parents' graves are. There is a section where the insurgents of the Uprising are buried, under crosses made out of birch trees. There are several rows of young people from the Uprising. I usually take flowers for her when I go. If you go there on August 1, there are lights from hundreds of votive candles."

The AK made one last desperate attempt to connect with the Soviet-Polish troops on the other side of the Vistula in the last part of September. With all the bridges gone, it was truly a desperate attempt. The forces coming from the East were unaccustomed to urban guerrilla warfare and given inadequate support by the Soviets. The result was a massive loss of life: 4,938 dead in the eight-day battle for the Cherniakov Bridgehead. Norman Davies comments that "The desperate scenes on the Vistula beaches on 23 September may be likened to the death-laden chaos which would have occurred in Normandy if the German defenders had stood their ground." After the failure of this effort, it was clear to the AK commanders that surrender was necessary.

> *"Further fighting has no sense. It's madness. Politically, we have achieved a great deal. Yet, since we have not received the assistance expected, we should save what is most dear to us, namely, the biological substance of the nation. This is all the more important because the whole cultural and scientific elite of society is concentrated in Warsaw. We won't be able to salvage much from the fabric of the capital, which as Gen. von dem Bach assures us, will become the scene of battles between the Germans and the Soviets. So we should aim to save our people at least. I am in favour of ending the struggle."* (September 28, 1944 speech by Chief Government Delegate)

"We knew that a ceasefire was coming," Maria says. "There was no food, no ammunition. I don't remember the announcement itself." But suddenly the guns were silent. It was strangely quiet, and people began to come out of the basements. "It was a funny feeling that you could walk through the streets, not have to go to an underground passage. People were around again. Everyone was talking about what to do, what to take with them, since it had been announced that the city would be evacuated." Despite asking friends for news of her family, Maria could not find out what had happened to them. The part of the city where they had been was in German hands.

"What I do remember was when it was announced over loud speakers that the Allies considered us a regular army and the Germans accepted that." Maria felt great relief that the AK would be treated as regular soldiers, eligible for the protections given to prisoners of war under the Geneva Conventions, and would be handed over to the Wehrmacht, not to the Gestapo and sent to concentration camps. "Civilian women would try to buy my ID card and AK armband in the street because they would prefer to go to a POW camp in Germany." Women soldiers, however, were given the option of leaving Warsaw with the POWs or with the civilians, so Maria had to reach a decision whether to leave her homeland. If she left with the civilians, she could stay in Poland and perhaps find her family, but she did not trust the Germans to treat former AK members well.

She talked to friends as she struggled with her decision. Some tried to induce her to stay in Poland. "A nice young piano teacher friend offered to take me along with her family; later I found out that she had been sent to a concentration camp and died there." The person who was of most help to her was an old family friend who had been the director of a Polish merchant shipping line before the war, and was then a high-ranking delegate of the Polish government in exile. The AK had chosen him to represent the Poles in the civilian camps after the Germans announced that the city would be evacuated; he was assigned to help administer the camp for civilians at Pruszkow. The Germans had guaranteed safety for his wife and daughter, and he offered to take Maria with them, saying that she was his niece, but admitted that it might not work. "He was the only one who put concretely in front of me what to expect if I were to go to a POW camp. He described what it would be like—behind barbed wire, underfed, cold, told what to do. He wanted to make sure I understood when I made up my mind."

But the decision could only be made alone. Maria lay awake all night trying to decide what to do. "The night was hell. I was trying to weigh the pro's and con's. I was worried about my sister. I felt responsible, but I did not know if she were alive since it was weeks since I saw her and her section had fallen. I was worried about my father, who was old and had emphysema. I didn't know what had happened to any of my family, whether they were alive, whether it was worth staying. To be behind barbed wire would not be fun. But if I went with the civilians, there was a chance I would be recognized as AK. I didn't trust the Germans not to send me to a concentration camp, and that would be much worse. Should I go to a POW camp where there would be Wehrmacht instead of Gestapo? I was afraid of the Russians and wanted to get to the west. I knew that if the Communists took me to Russia, there was a very small chance of getting out alive. If I went to Germany, there was always a chance to get out and be in the civilized world. I finally decided to stay with my unit."

Maria's godfather's wife was still in the part of Warsaw where Maria was and helped her prepare for the journey. She gave her a light fur coat for the winter. Maria took only a knapsack with her, a pair of leather ski boots, a pair of warm socks, a jumpsuit, a skirt and blouse. And, she says, "I got a change of underwear from a friend; I knew it was important so as not to get lice." Her unit was ordered to report to the intersection of Szpitalna and Zgoda Streets on October 5th to surrender.

On that day, Maria's unit assembled at the appointed spot, and the Germans escorted them out of the city. "We were walking four in a line with Germans posted on the sides, marching though Warsaw toward the west. We went to the university student housing complex, which was in ruins, and had to deposit all our arms. From there we walked through the streets toward Ozarow, a town outside of Warsaw."

Other observers and participants have described the emotional departure of the Polish insurgents from Warsaw on that day, among them Stefan Korbonski, a leader of the Polish underground:

> Bor [and his] staff were already at the head of the column. Fifty yards away . . . stood the motionless Germans with rifles at the ready, watching the deep ranks of the Home Army. The day was cold and I felt sad. I again shook hands with many friends, wishing them good luck and receiving similar wishes. At last, all the men in the column bared their heads, and the stirring words of the national anthem, 'Poland shall never perish', rose into the air. All eyes were wet, and voices quivered with emotion. The ranks moved forward . . . those young boys and girls, marching with soldierly bearing, their faces set in stony immobility. The muse of history was soaring above that column.

With this proud group Maria marched into captivity on October 5, 1944, leaving the city where she had spent the first 21 years of her life. Only her friend Krystyna accompanied her from the past into whatever future lay ahead.

Maria and Bogdan, her first boyfriend, Warsaw

Maria (far right) and girls from her unit on pass during the Warsaw Uprising

CHAPTER 9

Prisoner of War

The AK soldiers marching out of Warsaw after the city's surrender finally reached Ozarow, a long 20 miles away. Many were injured or sick; and all of them were exhausted and starving after their long ordeal. "We stopped to rest once in a while," Maria says, "once next to a field of tomatoes. They let us in to get them. I had never tasted anything so good. For 63 days, we never had anything fresh to eat. It tasted like heavenly fruit."

A factory in Ozarow was used as a transfer point for the POWs before their journey into Germany. By the time Maria and Krystyna arrived, it was already very crowded. Civilians were gathered by the barbed wire fence that surrounded the soldiers, and Maria, resourceful as ever, took the opportunity to throw a note over the fence. The farm her father owned was close by, and she hoped that the farmer who rented it would get word to her family that she had left Warsaw alive. The farmer apparently came by with provisions for Maria the next day, according to a girlfriend who was still there, but Maria had already gone.

On the next day, October 6, Maria went to the other building at the factory to look for friends. "Everyone there was red like beets in their faces," she says. "Some chemical in storage made them look that way." Krystyna, with whom she had gone to school and been with during the entire Uprising, was her only close friend there. Maria knew other members of her unit, of course, but only from drills in small groups prior to the Uprising. Krystyna's sister was in another unit, and the sisters wanted to go to a POW camp together. So Maria and Krystyna went to the commander of that unit and explained; he allowed them to transfer to the other unit, which left for the west at 2 p.m. "We couldn't even say goodbye to our own unit; everyone was packed in there like sardines."

The cattle car transporting the girls to Germany was supposed to hold six cows; there were sixty girls in it. They could sit, but not stretch out their legs. The journey took two days, as the train would stop to let military transport go by. A couple of times a day, it would also stop so that the prisoners could go off into a field to relieve themselves, while the German soldiers watched. The trains were made up of alternate cars of women and men, and the rest stops also alternated between women and men.

Maria had with her a scout knife her father had bought her; she managed to make a small hole in the wall of the cattle car with it so she could see out. When they got to Częstochowa, she could tell where she was. Some civilians came to the car and pushed tomatoes through the hole to the girls inside. Toward evening, they could hear heavy planes, bombers, probably the British or Polish air force. Reaching Opole, a city then in Germany but now in Poland, the girls could hear people outside the train being told to go to shelters. Heavy bombardment followed, but luckily the train was not hit. Maria began looking for her ski boots, which she had taken off and could not find in the dark. When someone asked why, she said "If they hit our train, maybe we can run away; it's easier to run in boots."

In the cattle car, Maria remembers, "Some were praying, some were singing. Some were crying, some laughing. When the rumor spread that we were going to Auschwitz, and during the bombing of Opole, all I could hear was crying and praying. But we had to face whatever was coming. We knew it was the end and were hoping that the war would end soon."

Just as the sun was coming up on a Sunday morning, they were unloaded in a little forest. A rumor quickly spread throughout the group of prisoners that they were at Auschwitz, that the Germans had not complied with the terms of the ceasefire agreement and had taken them to the death camp. Many started to cry. As they began to walk the miles to the camp, they did not know where they were. Finally, they passed a hill where there were some civilians being evacuated from Warsaw, who told them that it was not Auschwitz.

The POWs walked first through hills then out into empty fields, where there were three camps with thousands of prisoners, all surrounded by barbed wire. Maria's group was put in a camp with three small barracks, in which there were 2,000 or 3,000 women. Male prisoners were separated from them by barbed wire, with guardposts in between and German soldiers patrolling. Many of the women prisoners smoked, so they put notes into matchboxes and threw them over to the men. "It made the Germans mad; they tried to catch them. I don't know why they wouldn't let us just talk to them." This POW camp, or stalag,* was not far from Opole, in a town then called Lamsdorf (it is now Polish and is called Lambinowice).

There were French prisoners at Lamsdorf who had been there a long time. The representative of the Polish prisoners arranged for Maria and her friend Barbara Matuszewicz to meet with them briefly. Barbara was four or five years

* Stalag is short for "Stammlager," the German word for these camps.

older than Maria and had been in the university before the war; she had attended the Lycée Francaise in Warsaw and spoke perfect French. "We met by the barbed wire. We said, 'Don't worry, the war will be over soon.' They said, 'We have been here five years; after a year you'll get used to it.' We couldn't imagine this. We were sure it would be a matter of weeks."

The barracks were one-story wooden buildings with windows at each end. The interior side walls were entirely taken up by sleeping platforms. There were three levels of these shelf-like platforms, with a little straw on them. They slept, Maria says, "packed in like sardines. I was on the bottom, next to a woman my mother's age who was with her three daughters. She looked at me and asked if I had a mother who had attended such and such a school and whose name was Jadwiga. She had recognized me from my resemblance to my mother! She was a character, very intelligent but very tense and nervous. She was also a vegetarian and even in the camps would not let her daughters eat any meat or fish. We called her 'Mama Wisła,' or 'Mother Vistula' and her three daughters the 'tributaries' because they were always with her."

Now that Krystyna's sister, Nina, was with them, the two wanted to be together, so Maria bunked with Barbara, who had been in Nina's unit. "Barbara was extremely intelligent, very clever, and had a great sense of humor. After the war she went to France and got a Ph.D. in economics from the University of Lille. She was the oldest, so we treated her as the head of our little 'family' in the camp." Maria's new "family" consisted of five members: Krystyna, Nina, Barbara, Nola, and herself. "Nola was with us ever since the day we were moved across the Allee to Mokotowska and stayed at my girlfriend's apartment just before the end. Although she hadn't been in the unit with us, she managed to get an ID card when the city was evacuated and to leave with us at Ozarow. Nola was full of fun, like her Russian mother."

Conditions in the camp were hard. Maria reports that "The food was scarce and horrible—some potatoes, a soup of sorts, something like turnips that you usually feed animals with, something that was supposed to be tea but we used it to wash with instead since it was awful but our only warm liquid." There was no particular routine in this first camp, apart from the daily roll call and the distribution of food in big containers. The prisoners ate either in the barracks or outside; the weather was good enough that the food was often distributed outside.

The latrine was in a wooden building outside the barracks; it consisted of one long shelf with holes in it. "You had to be careful not to fall in. There was a story that one Italian died by slipping inside. There was no toilet paper or privacy. The Germans told us all to give them our money. Each one just gave a few notes but saved the bigger (and also more valuable) notes to use as toilet paper since we didn't want to give them to the Germans."

73

Asked what she was feeling during the early days of imprisonment, Maria replies, "I was relieved, I could stop being nervous about the Gestapo getting me." She had lived in fear of this for five years, since she was 16. "And I was happy not to be in the concentration camp. I was worried about what had happened to my family. I tried not to think about the future. Before they moved us further west, I was hoping we'd go back home and everything would be like it was before the war. I didn't realize that the whole of life would be changed."

After the POWs arrived at Lamsdorf, the Germans took pictures of them and requested basic information; then they were given numbers. Maria still remembers hers: POW #107088. Each morning and night, the prisoners had to stand in line outside the barracks for what was called "Appel," so that the German guards could count them. But until their information was processed and sent to Geneva, the procedures for receiving letters and packages from family could not be set in motion, so no one had news from home.

After about a month, Maria's group was moved to another camp, at Mühlberg, in Saxony. It was located in the countryside, in open, often muddy, fields. The camp was larger and more international. Again, men and women were separated, although there were AK men near Maria's group.

As before, Maria lived in a wooden, one-story barrack, but this one was raised up on blocks a foot or so because of the mud. There were only a few benches or shelves; most of the 250 women housed there slept on the floor. Maria and fifteen others made a little "room" at the end of the barrack by hanging up a camouflage curtain; in the curtained-off area a couple of them were able to sleep on platforms at each side. Maria slept on the floor. She remembers that Mühlberg had one distinct advantage over other camps: the POWs were not locked in at night and so could go to the latrine.

It was now November, and cold. Some of the prisoners got sick. A couple of Maria's girlfriends got a rash; and, out of fear of contagion, the Germans took them to a military hospital, where they had a much easier life. Maria herself had the flu but stayed in the camp. "I lay on the floor with a fever, dreaming of being in a nice clean bed with clean sheets after a shower, with a good book to read and a box of candies!"

When they first arrived the girls were searched, and any property considered contraband was taken away. Their living quarters were periodically searched as well. One friend of Maria's lost all her family pictures in a search, but Maria managed to keep hers. "It was always a matter of luck. They did what they wanted to. Once in Altenburg [her next camp] during a search by the Wehrmacht, they went into my knapsack, pulled my cigarette lighter and knife out, and took them both. I pulled the lighter back and said 'That's a souvenir from my fiancé,' and the guard was so flabbergasted by my defiance that he let me keep it."

One day a representative chosen by the Polish prisoners (one was chosen in each camp) came to see Maria's group and said they would bring them a French priest from among the prisoners of war. The girls got ready for confession, but the man they brought in was a doctor instead. He sat and talked and talked to them; he hadn't spoken to a woman in the five years he had been in prison. But some of the women didn't want to believe that he was not a priest and were angry that they were not allowed to go to confession.

Toward the end of November the female prisoners were told they were to be transported to a women-only camp. They worried that there would be no one to stand up to the Germans on their behalf. The English prisoners, who were on the POW list in Geneva and thus were receiving parcels (the Polish prisoners were not yet listed), gave them some soup, into which they had secretly put a laxative, trying to delay the transfer because of illness.

Maria woke up during the night, needing to run outside to the latrine. As she went toward the little building, she found the whole camp was moving; everyone was going to the latrine, wading through the mud from their different barracks. There were so many people that she couldn't get in. Everyone was sick. "For two days, the whole camp was moving about through mud and cold, all heading toward this little building, and the nervous Germans thought there was some sort of uprising!" After a two-day delay, the women were transferred to the new camp anyway.

Maria remained in the new camp, which was near Altenburg (in the vicinity of Dresden), from the end of November until the middle of January. When they got to the town, the prisoners were marched through it; Maria remembers that townspeople had decorated their doors with wreaths of dry leaves. "I didn't know why; maybe it had been for All Saints Day [November 1]." The new camp was smaller and only for women, in fact, only Polish women. The barracks themselves were smaller and divided into room-like spaces.

But there were more organized activities in the Altenburg stalag. Meetings at which the POWs elected their representatives were held in a theater/auditorium building, and there was a room on the side of that building which was given to the prisoners for recreation. Maria tells a story that reflects the prisoners' dogged, irrepressible Polish spirit. "I spent a lot of time making a big eagle [the symbol of Poland]," she says, "out of an aluminum box in which someone had been sent cookies. I ruined my manicure scissors making it. We put the eagle on the wall, but the Germans got furious and pulled it down and stepped on it."

Their day at Altenburg started with being given the so-called tea, which they used for washing. Then the prisoners had to line up outside in the cold for *Appel*, where they would stand as long as an hour to be counted. Their shoes were beginning to wear out—at the next camp they were issued wooden sandals. After line-up, they would be given bread, which they would divide up; but after a while, there was no more than one slice per person a day.

There was cold running water at Altenburg and small bars of gooey soap, but no shampoo. The water was very hard, so if the women washed their hair, the soap would leave a residue. One or two of the prisoners had special combs with teeth close together, like lice combs, which could be used to get the sticky stuff out. Others would borrow them. "They were scarce but important," Maria says.

"Once in a while they took us to get a shower in a special building. You had to undress completely, and they took all your clothes to disinfection. We would be standing waiting all naked to get under the shower. Camp maintenance was performed by Russian prisoners. Because Russia had not signed the Geneva convention, they were used for the worst jobs. Once while I was standing waiting for the shower with a girlfriend who had a big bottle of cologne, a Russian boy came and grabbed it—and drank it!"

To keep themselves occupied when they were not busy with chores, such as washing up or cleaning the barracks, some of the prisoners organized courses. "If someone knew Morse code, they would teach it. Languages. Some English. Some would organize a show. We tried to keep busy so we would not sit and cry all the time." By and large, people adjusted to life in the camp. However, "when people got letters from home," Maria says, "they would often get upset. You would long for your family and wonder what would happen."

In the late afternoon, the prisoners were given soup, "made," Maria says, "out of a stiff herb called *"jarmusz"* in Polish. It was used to decorate platters in Poland, like a decorative weed. There was no salt. No meat or fat. It was horrible tasting. In the last camp, they gave us pea soup once a week—five peas and twenty-five insects. I was so hungry but couldn't eat it. My girlfriend used to laugh at me and say 'It's not Friday, you are allowed to eat meat.' While we were in Altenburg, the Red Cross came to visit; a couple of girls pretended to faint to attract attention [to the hunger]."

There were some French prisoners at Altenburg. They were given more liberty. (Maria believes this was because of the cooperation of the Vichy Republic with the Germans.) The French could walk into town, and also had a hidden radio, so they could follow the news. Maria's job was to go early in the morning with two pails to bring back briquettes of turf to heat the barracks. Maria spoke the fluent French she had learned from her governess, so when the Frenchmen would come by, she would walk slowly so that she could get news from them. "I had to walk to a shelter where they kept the fuel, mountains of this black stuff, small like briquettes of coal. I would pick it up one by one so I could hear them whisper all the news, while the Germans kept yelling "Schnell! Schnell! [Hurry up!]"

The news from the Frenchmen allowed the women to know about the progress of the Allies. One sunny day there was an air raid. The women all ran outside, laughing, talking, and cheering, happy that the Allies were advancing. Angrily, the guards told them to get back inside the barracks.

At last, in December, Maria received her first news about her family, a letter written by her father in late November and forwarded to her from the camp at Mühlberg to Altenburg:

Ozarow, November 23, 1944

My dear Rysia,

> On September 7th [i.e., immediately after Maria's last visit home], we were forced to leave our apartment in Warsaw. We were taken to the National Museum (the assembly point) from where we traveled along the banks of the Wisła [Vistula] . . . until we reached the Western train terminal of Warsaw. From here, we were taken to a camp in Pruszkow. After two days in the camp, we were taken to Opoczno. We settled into very primitive surroundings in the neighborhood of Opoczno. Mother became sick from a lung infection which lasted two weeks. After she recovered from this severe illness, we moved to Opoczno. On October 15, we left for Ozarow. We learned of your travel through Ozarow from Mr. Bajkowski [their farm tenant]. I received a post card from you . . . with your address on it. I replied right away. I doubt if you received it, though, because it was not written according to the instructions. Although we are living in the coach house of our property, and everything here is very expensive, we feel well because we are at our own home. Ninka wrote to the Bajkowskis from Krakow . . . . Ninka is working at a casino. She is getting her meals and a hundred twenty zloty a month salary . . . . I sent Ninka some money. Did you know that Zbyszek died in a camp in Pruszkow? Kisses from both of us. Your Daddy . . . Much, much love, my dear child . . . .*

Thus Maria learned that her parents had survived the fall of Warsaw. But her cousin Zbyszek, who had stayed with them during the war, had been badly wounded fighting in the Uprising. Maria had seen him a couple of days before she left Warsaw, and he had a high fever. He died during transit to a POW camp.

Later, Maria heard how her sister Ninka survived. When the Germans arrived at the AK hospital where she was working, they dragged everyone outside and killed some of them on the spot; Ninka was lucky and managed to run away. Because the district where she was working fell to the Germans before the ceasefire

---

* Several letters Maria received as a POW were translated for this book by her son, Andrew Chudzinski.

agreement, Ninka was not sent to a POW camp. Instead she was taken to a camp outside Warsaw and then to Krakow, in the south, where she was forced to work for the Germans in the kitchen of a casino. She told Maria later that the Polish workers in the kitchen would spit in the salads they were making for the Germans. After Ninka had been in Krakow a while, a cousin found her and somehow got her out. She returned to the farm at Ozarow.

Soon after this first letter, Maria also received a parcel from home. She had asked for garlic and onion, which were like money in the camp, and for cigarettes, because she smoked a lot at the time. She was disappointed only to receive one onion, one head of garlic, and one package of cigarettes (her father didn't want to encourage her smoking). Not long after, a second letter arrived, sent in mid-December to Mühlberg and forwarded to Altenburg; it contained brief greetings from all three members of her immediate family:

> From Stefania (excerpted): "We sent a food package to you on the 8th of December . . . . Ninka is with us. Daddy is not feeling so well. He is coughing much. Ozarow is not the right place for him. He is very weak here. Maybe this letter will reach you by Christmas. So our very beloved thoughts will be with you on that day. We sent an opłatek [the holy Christmas wafer] in the package. Love and kisses."

> From Wacław (excerpted): "I am very sad that you are not with us like your sister Ninka is. She came from Krakow on the 30th of November . . . . Loving kisses. I wish I could see you as soon as possible."

> From Ninka: "My dearest big puppy. For two weeks already, I am living here and studying. I met with Renia and her husband in Krakow. Leszek [Renia's brother] is in an officer's POW camp. Fight with the lice, because I had them, too. Zbyszek is dead. Renusia [his wife] is at her family along with her child, her mother, and her grandmother . . . . I hug and kiss you sincerely. Constantly I am thinking of you. Nina."

Despite receipt of the opłatek and comparatively good news from home, Christmas was a difficult time for Maria and all the other prisoners of war. Everyone saved things out of their parcels to share. Although they were ordinarily locked in after 7 p.m. at Altenburg, they were told that they would be allowed to stay in the recreation room until 11 p.m. on Christmas Eve. "I was out walking," Maria recalls, emotionally. "It was a nice moonlit night, quite cold. Around us were low mountains covered with snow. Between the rows of barbed wire, the German sentry was walking, keeping guard, watching the activities in the camp. He was whistling 'Silent Night, Holy Night'. He was young. Probably he was reminiscing about good times with his family at home in the past, just as we were. A few minutes later I returned to the barrack. Right after me, a few German soldiers came running in and screaming at us. What a sudden change in the atmosphere! They counted us, locked the doors, and told us not to try to go out. We didn't learn until the next day that two girls had escaped and they were punishing us all for it." Apparently the two prisoners had walked ten miles before they were caught and brought back.

Locked into the barracks, everyone was shocked at suddenly being deprived of their plans for a nice evening. They were all intensely homesick. "Christmas Eve was the worst point," Maria reports. "We decided to create something that would remind us of a regular Christmas Eve supper in Poland. We tried to make a table and a meal. When we sang the traditional first carol, "Bog sie rodzi" (God Is Being Born), everyone was crying. I was thinking of my family sitting at the table assembled together, and here I was alone, behind bars. Everyone was thinking about their families and felt so sad to be missing that family moment."

The next morning the Germans let their prisoners out and counted them, standing in line. They were finally taken to the recreation room, where a French priest came and said Mass, although the prisoners were not allowed to approach him. One German soldier who spoke terrible Polish told them, "You have so many privileges here and you do not appreciate them." Maria was sent into town that morning to pick up some parcels at the Post Office. She remembers, "I could tell they had nothing in the little town. There was no food in the town either. There were a few paper Christmas decorations in the windows."

Later that day those who had parcels shared their contents with those who did not. "Everyone wanted American parcels," Maria recalls. "They had all the essentials—cigarettes, soap, chocolate, powdered milk, canned meat. The English parcels would have a can of celery or peas. But Mama Wisła, the vegetarian, would exchange American parcels for them—bacon for green peas, ham for celery, and so on." Everyone tried to be cheerful and to celebrate the birth of the Savior, but many tears were shed that day. The German guards were also homesick. As Maria went to the washroom, she again heard a young soldier whistling Silent Night as he patrolled.

As the Soviet armies moved west, the prisoners had to be moved further west. Both Mühlberg and Altenburg eventually became part of Communist East Germany. In mid-January 1945, Maria's group learned that they were to be moved again, from the southeast of Germany to the far northwest, a journey that would take seven or eight days in the middle of a very cold winter. The Germans emphasized these hardships, as well as the risk of being bombed en route, in an effort to get the women to sign waivers of their rights as prisoners of war and go to work in a factory (presumably a munitions plant). Forcing them to work, except for basic camp maintenance, was not allowed by the Geneva Convention.

They were told that they would have a warm place and more food if they signed the waiver document. Some of the girls did so because they wanted to stay in the east, closer to Poland. NCOs (non-commissioned officers) could not be forced to do so, however. When Maria left Warsaw, the papers she was given classified her at the NCO rank, and she refused to sign. "I still wanted to get as far west as possible, as far away from the Bolsheviks. I wanted to get to France because I knew French and to go to the university. That was my dream."

"We had a little group of five who were like a family—Krystyna and her sister Nina, Barbara, Nola, and myself. Three of us were NCOs, but the Germans told us the others (Krystyna and Nola) could be forced to go to the forced labor. Just then a friend of mine [in fact another sister of Bogdan] who was a doctor came to me and suggested that the others needed to be excused as not physically able to go to work. The two were good-looking, full of life. But they went at the end of the clinic. They walked in looking so healthy. There was a German colonel there who was also an M.D. But my friend said that one had a heart problem and the other chest problems. He could have checked them but did not. So my friend saved them, and they went with us."

The women were loaded onto trains. The trip to Oberlangen, in northwestern Germany, took eight days. "The winter was incredibly cold," Maria says, "and we did not have proper clothes, and no blanket. The cattle train would stop here and there, and we could hear bombardment." The prisoners tried to keep their spirits up by singing. At one point "we were locked in, on a side track, with no hygienic facilities, and not let out for two days. So we made a hole in the floor. A Polish woman who was our representative knocked on the wall of our car and asked how we were doing. 'We have to get out, we have to go!' we said. She said, 'Don't worry, I'm writing a report to the Red Cross saying that they are not observing the Geneva Convention.' It was tragi-comic. We have to get out right now, and she's writing a report to Geneva!"

At last, the train arrived at Lathen, close to the Netherlands border, in the province of Oldenburg. The prisoners had to walk about twenty kilometers to the camp, through bare, tree-less fields. As they walked, they could hear explosions from the front line, but their German escorts told them, "Don't be so happy; that's been going on for six months."

They arrived at Oberlangen, or Stalag 6C, in the evening, when it was already dark. Another prisoner who spent time there has described the area in which Oberlangen was located as "desolate, flat lowlands near the Dutch border, in the middle of nowhere, surrounded by miles and miles of peat bogs crisscrossed with ditches and canals." Like the other camps Maria had now seen, it was surrounded by wire and had watchtowers for the guards. Maria recalls that, "There were two rows of barracks, and a large space in between. Only one row was filled; later the other side filled up. Polish girls from different stalags were being brought here.

Only Polish girls were POWs there." Indeed, Oberlangen was the main camp for female AK soldiers, 1500 of whom were imprisoned there.

At one end of the barrack to which Maria was assigned there was a washroom. "The windows were broken; snow was inside; and the water was ice." But after eight days in a cattle car, Maria was desperate to get clean somehow. She went to the so-called bathroom by herself. "There were high stone sinks; snow was covering part of the sinks and there was also ice. The water was just drips and would freeze right away. I climbed up and got inside. I soaped myself and start to wash in the icy water. Suddenly the front doors opened and a group of German soldiers with one SS woman walked in unexpectedly. I stood there like Venus, trying to cover myself. But I was covered with soap and, because of the difference in temperature, I was steaming, covered with a thick mist like a fog."

The barrack in which Maria lived at Oberlangen was very large and, apart from two small round metal stoves, had no heat. All the prisoners had for fuel was turf that they gathered in the fields around the camp. "We could be forced to work only to maintain the camp. We were assigned periodically to go pick up turf with Germans guarding us. It was already dry in the fields, and we would pick up pieces like little brick squares and load them onto a little train with an open deck. Each morning, a couple of girls would go with buckets to bring turf into the barrack to burn."

"We were only getting one slice of bread by then, and it was so gooey that we would stick it to the side of the stove to make toast out of it, so it was edible." There were wooden benches with a little straw on them for the 250 women to sleep on, two to each bench. Maria slept on a shelf with Barbara, who was "rich" because she had a blanket. "The blanket could cover both of us but we had to turn at the same time since there was so little room." The latrine, as always, was outside.

Soon after arriving Maria received one more letter from her father. It was sent on December 30, 1944 to her at Altenburg but forwarded to Oberlangen. In it Wacław recounted the difficulties they were confronting in Ozarow:

> ... Ninka came home and is with us since the 1st of the month. She arrived without any warm clothing, and only in a borrowed light coat. In order to clothe her properly, we would have to spend a large sum of money. This would be very difficult for us. For the last four months we are living without any income. I have no work and there are no possibilities of earning any money at this time. Ninka's education is also pretty expensive. I couldn't get anything out of Bajkowski (he leased land from me). He maintains that he had a very poor year, because he could not sell his crops. In spite of all the difficulties, I will still be sending you more packages .... [T]here are many difficulties with the sending of the packages. The post office in Ozarow is not functioning. The post office

in Pruszkow, seven kilometers from here, accepts only a limited number of parcels, and quite often you have to waste two days to get the packages through. We walk to Pruszkow. It is not always possible to do this, due to the weather and my emphysema. I am happy, my lovely child, that you are healthy, because I am not so. Kisses, Daddy.

This letter describing the hardships the Chmielinskis were having at home was written while the Germans still controlled Poland; soon afterwards Soviet troops reached Warsaw. Once civilians were permitted to return to the ruined city, Maria's parents did so, staying in their former apartment, even though it had been heavily damaged. The new regime was organizing the administration of the city, and Wacław found work once again in the legal department at city hall. But living conditions were so bad in Warsaw that he sent Ninka away to a boarding school for girls at a convent. She still had a year or so before graduating from high school. Maria did not hear this news until much later. Once the Russians occupied eastern Poland, communications with that part of the country ceased for some months. This letter was the last she received for quite a while, and when the mail did resume, it was heavily censored.

The winter of 1944-45 was difficult in all of Europe. After the invasion of Normandy, the Allies' march to the East had bogged down; the weather was severe, and supplies scarce. "It was cold, extremely cold," Maria remembers. "It's horrible. Whenever you get a cataclysm, on top of it you have bad weather. God doesn't sympathize with us." When March arrived, however, there were suddenly a few warm days. The prisoners sat in the sun and began to experience feelings of happiness again. They sang; they organized more courses. Unfortunately, along with the sun came fleas. "I had to get up during the night," Maria says, "take off my jumpsuit, shake it outside, in the nude, and then do it again a few hours later. I was eaten up. My girlfriend would say 'Come back to bed,' but then they would jump onto her instead."

The prisoners had to work on maintaining the camp. "The worst," says Maria, "was when you had to go clean the latrine. It was horrible because there was a special closed wagon that we put the stuff in. You had to fill it with shovels from the latrine, and you smelled so bad for weeks. There was no way to get your clothes and yourself clean properly." The jobs she preferred were ones that would get her outside the camp, either to gather turf for heating or to pick up potatoes from where they had been buried.

One day Maria went out to pick up potatoes with a woman who had been a singer-actress in Poland and had known her father's secretary. The woman got quite emotional. "Your father would cry if he saw you here," she said. But Maria had taken off her panties to make a sack in which she could hide some potatoes when the guard wasn't looking, hoping to smuggle them back into the camp.

Practical as always, she told the other woman, "Stop crying, and put as many potatoes as possible into your pants." A nice older guard was watching them that day, and he walked with them to the house of a farmer who kept pigs. They were cooking potatoes for the pigs on an open fire outside the house. "We put some potatoes in the fire, with the dirt on them, instead of cleaning them first, but I was so happy to have a warm potato. There was no salt, no butter, but I was so happy." Maria was wearing a scarf, and the farmer's small daughter said she wanted it. Maria said she could have it if they would give her some eggs. The farmer refused, but the girl's mother begged; finally they gave her two eggs. "It was hard to get them back to camp. When we returned, they lined us up and checked us, but they didn't find the bag between my legs. My four girlfriends were so happy and excited to have two eggs between the five of us."

Because the Allies were approaching, the guards told the prisoners that they would move them toward the interior of Germany before Easter. Easter was at the beginning of April that year. The women tried to decide what they could do to avoid this fate. They had heard that prisoners in the east had sometimes been sent on death marches of hundreds of miles as the Allied troops advanced. But the prisoners soon noticed that the soldiers themselves appeared to be getting ready to escape, loading up the carts used to bring in turf with their luggage. They had apparently changed their mind about the move because things were going so badly for them. Explosions could be heard from the direction of the Dutch border.

On Saturday, April 12, 1945, a nice, sunny spring day, some of the prisoners were outside the camp, picking up turf and dry wood in the forest. They were singing Polish songs. The area was close to the Dutch border, and Holland was in Allied hands. An Allied reconnaissance patrol, which happened to be a Polish unit under British command, had been sent into the German territory to check the area. They stopped at a farm near where the prisoners were working and heard them singing. The farmer told them there was a women's camp nearby. The Polish soldiers returned to their unit and reported this news, and their commander quickly organized a unit of Polish volunteers to liberate the camp.

"It was so unexpected," Maria remembers. "I heard some shooting going on in the afternoon, so I went outside to see what was going on. These men in Allied uniforms, less than twenty of them, were running up the stairs to the watchtowers to take over from the German guards. We thought they were American or Canadian, so we called out 'Hello, boys!' They shouted back in Polish, 'You forgot your Polish already?'" Only then did the prisoners realize that they had been liberated by a Polish military detachment.

"The battle was a matter of minutes," according to Maria. "One of the Germans was killed, but the rest surrendered. Suddenly everyone was assembled, singing and happy, and the commandant of the camp was giving a report to the officer who was in charge of the liberation unit. They just opened the wires all around the camp."

Leokadia Rowinski, another prisoner at Oberlangen that day, reports the following interchange between the commandant of the camp and the colonel who liberated it:

> Commandant: "Colonel, I respectfully report a battalion of women from the Warsaw Uprising. There are 1,716 soldiers present, 20 in the sick-room, and 9 infants."*
>
> Colonel: "Soldiers of the Home Army, comrades-in-arms! This is a historic moment of two Polish Armed Forces meeting on the German soil. May this day remain in your memories forever as the fulfillment of your dreams and your efforts. You are now free! Long live Poland!"

The colonel saluted, and the red-and-white Polish flag was raised on the flagpole, from which the German flag had just been removed. The group then sang the Polish national anthem, the first line of which means "Poland has not perished as long as we still live."

Asked what she looked and felt like on that day, Maria replies, "I was dressed shabbily. My shoes were gone, I had wooden shoes like the Dutch, some socks, and a jacket. All of our faces were swollen so we did not look as thin as we were, swollen from hunger. My thick dark hair had seldom been washed. We were allowed to shower once a month, though we tried to wash ourselves with the morning tea since we couldn't drink it. All of us smelled so bad that we didn't notice. But it was one of the nicest days of my life, that we were finally free. The moment of liberation was euphoria."

In the summer of 2000 Maria went by car with a friend from Warsaw to Rome. On the way back they passed close to Altenburg, one of the places she had been imprisoned. Her friend proposed that they stop and visit. "It had completely changed since the time I was there," Maria reports. "We saw the theater where the command used to sleep; it was all redecorated. There used to be a big open space where the prisoners' barracks were but all I could see were dilapidated old houses. It seemed impossible that they would be dilapidated in 50 years, but, then, this had been part of East Germany. We went in to a little café to ask if there had been another theater; maybe I was wrong about the location. A man was there. I told him 'I was here as a POW in 1945. Is there another theater?' He said, 'No, there never was another theater. But I can't help you; I was born in 1950.' I was already a piece of history . . . ."

---

* Babies were born in the camp to women who had gotten pregnant during the Uprising.

CHAPTER 10

Warsaw, Summer 2002

On July 13, 2002, I arrived in Warsaw, after an all-night flight from West Africa. I had arranged via the Internet to be met by a taxi, and a kind older man stood there holding a placard with my name on it. We set out for my hotel in the center of the city, close to the area where Maria had grown up.

It was a beautiful, hot Saturday afternoon, close in time to the season when the Uprising took place. Warsaw is a city of parks, and people were out enjoying them. I was surprised to see how prosperous, well-dressed and "western" everyone looked. I'm not sure what I expected, but not that. Except for some Communist-era socialist-realist style buildings, the city has been so meticulously rebuilt that you would not dream it had been totally destroyed.

I had asked Maria to recommend a hotel that she remembered from her youth, and she said that I should stay at the Europejski. The exterior of the hotel was still reminiscent of the luxurious place it had been in the early part of the twentieth century (it was built in 1857), but the interior had been rebuilt in the dreary style of the Soviet era. My room, down a very long and winding corridor, was small and contained only the essentials. Nonetheless I gratefully subsided into the single bed for a nap.

Later in the afternoon, I went to the lobby to meet Maria's sister Janina. She is a nun. After her education in the convent school, Ninka became determined to join that religious community. She has been a member of an order of Ursuline nuns* for more than fifty years. Waclaw was not happy about her choice and insisted that she wait until she completed university to take her vows. He wrote to Maria, "I have already lost one daughter; now I am losing the other."

As I descended the steps into the lobby, a white-haired woman in a gray habit stood up to greet me. She looked very plain and seemed older than Maria.

---

* Specifically, a Grey Ursuline, belonging to an order founded by Urszula Ledochowska in Poland in 1920.

85

What impressed me most were her wonderful eyes and kind face. Because the only language Nina and I share is French, and mine is rusty, she brought along a friend who worked as a guide and spoke English, though not very well. Her friend had trouble understanding my American English, so often Nina and I struggled to understand each other in French.

They asked where I wanted to go, and I immediately said "Foksal. I want to see where you both grew up." So we set off, past the statue of Copernicus near the university and down Nowy Swiat. It was bustling, and filled with expensive-looking shops. Our first stop was the Church of the Holy Cross, where Maria's parents were married and her mother's funeral took place. The huge statue of Jesus bearing his cross stands again in front of the church. I recognized it from photos of Warsaw in 1944, when the church had been destroyed but the statue remained partially standing for a while, making it appear as though the load Christ bore included all the evil of that time and the suffering of the Polish people.

The two women took me inside the church and showed me the pillar with the urn that contains Chopin's heart. I wondered how this body part survived the destruction of the church. From my reading, I knew that the interior of the church was the scene of fierce fighting between the Germans and the insurgents during the Uprising. You would not know this today. The huge gold altar is surrounded by Baroque figures and portraits; the side aisles are full of more paintings and decoration; and at the back of the church, overhead, there is a wonderful white and gilt organ.

Our next stop was the Café Blikle, at the intersection of Nowy Swiat and Foksal, the elegant coffee house where Maria and Nina went as children for cakes, and where famous actors and singers performed during the German occupation. We went in and immediately stepped back a century. Nina insisted that I eat, so I ordered blini with smoked salmon and Polish beer, all of it wonderful. I was exhilirated to be in a place that had come to exist so vividly in my mind.

When I had finished eating, we proceeded to Foksal 13, where the Chmielinskis had lived. It had obviously once been quite wonderful, but now is a terrible ruin. Although the building miraculously survived the war, it was heavily damaged and has never been restored. A few people were living in it nonetheless. A little girl was playing in the filthy courtyard with a stray cat. Nina, who appeared to have a special affinity for children, made friends with her. Everyone seemed to trust Nina, in her simple nun's habit.

Soon we were on our way up the crumbling interior staircase, which smelled like garbage and urine. Yet there were still remnants of elegant lintels over the doors and stone decorations on the stairs. Nina pointed out the rooms that had formed the family apartment. Everything was so different that it was hard to get a sense of their affluent former life. The experience did, however, convey some sense of what it must have been like to live in a partially destroyed building, as so many did during and after the war.

When we went outside and looked at the facades of other buildings on the street, buildings that had been restored, it was possible to sense what a lovely street this was when Maria and Nina were children. The apartment houses all had huge windows looking onto the street, and the facades were beautifully decorated; one had an alcove with a medieval-looking statue of the Virgin in it. Foksal 13 also had huge windows and now-crumbling balconies overlooking the street.

I asked to go to the end of the street, to see the park by the Zamoyski palace where Maria played as a child. The building is now in the hands of a private foundation, and an elegant affair of some sort was in progress. A guard tried to stop us, but Nina talked with him long enough to allow me to sneak into the huge garden behind the building and get an idea of how lovely a place it had been.

We then hopped on a bus up Nowy Swiat and the Royal Way, past several beautiful palaces, and got off in the bustling square at the entrance to the Old Town. Remnants of the ancient city wall were visible. The huge statue of Zygmunt III (the Polish king who had established Warsaw as capital in 1609), once toppled by the Nazis, dominated the square. Lovely old (though I know this is not true; everything here is, in a sense, a reproduction) townhouse buildings lined the square, with umbrellaed café tables in front of them. With its red façade, the once-destroyed royal castle stood in all its former splendor, with a concert taking place in its courtyard. Later, when I visited it, I marveled both at the art work that had been saved and at how much had been stolen or destroyed. The beautiful Canaletto paintings of 18th-century Warsaw, which had been used as blueprints in the restoration of the city, once again hung on the castle's walls.

Narrow streets led off the square at inviting angles. Nina led me down one of these streets to a church where a Mass was taking place—the cathedral, though it is not particularly large or impressive. After the service ended, she showed me where various famous people were honored in the church. Paderewski, the famous pianist and Polish nationalist, was buried in the undercroft. We then walked to Market Square, which was full of Saturday night crowds. The square, bounded by lovely multi-colored town houses and filled with open-air restaurants, has a statue of a mermaid at its center, a traditional symbol of Warsaw. The beauty of the square was marred by giant posters advertising the commercial sponsors of its restoration.

I asked to see the Vistula. Nina led me down several narrow streets to an overlook, where the river can be seen winding through the city, with Praga and other suburbs on the opposite shore. The river was quite narrow, an easy distance for mortar shells. On our way, Nina stopped to show me a wall plaque commemorating those who had died on that spot during the Uprising. Warsaw is full of such plaques. One of the most moving to me was located on Nowy Swiat, not far from the Café Blikle; it marked a place where thirty people were lined up and executed by the Gestapo. The contrast with all the happy, prosperous people celebrating their Saturday evening was jarring.

I got up early the next day to walk through Old Town when it was empty of crowds. I wanted to imagine the brave souls who had fought for weeks to defend it. I walked slowly through the empty streets trying to hear echos of their struggle. But it was only a pretty area of an historic city, recovering from its busy Saturday night.

I then walked—quite a distance—to the site of the 1943 Warsaw Ghetto Uprising. The enormous area where the Ghetto had stood prior to the Jews' last desperate attempt at resistance is now a park, with an heroic-style commemorative statue at one end. The place where the Jews were deported to extermination camps is marked. But on this bright Sunday morning, the park was filled with sunbathers and a few tourists. There were even souvenirs of the Ghetto for sale, primarily reproductions of historical photographs. Try as I would, it was hard to reenter the past on the spot where so many lives had been lost. The sun was shining; people were happy and, despite my reverence, so was I.

On my way back to the hotel, I passed the monument to the fighters of the Warsaw Uprising, completed in 1989. It is a series of sculptures, surrounded by a colonnade. The symbol of the Uprising—an intertwined "P" and "W" for "Powstancia Warszawa" (Warsaw Uprising in Polish)—appears at the top of each column. Two huge blocks of stone lean against a group of statues of soldiers defending the barricades, as though the city were falling on them. The other group of sculptures represents insurgents emerging from the sewers; one of them is a woman. Perhaps because of the inclusion of the woman, perhaps because of their posture straining to release themselves from the sewer, I found this sculpture strangely moving. I asked a Japanese couple who happened by to take a picture of me in front of it. Later, I read that during the 1994 celebrations marking the 50th anniversary of the Uprising the President of the Federal Republic of Germany officially apologized to the Polish people at this monument, both for the attack upon their nation in World War II and for the brutal suppression of the Warsaw Uprising. Fifty years seemed like a long time to wait.

I had Sunday dinner at noon with Nina at her convent, just the two of us without an interpreter. I had never been to a convent before, and I didn't know what to expect. Perhaps a simple soup and some bread served in an ascetic room. To my astonishment, Nina led me to a room that was furnished rather like an upper-class Victorian parlor cum dining room. The two of us sat down, while an elderly nun served us a multi-course meal on beautiful china, soup tureen and all—a small-scale version of dinner at the Chmielinskis' home in the 1930s, with Nina presiding graciously. To the extent I could, given the language barrier, I pumped her for information about the past. She seemed most eager to tell me about the hardships of the period under Communist rule, especially for the church, and about the order of nuns to which she belonged. These were, after all, the experiences that had most affected her adult life.

The next day I took a quick trip to Krakow, to experience an ancient Polish city that had not been destroyed (Frank, the German governor, ignored Hitler's order to do so), and to visit Auschwitz-Birkenau. Krakow is beautiful—its medieval market square, Cloth Hall, Renaissance royal castle and Gothic cathedral all intact—giving me a sense of the world that Maria had experienced as a child. I stayed in a hotel she recommended, the Francuski. From my window I could see ancient buildings and the city walls; lying in bed I could hear the clop, clop of horses' hooves, as tourists were driven through the ancient city in nineteenth-century carriages, and I could easily imagine myself back in time.

Back in Warsaw, what remained to be done was to retrace Maria's footsteps during the Uprising. Having carefully reviewed my notes of our most recent conversations, I set out with a map of the city center in my hand. I decided to proceed chronologically. I returned to Foksal, where she set out on August 1, 1944. I walked past the house where she stopped to say good-bye to her friend and located the building where her unit had spent the first night under fire. It was only when I reached the Plac Dabrowskiego that I was able to escape the everydayness and begin to imagine Maria's experience. The small square across which Maria and each member of her unit had run, ducking to avoid German sniper fire, was no longer empty. It was now a tranquil little park, with trees, decorative street lamps, and benches. I sat on one, contemplating how one would be exposed to enemy fire from the taller buildings. I wondered if I would have had the courage to expose myself to such danger. Mostly, however, I was overcome by the contrast between the peaceful little park, glittering in the sunlight, and the violence that had taken place there.

I walked through the park to the building on Szkolna, Maria's first "home" during the Uprising. It was easy to see how grenades could be thrown from its windows at tanks in the boulevard below. Finding the Adria, where she stood guard, proved more difficult. I knew from Maria that it was opposite the Philharmonic Hall and that it was a wonderful old building in the classical style. I also knew, roughly, its location. But I saw no building that looked like a symphony hall. I walked around and around the area. Finally I paused for a moment to think. I could see some writing on the large, rather ugly stone building across from me. Crossing the street, I saw that it said "Sala Koncertowa." Looking for a classical building, I had been circling the concert hall all along. It had been rebuilt during the Stalinist era, but in the socialist realist style of that time.

Now I had to find the Adria. "Opposite the Philharmonia" filled quite a lot of territory. After my experience with the orchestra hall, I assumed that the building would not exist in the same form. Again I walked and walked. Just as I was giving up, I looked back down one street and was astonished to see a sign jutting out from one large building, bearing one word on it: "Adria." As I returned to it, I saw a seven-story stone building, with classical columns on its façade. It still housed a restaurant of that name on the first floor. So here was the place where Maria was stationed as a guard for the first month of the Uprising—now just a nice old building in an ordinary, rather dull-looking city street.

For reasons of time, I decided to go only to places that had played a striking role in Maria's experience during the Uprising and which might have retained their former appearance. I sought out the Plac Napoleon, where she spent a week lying on the ground with a flag to show the wind direction to Allied pilots overhead. It had been renamed, I knew from Maria, in honor of the Uprising; it was now the Plac Postancow Warszawy, or Plaza of the Warsaw Uprising. This turned out to be a very large, rather ugly space, with cars parked throughout it, surrounded by huge and quite homely buildings. It was starting to rain, and I began to question my undertaking. What I was looking for simply did not exist anymore. But as I started to leave, I came upon a large horizontal plaque, about one foot above the ground. It stated (insofar as I could decipher it) that it was placed there in memory of those who had fought in this area of Warsaw during the Uprising. Bunches of freshly cut flowers had been laid upon it. I was clearly not the only person coming here to remember.

Time was getting short, and it continued to rain. I decided to abbreviate my tour and to visit one last place, the corner at which Maria's unit had been instructed to gather on the day they left Warsaw and became prisoners of war. The corner of Szpitalna and Zgoda, which come together and intersect Chmielna at an angle, still has some open space, where one could imagine soldiers mustering for their last march. But the corner is otherwise taken up with a large restaurant/bar on an American Western theme. It is called "Bonanza," and life-sized models of cowboy horses stand in the windows, which are emblazoned with an advertisement for "darts" and "billiards." Not only have the Germans been chased out of Warsaw, but so has the influence of the Soviet Union.

I was feeling jangled by my tour. To comfort myself, I walked back to the Café Blikle and ordered a wonderful Austrian-style pastry, sitting at my little table until the last bit of cream was gone. Thus fortified, I began the walk back to my hotel to pack for the trip home. As I passed in front of the Church of the Holy Cross, I heard the sound of singing, and went in. A Mass was in progress. Though it was a weekday, the church was full. I took a seat in the back and listened to the people around me singing the responses to wonderful tunes I had never heard. I knelt down and said a prayer for the courageous people who had died in the summer of 1944.

CHAPTER 11

The Air Force

After heavy losses as a result of the German offensive in the winter of 1944, the so-called Battle of the Bulge, the Western Allies resumed their march to the east and crossed the Rhine in March 1945. The Russians, meanwhile, had been sweeping westward and by that time controlled all of Eastern Europe, having taken Warsaw in January. After Hitler's suicide, the Germans surrendered unconditionally on May 8, 1945, since known as VE, or Victory in Europe, Day.

The soldiers of the victorious Allies returned home to festive welcoming celebrations, to rebuild their lives and, in many cases, their devastated countries. Western Europe was also filled with refugees, including those liberated from German POW and concentration camps, those taken to Germany from Eastern Europe for forced labor, and others uprooted by the movements of armies. Camps were set up, but it took years to process all the displaced people.

In Poland, the Soviet Union moved quickly to consolidate a Communist regime. The AK having been effectively crushed, at least in the cities, the Poles who had fought in the Communist resistance and with the Soviet army predominated in the interim government established in early 1945. By May, surviving leaders of the AK were denounced, tried and imprisoned for allegedly "collaborating" with the Nazis. Thousands of AK members were imprisoned, deported, or killed. Soviet-style rule was imposed upon the country. Thus the Poles, despite being on the winning side, exchanged Nazi oppression for a totalitarian Communist state that crushed nationalist dissent.

After the prisoner of war camp at Oberlangen was liberated, the former prisoners remained there for a few weeks before being moved to a larger camp in nearby Niederlangen, where the barracks were somewhat more comfortable. The camp was now run by the Polish women themselves. They organized, had their own guards, and, most important of all, got supplies. Food was the big thing. Maria recalls that "After liberation, the Polish soldiers would bring us candies, but we said we wanted bread."

Maria was very popular among the women in the camp. She was chosen to supervise a 250-woman unit and ran the communications department. The new displaced person camps were carefully controlled, especially until the war with Germany ended. Before then, some girls taken out for a ride by Allied soldiers were killed by German snipers. Precise numbers of the residents were important because they were the basis for allocations of food and clothing by the occupying forces. "I had to oversee the switchboard, for military purposes, to be in touch with other units, to arrange shifts for the girls, distribute food to them, and administer two and one half barracks. I had to give an account of how many women were there, how many were sick, if any had run away, and if any had been given passes to get out of camp. I got all the best staff because I had been an officer. I was also getting better clothes from the Polish in England; they were distributed according to ranks. When I left, I left a whole locker full for my girlfriends."

Maria's friend Nola caused a stir during this period. "She had gotten married in November 1943, and her husband was a prisoner of war in a camp for officers in Bavaria. When the camp was liberated, he got a permit and bicycled for 17 days to get to Nola. But she rejected him, and he became suicidal. I spent time convincing him that there was still life ahead." Maria obviously succeeded because, she tells me, "He remarried and I was godmother to his second son in Chicago."

The key question for Maria and the others was what to do next, now that freedom—and by May 8, the end of the war in Europe—had arrived. All through her period in captivity, Maria expected to return to Poland. "We were waiting for the end of the war and then we would be free to do whatever we wanted to. We didn't figure out that would be impossible because of the type of regime in Poland." It must have seemed strange to be on the winning side of the war but not be able to go home. When I ask Maria how she felt, she replies "While I was still in Germany, I was so busy I hardly had time to sleep, and things were so uncertain that I just didn't think about it until I got to England and had settled in."

Maria's cousin Franek, Zybszek's brother, was in England, where he had been working in the foreign office of the Polish government-in-exile. When he saw Maria's name on the list of POWs published in a Polish newspaper there, he wrote to her and said that his friend, a doctor, would come and try to bring her to England. But this seemed very uncertain. So when another opportunity came up, she jumped at it.

A friend told Maria that a group of Polish Air Force people would be coming to make a list of women they wanted to enlist in the air force in England, but they could only designate relatives. "My cousin is coming," she said. "I will say you are my cousin." When the friend's relative in the Air Force arrived, Maria describes, "We went for a walk outside, and the fellow said, 'I will present you as my niece. Give me your data, and I will give you mine.'" And so Maria's name was placed on the list of Air Force families. "I never intended to be in the Air Force," she says, "but I wanted to get out of Germany and be able to continue my education. It took some people years to get out of the displaced persons camps in Germany. My family wasn't in the military. Indeed, they were against military service, with its different perspective on the world. Career officers, my family thought, were people who didn't want to face the world." Now a daughter of this family was about to join the career military in order to get out of Germany quickly.

"Germany was in chaos; there was no future there. I had no one to rely on in France, though I spoke the language. But in England I had Franek, and there was already a Polish life and community organized there, so I knew I could survive while I learned English. I grabbed the first opportunity to get there. I had always thought of England as imperial, a strong country, which had never been occupied by the Germans. I figured everyone would be rich, and was shocked when I saw real life there."

Thus began Maria's affiliation with the Polish Air Force, an affiliation that would play a major role in her life, then and later. Although it was officially part of the British Royal Air Force (RAF), the Polish Air Force had its own administration. It had played a critical role in the Battle of Britain. Maria became a member of the Women's Auxiliary Air Force, or WAAF, and wore Polish insignia—a Polish eagle on her hat (which she proudly showed to me) and the word "Poland" on her sleeve. Later, the Polish Air Force was merged into the RAF.

Most of the former prisoners of war who were selected for the Air Force had higher education of some sort, as did Maria. Eighty-four of the 2,000 women in the camp got into the air force. Their commandant thought that they were disloyal to Poland. She regarded the women as fighting troops, not as auxiliary, and told them that it was their job to fight to liberate the Polish territories taken over by the Soviet Union. "I said, 'Uh, huh'," reports Maria, in the modern idiom. "One girl said straightforwardly, 'I'm not going to fight for the eastern territory, in spite of the fact that my family had an estate over there; I'm not foolish enough.' The commandant said she would court martial her when the troops came."

The new Polish Communist regime also tried to convince people to go back to Poland. However, the new government didn't trust the nationalists who had been in the AK, so many former AK members were arrested when they did return. Most of the women who had been prisoners with Maria resettled in other parts of the world. "Some eventually went to Italy to work with the Second Polish Corps there, and organized high schools there, in Northern Italy. Some went to where other Polish troops were stationed in Germany and worked in canteens or libraries. And some were lucky enough to be accepted into schools of higher education in Western Europe."

At this crucial turning point, Maria went on without her childhood companion, Krystyna, who had been with her throughout the Uprising and imprisonment. Krystyna remained in the POW camp and eventually went to Belgium, where her sister had been admitted to a program in art history at the University in Brussels. Krystyna herself studied at the School of Commerce at Antwerp, where she met and married a Polish man with whom she emigrated to Australia and raised six children. (Maria went much later to visit her in Melbourne, and they would have long telephone conversations.) The only friend who managed to get into the Air Force and go with Maria to England was Nola.

Because it was officially prohibited to recruit in Germany, for fear of offending the Soviets, the new recruits were taken to the Netherlands for briefing, medical exams, and to be issued papers. Maria thus arrived in Enschede, Holland on June 1, 1945. "Everything was so nice and clean in Holland," Maria remembers. "There were rhododendrons all around. And houses you could see through, from the big front window to the back. I would walk around and look at people's homes, since I missed privacy so much." The women were housed in a big rented house while going through their medical exams and briefing. Girls who didn't pass the physical—including the woman who introduced Maria to her cousin to get her into the air force—were sent back to Germany.

What Maria remembers most about her stay in Holland was eating. "When we got to Holland and ate constantly, we got fat again. There was a big house of the Navy Army Air Force Institute, or NAFI, where you could eat cheaply. Our biggest pleasure was to eat. We would have breakfast at home, then go to NAFI for a snack, home for lunch, then have an afternoon snack at NAFI before going home to dinner." In the evenings they sometimes went to the movies, where people in uniform were allowed in free. Not knowing English, it was hard to understand the dialogue in many of the movies they saw. "The movie *Laura* was playing for a week," Maria recalls. "We would get home and have big discussions trying to figure out what was going on in it: was she his wife? his fiancé? his sister?"

While in Holland, the Polish authorities asked the women to write down what they knew about the Polish underground. Based on their experience and training, the women were mistrustful. "We tried not to write very much because it could cause problems for our families over there. We just wrote the obvious things since we had to write something. This was a good thing because the commandant for all the Polish air force girls took all these papers and was supposed to give them to the higher command. She left the camp and stopped in Paris on her way to England, and left her briefcase in a taxi!" This woman's husband left the forces in the west soon after and returned to Poland. He joined the military and did espionage work for the Communists; when he went back, he disclosed what he knew about the underground to the authorities, and was rewarded by eventually becoming a general in the Communist forces. So the women's instinctive caution was correct.

Starting life again in a new country, where she did not speak the language, was a big step for Maria. She was only 22 years old. "I was so young that the transition was easier," she says. "I was looking forward to going to England. I had never been there and imagined it as a big strong country with everything plentiful, everything the best. So I was surprised when we had a briefing before going and were told that the food was not plentiful or tasty and the cakes and pastries were horrible. I couldn't believe it."

After the new recruits had been in Holland for three weeks, the British sent three Dakota airplanes to pick them up. "It took two hours for the prop planes to fly to Croydon, twenty people in each, a military plane with a bench around the side for seats. Then they put us in cars and we drove to London. I didn't like it at first. Buckingham Palace looked to me like a stable. London was homely, not like European cities with their beautiful architecture. Later I came to love it, to appreciate the small squares and green spaces, the residential areas. It's a cozy city." When they got to the countryside, Maria thought England was more attractive. Their destination was the recruiting center near Wilmsloe, in the rolling green hills south of Manchester.

They arrived in Wilmsloe by train. The recruiting center, run by the RAF, was a half hour's walk from the village and consisted of barracks with no trees around them. Maria's first reaction was "Oh, no! A camp with barbed wire and guardposts again! You couldn't go out without a pass, and we got none for the first two weeks, since we were just recruits." There were three barracks assigned to Maria's group of about 84 women. They were issued uniforms and began their military training. Every morning there was an inspection in the barracks. "Your buttons and shoes had to be shining. Three pairs of shoes had to stand at attention under the bed when they were inspecting the barracks," Maria says. "Your jacket had to hang just so; the gold buttons on your overcoat had to be cleaned every morning. The floor had to be shiny, shoes in a row, and your uniform with shiny buttons. When the officer walked in to inspect in the morning, you stood by your bed and had to turn around so he could make sure you were in proper shape. If something was wrong, you would get demerits. Once in a while, if you were the orderly, you were supposed to go out into the meadow and pick flowers to put in a vase inside the barrack. But there was a catch to it. If you went in the morning, there was dew and it would spot your shoes, which the officer would notice when he went to check. When you returned, the floor had to be shiny, so to avoid making marks, I would jump from one bed to another." Maria found the regular military discipline rather trying.

It was also uncomfortable to wear uniforms all the time. It was summer, and the jacket was made of wool. The hat had oilcloth inside and was hot and sticky. The women were issued several blue shirts with button-on collars that were starched so stiff that they left a mark on the wearer's neck. A black tie completed the outfit. "They also gave us really long underpants and ugly thick hose with seams. We would put it on the wrong side out since we thought that looked sheerer; but if you were caught by an officer, you got a demerit." Maria had no civilian clothes, and wasn't able to buy any for some time, so though the uniform was uncomfortable, she wore it day in and day out.

The time at Wilmsloe was spent in training. Everyone new to the service had to go through eight weeks of training, learning drills and the King's Regulations, which governed military discipline and procedure. "We were being conditioned and disciplined for service and taught the proper attire and behavior to represent the army of the King. Your jacket could not be unbuttoned; you had to wear the proper tie, etc., etc., etc. We had to be on the parade ground for drill, and were supposed to be learning English to pass an exam on the King's Regulations for service—how to behave, what's permissible, what to do." Maria memorized the regulations without knowing a word of English. "You had to wear a hat all the time when you were out of the building, and salute anybody with a higher rank than you. We were at the bottom, so we had to salute everybody!" (She laughs.)

"We had to march to the mess for meals. The food was lousy, but we in the service had better food than civilians, because everything was rationed and what was available was poor. And English food is bad anyway. Dinner might be hot sardines on hot greasy toast." She describes being excited at the prospect of having cocoa for snack one day, remembering cocoa at home, made with sugar and whipped cream. "But when we got to the mess, what they gave us was made with water; there was no sugar and, of course, no whipped cream."

After two weeks of this misery, Maria was entitled to a pass for a few hours. Her cousin Franek in London wrote that he wanted to come visit her, and he arrived on the first day she was allowed to apply for a pass. It was a long hot walk into town, in July and with practically no shade along the way. But Maria had no money for a bus even if there had been one. Because the paper work involved to receive a pass had taken some time, she arrived at the station after Franek's train was scheduled to arrive. "When I got to the station, how was I to find out which platform to go to? I went to the window on the first floor and tried asking in French, in German, and with gestures. They finally told me it was Platform 3, but then I didn't know if it was the right train or even the London train at all because I was two hours late. Luckily the train was two hours late, and my cousin came out of it."

Alone and uprooted, Maria was comforted by the connection with a member of her family. Franek was ten years older than she and had been in London for some time, and he stepped into a protective relationship to his younger relative. Being in the diplomatic service, he was also able to get some news from home during the period when Maria was cut off from all communication with her family. The visits with him helped to ease the pain of homesickness that began to afflict her in this new land.

Maria was also determined to get along in her new surroundings. The first task was to learn the new language. "I realized if I didn't learn English fast, I would die. It was so tangible that day no one could help me on the train platform." English could also prove necessary to get a good work assignment after the weeks of training. While still at Wilmsloe, there was a meeting to assign positions to the new recruits. "They took us to a large room, where a number of officers were sitting at a desk. We were to be interviewed and assigned a trade. I walked into the room, still wearing the little "Poland" badge on my sleeve, and saw a woman who had "Belgium" on hers. I went up to her and talked to her in French. So she put me down as a translator, and I was given a Clerical General Duty rank, so I didn't have to do any physical work." At the same time, Maria focused her attention on trying to learn English.

After eight weeks at Wilmsloe, Maria was posted to Headquarters, Maintenance Command, at Andover Amport in Hampshire, not far from Salisbury. Because she was picking up English much faster than the other recruits in the English classes at Wilmsloe, she was sent to a British station. Still, she was disappointed not to be posted to London, where she could continue her studies. She went to London on a weekend pass to complain about the posting, and the authorities said that they would see what they could do, but all the London posts were filled right then, so she needed to go to Andover Amport.

When Maria got off the train at Andover Amport, a colonel, a captain, and a clerk from the small Polish liaison office there met her and took her to the WAAF station. She was the only Polish woman there. Trying to be friendly, the English women brought her a drink of spoiled milk, mistakenly identifying it with the yogurt-like milk drunk in Poland. Maria lived in the barracks with the British women, but felt isolated and lonely. She found it very difficult to understand their accents, and her background and experiences were very different from theirs. The result was that she had quite different interests and perspectives. Maria wanted to get more education, to read, go to plays and museums, and travel, while the other women were obsessed with movies, clothing, and boyfriends.

At Andover Amport, Maria was assigned to clerical duties. She would type administrative materials to go to the Polish squadrons on an old typewriter. "You had to bang really hard to type, especially with many carbon paper copies in there," she says. Maria had learned the basics of typing when she attended the underground school of commerce and economics in Warsaw during the war. Because its "front" for evading the Nazi prohibition on higher education for Poles was as a vocational school, a certain amount of typing and shorthand was in the curriculum. But, Maria reports, "the teachers would say, 'Don't worry. You'll be directors, you won't need to know how to type.'" Ironically, when history changed her fortunes, the typing skills came in useful.

The station at Andover Amport was on the grounds of a manor house requisitioned for the purpose. Maria was given an old bicycle to use and began to explore the beautiful countryside surrounding it. It was August, already a year from the start of the Uprising. The evenings were light, so she would go for rides after work. Soldiers were returning home from the war to towns all over England. "I would pass little villages," she says, "with banners saying 'Welcome home!' and my heart was breaking. I couldn't go home, I couldn't even write a letter. Postal service was not functioning between the Eastern and Western blocs then. It seemed so unfair."

Her journeys through the area near Andover Amport yielded some amusing moments as well. "One day I was going through the countryside where there was a manor or palace, then a wild garden. I stopped in the park where there was a cemetery and started reading the headstones. One said 'Beautiful Betty, such a nice mother and wonderful grandmother to many grandchildren, 30 years old!' I couldn't understand this. But when I returned to the barracks and asked, they explained to me that it was a dog cemetery!"

On weekends, the WAAF's would take the bus into the nearby town of Andover and see movies. "One day they came back and said 'We saw such a good movie, you have to see it.' So the next weekend, I walked all around the town looking for a movie called 'Abyssinia.' I found nothing like that. When I got back, they told me it was 'I'll Be Seeing You' with Joseph Cotton!" Maria had particular problems understanding the English women who spoke with Cockney accents; she would have to ask others to translate for her.

One advantage of the posting to Andover Amport was that it was easy to get to London by train, so Maria could begin to explore the city. She had almost no money but would stay with Polish friends who had been assigned to London. And, of course, she would see Franek, which helped relieve her loneliness.

On one of her first trips to London, Maria was in Trafalgar Square on August 15, 1945—VJ Day. She couldn't understand the announcements over the loudspeaker, but she quickly picked up what was happening from the overjoyed reactions of all the people around her. World War II was now over in the Pacific as well.

In early October 1945, Maria's request to be posted to London was granted, and she was assigned to Headquarters, Fighter Command, in Stanmore-Bentley Priory, from which the Battle of Britain had been directed. It still was the command center for the many air force units stationed around the British Isles. The Headquarters was on the grounds of a large country mansion in a suburb of London. There were formal gardens surrounding it and small barracks for the officers, both English and Polish. "It was different from Poland," Maria says. "British architecture is different. There were not so many monuments and statues.

It was more austere, not so fancy." The WAAF's stayed in houses that had been requisitioned in the village of Stanmore, down a hill from Bentley Priory.

Maria was at Stanmore from October 1945 to February 1947. She worked with 40 other people, mostly officers, in the Polish liaison office. "There were five former POW girls in there. I was a general duty clerk; I did typing and general office work." But being near London allowed Maria to take some classes in town. She quickly joined a French conversation club because it was the only thing she could take up in the middle of the course, and the Polish commander of her office sometimes gave her a lift into London because he knew she was going there almost every evening. Military personnel like Maria got free tuition and train passes to pursue their education. The French class had an added advantage; it allowed her to share experiences with other foreigners trying to adjust to life in England. "There was an old teacher, a Frenchman who was married to an English girl. He said 'How hard it is to live here. I'm used to gesticulating with my hands, and it's not polite in England—so I put my hands in my pockets to keep from gesticulating. Then my wife says that's not polite. I can never win.'"

Maria traveled frequently into London, and began to wander farther afield as well. In January 1946 she got a two-week pass and went to Paris, with only ten pounds to her name. "Franek laughed at me and said he would be waiting for a cable that I was in jail for an unpaid bill, but I came back with one pound. I stayed at an RAF hotel, a few blocks from the Opera, free of charge. I went to Notre Dame, Versailles, the Louvre, all the museums and churches. When I went to classical plays, I would be the only one there in uniform. After the war, people didn't like uniforms, but I didn't have anything else to wear. I could speak French, so the waiters and the concierge liked me; I was always running to the theater and coming back late, and he would open up for me." And even though the French did not have more food than the English, Maria reports that their flair for cooking made more palatable meals out of what they had. "English people," she says, "have a talent to spoil the food."

Being on the Continent also allowed Maria to see friends from the past. She visited the French governess who was with her family up until the outbreak of World War II. "Madame seemed so small," she says. Maria also visited friends from Poland who were now scattered in Western Europe. She went to visit Barbara, with whom she had shared the bunk and blanket in the POW camp, near Lille, boarding a night train to get there. When she found that she was the only woman in a section filled with rowdy American soldiers, Maria hopped off and managed to reboard the train in a section for officers, where there was a protected area for women. She got to Lille at 4 a.m. and had to wait in a smoky, crowded restaurant across from the station until the first bus came at 6 a.m. Barbara and her friends were going to the University of Lille. In the evening they held a party with all the young Poles nearby. "Everyone asked me if I was flying since I was in an Air Force uniform. I would laugh and say 'yes.'"

From Lille, Maria went to Brussels, to visit another friend for a day or two, and then on to Antwerp, to visit Krystyna, who was studying there. "It was nice. I was happy to see her and be with her again. She was telling me all about what had happened to her, what she went through. We talked about our families and how we missed them, about our experiences and ideas about the future. We went to a café together that evening, and everyone was playing the piano and singing."

The trip to the continent allowed Maria a chance to connect with persons who shared her past and who understood both her background and wartime experiences, with whom she felt comfortable. This experience contrasted with her discomfort with the Polish women with whom she lived and worked at Stanmore. When she got back, her colleagues simply couldn't understand why she had spent the small amount of money she had on travel, rather than buying civilian clothes. Maria said to them, "Dresses I've had in my life and I hope I will have them again, but I'm not sure I'll have the opportunity to visit the Continent." The other women were from a different social background in Poland, and it took a long time before they accepted her. Her life had been much more comfortable than theirs, and her expectations of what life would hold remained higher. She was an oddity to them. "It was hard for a year," she says. "They wouldn't include me, so I was lonely even among them. I had been so sheltered in my life; we had lived in an enormous, expensive apartment; I spent more on clothes than others made in a month. The other girls were from the working class. The way I acted and thought was so different. If it were now, I could get along with all of them."

Although she mostly lived in what she refers to as a "Polish ghetto," Maria did have one good English friend. In May of 1946 Marion Windsor invited Maria to go with her to the Scilly Isles, off the coast of Cornwall, in the southwest of England. Maria leapt at the chance to see more of the country. She earned three free railway passes a year, and by now had been a WAAF for almost a year. So the two women took the train to Penzance and then a ferry to the small island of St. Marys. "When we got to the top of the hill, you could see water all around. There were cows and horses, only one car. There was one store where they had everything and nothing. One or two small hotels. Only honeymooners and actors went there. We were lucky we got a room. There were fields of flowers—hyacinths, tulips, daffodils; a tiny plane would fly them to florists in London. There were small coves where we went swimming. Once we met an old fisherman who came there to shop from another island on a tiny boat; he had never been to the mainland. We walked around a lot. One day we saw a cow with calves, and I said 'Look, there are the cow's children.' Marion laughed at me! The farmers thought I was Welsh because I couldn't speak English right."

Despite her happiness at traveling, Maria could not escape her homesickness, loneliness, and the feelings and attitudes drilled into her by the war. "We were so used to being very careful what we would say. After I had been in England for months, I came to London and went out to lunch with my cousin. He asked me to tell him what it was like in Warsaw during the war, what I had been doing, how people were behaving. I thought, 'How can he ask such a question in a public place? Is he stupid?' Then I looked around and suddenly realized I was not in occupied Poland but in the free world; we could say whatever we wanted to. But it was very deep-seated to behave with care." She found it hard to adjust to ordinary life after living under stress for so long.

Maria had come through the war years, the Uprising, and life as a prisoner of war with amazing calm. But one day in the summer of 1946 the feelings she had suppressed in order to survive caught up with her. She came into London from Stanmore to see the dentist and arranged to meet some ex-WAAF friends after her appointment. "It was a nice sunny afternoon. I was walking down Oxford Street and started to feel funny. I went into Selfridges to keep busy, but it got worse. I was short of breath, hot. I jumped into a bus to Piccadilly Circus but I felt weak, like I was going to faint, and very nervous. It is hard to explain. When I got out, I decided to walk fast, thinking that might help. But I felt like I was having a heart attack. I was passing a movie house and grabbed the bellboy who was outside and asked him to bring some cold water, quick. He ran inside and brought a beer glass full of water."

"I had had this feeling once before when I went to a piano concert at Wigmore Hall in London. I felt so funny, panicky, but one of the attendants put me into an empty box and I recovered. After that, I was afraid of distance. If I was walking, I kept close to houses where I could get in if the feeling came. I was also frightened of being alone. Once I went to the movies in Harrow with an officer but had to sit at the corner of the row or I would get panicky; I needed to be able to get out."

On the day of her anxiety attack in Piccadilly, Maria's friends arrived and took her to a chemist's shop, but the pills he gave her didn't help much. The women called the Air Ministry Headquarters, and after several hours an ambulance arrived to take Maria to a health department office, where they left her in an office all alone. "Suddenly someone called 'Corporal, come in.' I looked around, and no one else was there. Then I remembered it was the day of my promotion! They put me in an office and gave me some pills and a glass of water. After a couple of hours they told me to go home. I said that I couldn't go alone. So I called Marion Windsor, who was already discharged and living in London, and she took me back to Stanmore on the tube."

Maria went back to work but kept getting more attacks of this sort. She was admitted to the RAF hospital in Uxbridge to recuperate. "If I had been British, they would have sent me home for a month's vacation. But since I was not, they sent me there for several weeks and gave me tranquillizers." It seems clear that Maria was having a delayed reaction to the war and the fighting she had been through. Once she had adjusted to her new life enough to relax a little, all the feelings she had so carefully controlled came out. Today we would probably diagnose this as Post Traumatic Stress Disorder, but such reactions were poorly understood at that time. In Maria's case, this was compounded with the stress of starting a new life in a strange country, and the loss of her home, homeland, and family. These alone would be hard for anyone to manage. It was hard for me to imagine the sparkling, social, optimistic woman who had become my friend in such distress. It is a testament to the depth of horror and dislocation absorbed by so many survivors of this period that someone as grounded and resourceful as Maria was incapacitated by her experience.

"There was a nice park around the hospital. I would walk in it and sit. I was thinking how horrible it was that I can't spend summer in my country, how I used to spend summer vacations in nice places. I was worrying about my family and what they were doing. I was so homesick. I felt how unjust it was that others could go home, wear civilian clothes, get discharged and have somewhere to go. I thought about everything I left behind. The main thing was my family and way of life. I didn't know what to do, except that I shouldn't go back to Poland because of my history in the AK. I had already heard stories of AK veterans' being arrested by the Communists. I worried about what I could do. I would have liked to get out of the service. The lack of privacy was getting me down but I didn't want to be alone in a big city. I couldn't see the future."

"I read as much as I could. It was summer and the days were long. Nurses were in charge of the convalescent ward where I was. The head nurse seemed like an old, skinny, typical English woman. One day I was reading a Polish book describing life in the countryside of Poland and Lithuana. I was very involved in it; I had a picture in my mind of surroundings—the Polish forest—so different from the one I was in. And I was feeling 'I cannot go home, I can't even get in touch with my family.' Suddenly I heard a voice above me asking 'And how are you, dear?' I looked up at this skinny woman; it was like she came from another planet. I was so surprised I couldn't even place where I was. My mind was so far away. Everyone else at the hospital was so British. People were nice to me, though." Maria stayed at the Uxbridge RAF hospital for the rest of the summer of 1946.

CHAPTER 12

Resettlement

The large number of Poles in England after World War II (about 150,000) posed many problems for the British government. A Communist government was in power in Warsaw, and in July 1945 recognition was withdrawn from the Polish government in London. The Poles who remained were anti-Communist, at a time when pro-Soviet feeling was still strong because of the role the Soviet Union had played in defeating Hitler; and the new Labour Government was delicately building its relationships with the new Europe.

English popular opinion did not favor integration of the many foreigners present in the country during and after the war. Quite apart from a native xenophobia, and despite a labor shortage, Britons felt threatened by the competition of non-citizens for jobs, social services, and the scarce supply of housing. Consumer goods were also scarce; bread and potatoes, for example, were rationed for the first time in 1946 and 1947. A Gallup poll in June 1946 showed that 56% of Britons disapproved of allowing the Poles to settle there, despite earlier feelings of gratitude to the Polish flyers who had valiantly defended London during the Blitz.

The British government decided to disband the Polish armed forces in March 1946. Poles were encouraged to return to their homeland, and would be assisted in doing so, although none were to be coerced. For those who remained in England, a Polish Resettlement Corps (PRC) was established in 1947, to provide education, social services, and assistance in returning to civilian life, either in the U.K. or abroad, within a two-year period.

Only Poles who had served in Polish forces under British command before June 1, 1945 were eligible for the PRC, thus excluding many Polish refugees released from Nazi concentration, forced labor and POW camps, including some 67,000 veterans of the AK. (Maria's eligibility for assistance rested upon her recruitment into the Air Force in May 1945.) Those who left the service were housed in camps vacated by the military throughout England, provided with medical care and instruction in English, and assisted in finding employment, either in work corps organized to address the labor shortages in agriculture and mining or in private employment. Professionals and other skilled workers, however, faced serious problems finding work, and many had to be re-trained in less skilled occupations. They also met with discrimination against the employment of non-Britons.

The British government subsidized higher education for the former Polish troops, to fit them for civilian employment either in England or other countries. Emigration was encouraged, with the government paying the cost of passage abroad and lobbying other Allied nations to accept the Poles, so that many fewer would settle in Britain. Long waits greeted those who wanted to emigrate to Australia or the U.S., although Canada admitted several thousand in 1946 and 1947. Entry into the United States was eased in 1950 under a bill enacted to admit 20,000 Poles over a two-year period. Poles living in the U.S. had vigorously lobbied Congress to pass the bill.

Poles who were in Britain during this time faced a good deal of hostility from the English. Government officials complained of being "saddled" with the "burden" of thousands of Poles, and Poles reported discrimination and, despite their heroic service during the war, verbal abuse. Many also said they found English society rather sleepy and dull. In short, despite a good deal of concrete economic assistance to the Poles who found themselves on British soil after the war, England was not a very welcoming place.

Whether from the rest or simply from allowing herself at last to experience the feelings of deep sadness within her, Maria eventually got well and returned to her station by the end of the summer of 1946. She continued to be lonely, however, and to feel different from the women around her and their values. She still had her cousin Franek, though, and would meet him every week or so. "He would take me out to dinner; he belonged to a nice club. He was more experienced than I, 10 or 11 years older and had spent a lot of his life in the west. He was the only person with whom I felt I shared part of my heritage."

Various classes were offered at Stanmore, so Maria signed up for sewing. Once the war was over, officers were not required to wear uniforms all the time, but Maria had been doing so because she did not have any other clothes. She built upon the sewing lessons her French governess had given her as a child and learned to make herself a skirt and a blouse. The big obstacle was obtaining material; it was rationed and Maria was ineligible for coupons. But she discovered some Polish Jews who were selling cloth on the open market in Watford. They spoke to her in Polish and said to come back later, when the English girls were not there. She bought enough material for a skirt, blouse and jacket from them without a ration coupon—using the black market as her family had done to survive during the war.

In early 1947 the RAF began to close the Polish liaison section at Stanmore. As a result, Maria was transferred to a camp near Melton Mowbray, a town in the Midlands, near Nottingham. Although Maria had not yet signed up for the Polish Resettlement Corps, she was posted at a PRC camp for Poles who were to be discharged. While Melton Mowbray was still an airfield, the base also had Quonset huts for émigré families, along with barracks for the staff.

"Melton Mowbray was a horrible station after the comparative luxury of Stanmore, where we had been in a nice barracks with central heating, radio, and a small indoor washroom. The winter was the coldest in years. All the plumbing pipes at Melton Mowbray were on the outside of the buildings and so were freezing. The WAAF side had no running water because of frozen pipes. We had to go to the men's side to shower and bring back water in a hot water bottle for the morning. Although the rations were the same, the food was lousy. They gave us horrible meals. The water was full of chlorine; you could taste it in tea or porridge."

When Maria knew she was to be posted to Melton Mowbray that cold winter, she saved up as much vacation time as possible. She had a month's worth by the time she arrived. As soon as she went through clearance at the new station, she filed an application for leave. So after a few days in the freezing cold, she left for London, where she stayed in a hotel. Her cousin Franek brought her sandwiches because she couldn't afford restaurant food. She succumbed to that year's flu epidemic, however, and while she recovered, moved in with a girlfriend who was awaiting repatriation to Poland. Franek continued to visit and bring her food.

London was also miserably cold that winter, so when Maria got well she decided to go to the southwest of the country, where the weather is always milder. She spent a week in Torquay, in South Devon, where almond trees were in bloom. By then, Maria had a skirt, blouse and jacket she had made, along with a pair of civilian shoes. She felt much freer in the civilian clothes. There is a picture of her in Torquay with a friend who lived there, posing in a park with palm trees in it. Another photo shows Maria against the backdrop of the rocky coast, wearing only a skirt and blouse. She looks happy and free.

When Maria returned to Melton Mowbray in March, it was warmer, and there was water on the women's side of the camp again. But she was increasingly dissatisfied with her lot. "My one close friend, the one I visited in Torquay, had left the military and gotten married. The other girls I knew had no ambition and were not thinking about the future. I could no longer see the future, or any advantage to staying in England. I didn't aspire to just earn enough to eat; I still had an image of the life I had lived."

To make matters worse, Maria's cousin Franek decided to return to Poland. The role of the government-in-exile was finished, because the Communist regime had supplanted it. When his brother Zybszek had died at the end of the Uprising, their mother had been left alone. (Maria's uncle had died near the end of the war.) "She kept writing about how desperate and lonely she was," Maria says, "that she had no one to consult. Their country estate had been taken away by the regime. All his friends advised against it, but Franek believed that he should go back to take care of her. He went back to Poland to my despair. I was heartbroken because he was like a brother to me. I couldn't talk to him about my concerns or about the future any more." When he left, Maria lost her only connection with the past. Franek died in Poland in 1954. She never saw him again.

Maria now had to face the decision whether to join the Polish Resettlement Corps, in which case return to Poland would be out of the question, or to go home. Her father was sick, and she thought about going back. The struggle within her was like that on the night during the ceasefire at the end of the Uprising when she wrestled with the decision whether to leave Warsaw with the AK for Germany or to stay in Poland with the civilians.

"I was working for this old Polish officer, who was telling me to sign or be deported to Germany. I did not know what to do. Should I stay in the west and have an uncertain future but be free of what was happening in Poland? Or go back because my father was old and sick? I couldn't make up my mind, and he was after me every day, asking 'Have you made up your mind yet?'" Then Maria's father wrote to tell her to think hard before coming home. As she recalls, he told her, "I would love to see you. You know that the house is always open and you are always welcome. But think twice before you decide what to do because our democracy doesn't resemble others in the west. I want you to be aware of this fact. It might be dangerous." So Maria finally decided to stay in the west, and she signed up for the Resettlement Corps.

This decision did not resolve the question of what she would do. "I had no money. When I was discharged I would be very lonely. I didn't know what kind of work I could get, or if I could live decently. Most of my girlfriends just got married, some because they were in love, others just to establish themselves. I had boyfriends, but I didn't want to marry them." Indeed, Maria had spent her whole life either living at home while at school, or as a prisoner, or in some form of military service. She had never lived on her own or made her way as an adult in civilian life. On the other hand, she was still young, healthy and attractive, had been well educated, was very sociable, and, unlike some of the Polish refugees, had learned English rapidly, with little formal instruction. These, and her natural resourcefulness, were her only assets.

While doing office work at Melton Mowbray, Maria began to date a British man named Ken, who was the adjutant of the station. "He was young and good-looking. He was very nice, very thoughtful. He was concerned about all the details to make me feel comfortable. For example, if I was going to London for the weekend, he would call and make a booking for me and take me by car to the railway station. But when I found out he was one year younger than I, I felt ashamed; this was unacceptable then."

There wasn't much to do in Melton Mowbray on dates. "Unlike Polish provincial cities, it was very boring. In Poland, it was livelier in the cities outside Warsaw; there were restaurants, movies, concerts. But in England, everything closed on Saturday at 6 p.m. and there was no place to go, even for tea. The movie house was closed on Sunday. There was simply no entertainment. It was boring."

Maria and Ken did go to the small town nearby for dinner at the restaurant in the one hotel there. On weekends they would visit Newstead Abbey, the ancestral estate of Lord Byron, in Nottingham. "There was a long walk from the highway. It was beautiful, with forest on one side and rhododendrons blooming all over. Next to the castle was the official park, then a wild park, which had a pond with swans. One day we saw a battle between two swans, a big fight up in the air. We would take long walks in the countryside there. It was my favorite place. It seemed so romantic."

Although Maria dated British men, she never seriously considered marrying any of them. There seemed to be a cultural gulf between her and the English, which she describes in an oblique fashion. "There was a little pamphlet called 'How To Be an Alien' written during the war by a Hungarian who became British. It was short but well done. One chapter was called 'Sex'. It said that in continental Europe, they recognize sex life, but in England it looks like this: what followed was a drawing of a hot water bottle! (Everyone went to bed with hot water bottles because there was no central heating.) At the end of this book it says they were sitting at a party discussing the latest news about the war. This guy, who was already a citizen, said 'Oh, our planes shot down ten German planes today.' A British lady looked at him and said 'I'm sorry. They were *our* planes.'" After three years in England, Maria was sure that the English would never really accept anyone who was a foreigner. "I knew that, behind my back, every one would always be saying I was a 'bloody foreigner.'"

The few Polish girls Maria knew who did marry Englishmen had unpleasant experiences with their new in-laws. "One, who was pregnant, married a British boy in the service; he was so in love with her. His family were well-to-do industrialists in the northeast of England. When he got out, they would hardly let him visit her. His family wouldn't accept her, and he didn't have the means to support her on his own. She stayed in the family camp for a year or so."

Maria also knew she would get bored living in England, at least in the countryside, because life was so slow compared to her cosmopolitan childhood and wartime adventures. Her initial expectations that life in England would be similar to that in continental Europe were sadly disappointed.

Although clearly not destined to marry because of the cultural gap of which Maria was so keenly aware, Ken and Maria nonetheless gave one another good advice about the future. Maria went to London once during that year for a short vacation and found a job as a seamstress. She came back and told Ken that she was going to apply for a discharge. "He said 'What are you doing? Are you crazy? It's not for you. Forget about it.' So I backed out." The next year, when Maria had moved to another station, they continued their conversations in long letters to one another. "I told him not to stay in the service, he was too intelligent, he should go to law school. So he went after we broke up. Much later I found out that he had graduated cum laude and was a solicitor."

After a year at Melton Mowbray, Maria was again transferred, first to Framlingham, near Ipswich, and then to a camp called Dunholme Lodge, near Lincoln, through which all Poles getting discharged had to pass. It was there that she met Brunon Chudzinski.

CHAPTER 13

Brunon

At Dunholme Lodge, the airfield had been closed. The station now processed former soldiers returning to civilian life. Maria worked in the employment section. Each morning she used a loudspeaker to call out names from a long list of officers waiting to find work, telling them to report to the employment section. In the spring of 1948, Brunon Chudzinski (known as "Bruno") came into her section to apply for a new I.D. card.

Bruno came from a village in Pomerania called Sulnowko, where his parents had a small farm. "They were better than peasants," Maria says, "but only a little. His sister later told me he was too lazy to work in the field so they sent him to school. He was very intelligent and ambitious. He could study anything, do whatever he wanted to accomplish. Somehow he got to officer candidate school, for cavalry."

Bruno graduated from military school in 1939 and was assigned to a cavalry unit in the northeast of Poland just before Germany invaded. When the fighting started, almost everyone in his unit was killed. After Poland was defeated, he crossed into Lithuania, but before long the Russians arrived and interned all the Polish soldiers. He was taken to a POW camp in Russia. "One day," Maria tells, obviously from stories repeated by Bruno, "they showed a movie with a Polish Communist who was glorifying the Communists, and the Polish prisoners were noisy and showed their opposition. Two days later they put the whole camp on a train and took them to Archangel, then by boat to some wild place where they had to build an airfield. They were told that when the people before them couldn't work any more, they were taken on ferries to the northern sea and sunk."

When Hitler invaded the Soviet Union in 1941, the Polish prisoners of war were released, pursuant to an amnesty agreement with the Polish government-in-exile. (Bruno later proclaimed at a law school party in Chicago—to astonished faculty—that "Hitler saved my life.") General Sikorski, leader of the Polish government in exile, wanted a Polish army to be organized in Russia and to remain there until the soldiers could fight their way back to Poland. However, General Władysław Anders, a Polish general released from prison under the amnesty, did not trust the Soviets and began to organize what became known as the "Anders army" in the south of Russia.* Bruno and a friend made the difficult journey from north of Archangel to join the Anders army in the south.

The soldiers then traveled overland from Russia to the Caspian Sea, to what was then Persia (modern-day Iran), and from Teheran to Bombay, eating whatever they could find—so many dates, Maria says, that Bruno would never eat them again. Bruno left India by boat, sailed around South Africa, and, escaping the U-boats, arrived in England in 1942. He promptly enlisted in the air force and after a few months training became a very good fighter pilot. "His rank was flight lieutenant, like captain, and he was flying Spitfires," says Maria, pointing to the picture of a Spitfire over her couch. "He was eventually transferred to a squadron in Italy that was a reconnaissance unit, so he would fly over the war lines taking pictures and directing the fire. Once he returned, and the mechanics asked 'How did you manage to come back?' The plane had holes in the wings."

"Later Bruno was given a whole unit to take from Italy to Cairo. He had all kinds of problems on the way, but managed to deliver everyone safely. He could've been in big trouble, though, because he flew at night, which many members of his squadron did not do because they were inexperienced." When the Cairo mission was over and Bruno returned to his unit, the war in Europe had ended. Deciding that it was time to study, he applied to the Polish University College then attached to the University of London, passed the entrance exam, and began a course of study in commerce and economics.

Bruno found it very difficult to live on the 20 British pounds a month he was given as a scholarship. After some time, he became quite ill with amoebic dysentery, a result of his journey through Russia to reach the Polish army. The only food they had had for a period was salted herring, with unsanitary water to wash it down. Because of the dysentery, Bruno left the university. He was sent to a Polish hospital in Wales for treatment. When he was released in early 1948, he decided to try to return to the air force, because he couldn't live on his scholarship. Although it was very unusual, he was allowed to re-enter the service, and went to be processed at Dunholme Lodge.

Maria remembers Bruno from April 1948: "He was full of life. I used to pass him when going to a different mess; he was always smiling. He was slim and looked great in his officer's uniform. He would always call me beautiful and

---

* One division of the military corps General Anders put together went to Palestine, Egypt, and then Italy, capturing Monte Cassino in 1944, thus clearing the way for the conquest of Rome. He is buried in the Polish cemetery at Monte Cassino.

make small talk. So we started to date. We would cycle out into the country together. On Saturday we would go into Lincoln on the bus for lunch and to go to the movies. We'd stop for fish and chips in a village on the way back, served on what we called "Polish china," that is, newspaper. At other times we used to go into the country with friends, where there was a tavern, to drink and watch people playing darts."

Photographs of Maria and Bruno from this period show a laughing couple on bicycles in the countryside with the wind blowing their hair, clowning around for the camera. Bruno is tall, dark-haired and handsome. Maria has long thick dark hair; she looks happy and full of life. Other pictures show a New Year's Eve celebration in what appears to be a Quonset hut; they are cooking with friends and then posing in front of a Christmas tree with everyone wearing funny hats. Bruno looks wonderful in a turban, Maria in a mortarboard. Other photos show the couple cuddling on a park bench and, in yet another, in tall grass, obviously enjoying themselves and one another.

By the time Maria left for London in January 1949, Bruno was her serious boyfriend. She obtained a final discharge from the air force in February of that year. Bruno got his about the same time and came to London. Maria rented a room with a girlfriend in South Kensington and began to look for a job. She got one at the YMCA headquarters, where she was assigned to calculate the expense incurred for each worker in all the hostels in Wales. She learned to calculate in her head so well that, years later, her supervisor would give her his budget to check.

Maria had to count every penny she spent because she barely earned enough to survive. "I would lie awake in bed wondering when I could ever save some money. I hardly had enough to buy lunch, and would just eat an egg at a snack bar." To make matters worse, after a few weeks in London, Maria came home after work one day to find a note from her roommate saying "I'm going to Nottingham, where my sister is." Alone, Maria had to look for a smaller furnished room, which was hard to find given the housing shortage in England at that time. She moved often. "Bruno would help me move from one place to another. He lived at a house for air force veterans not far from me, and we would see one another every day. He was very helpful to me. In the last place I lived there were lots of mice. It was very small; you could reach each corner of the room sitting on the divan bed. Mice were coming through the fireplace at night. One day I turned on the gas fire and one got burned; Bruno threw it out the window for me."

"We tried poison; it didn't work. We borrowed a cat, who messed up the floor, and the mice were still running over me in the bed. I had saved up coupons to buy one wool dress; the mice got into it and chewed a hole in it. I was fighting all the time with the mice. I'd wake up and find a mama with babies still without fur on my bed. Finally a new owner put a metal bolt over the fireplace, and that was the end of the mice."

Bruno was also working at the "Y," though at a different location. "But he was determined to go back to school, to get a scholarship again. Others just went to learn practical jobs, but he was ambitious to study. I liked this about him." Although Maria also wanted to study, she was stuck for a while in jobs she hated. She was miserable at the Y because she had a boss with a difficult personality. She worked at the Polish Air Force Association Club as a waitress for a few months. For a couple of months she even worked as a seamstress, doing alterations. She kept her dream of returning to school, of continuing with the study of commerce and economics she had begun in Warsaw during the war and eventually attaining a managerial position, even if she had to begin as a clerk.

In the spring of 1949, one year after they had met, Maria and Bruno decided to get married. "We decided it would be better to get together. The society there was so different from how it was at home. We were cut off; we got few letters. We were both alone and we weren't going back." Their solution to deracination was to establish a family of their own.

When Maria wrote to her family about their decision, her stepmother went to a seamstress and had a dress made to the measurements of the clothes she had left behind in Warsaw. "Rita Hayward got married that May to Aga Khan, and they [her parents] had a similar dress made. They sent it in two parcels, one with the gown, the other with the lining."

Maria and Bruno were married on July 30, 1949 at the Brompton Oratory, a Roman Catholic church in Kensington, by a Polish priest who had been attached to Bruno's squadron in Italy. They were surrounded by forty or fifty friends, mostly acquaintances from the Polish air force in England. Only two of Maria's relatives were present—Zybszek's uncle, the equestrian whose fame had saved Zybszek's life the day he was taken by the Gestapo, and one of the male cousins who had been with Maria at her aunt and uncle's estate when the war broke out; both had been in the Polish forces in Great Britain. Maria was 26 years old and Bruno was 29.

Maria showed me a scrapbook of pictures from her wedding. It includes an elegant wedding invitation in both English and Polish, announcing the ceremony at 11:30 a.m. The photos show a beaming Maria in a beautiful long white dress and short veil, carrying an enormous bouquet of white carnations. Bruno looks happy yet solemn next to her, in a dark suit with a white carnation in his buttonhole. Despite the happy looks, Maria tells me of her fears in the days before the event. "I went shopping with someone who told me she had been married ten years. I got cold feet and threw my dress around, thinking of spending ten years with the same man! We were married fifty years."

The wedding consisted of a brief Catholic service without a mass, followed by a civil ceremony. Instead of being required to go to a government office for the civil ceremony, Bruno gave a tip to the clerk, who came to the church sacristy and performed the civil marriage right after the religious ceremony. After the wedding they went to a hotel for a formal dinner with friends. I met several of these friends, fifty-some years older, in Chicago.

On the day of the wedding Maria and Bruno moved into a one-room apartment in the Earls Court neighborhood of London, where they lived for two and one-half years. "At midnight we were walking with pots and pans down the street. I went to my old place to get frying pans for breakfast. I still didn't know how to cook, not the slightest idea. Bruno did, but somehow he became too dumb to cook by two weeks later, after he showed me how to make a few things, such as to fry a fish." The room in which they lived was large, but the bathroom was on the landing below. There was one sink inside the apartment, and the kitchen consisted of a table and a small electric burner. "Eventually I learned how to function," Maria says.

Maria and Bruno did not have the money to go on a honeymoon until the following year. Finally, in the summer of 1950 they went for two weeks to the Isle of Wight, off the south coast of England, for their wedding trip. Apart from one long weekend, this was the only vacation the two had together in England because they were working and studying all the time. "We stayed in a nice place, a lovely little manor in Ventnor that used to belong to a lady portrayed in a novel by Charles Dickens. There was a guestbook Dickens had signed." A photo shows them sitting on the lawn outside a magnificent mansion. Maria describes the weather as having been somewhat cold. "We used to take long walks in the hills or by the sea. When it was sunny we were at the beach, but wearing sweaters. Later on it got warmer. We spent all day by the sea, and went out walking after dinner. Ventnor was quiet. There were no evening activities. When we came back home after the evening walk, we would read or talk to other guests." Maria says that she felt sad to go back to London at the end of their time away because she enjoyed the time in the countryside so much.

Maria's scrapbook from the period after her marriage to Bruno shows that the couple had a very active social life in London. It is filled with pictures of them drinking wine or beer with friends, of dances at the Polish Air Force Association, at friends' weddings, and on excursions out of town—at the beach, on picnics, swimming or rowing, at Hampton Court, or Windsor Castle. Maria especially liked the huge formal gardens outside Hampton Court Palace. Bruno, unfortunately, also liked to go to the racetrack.

After their marriage, Maria continued to work, although she still dreamt of studying. In 1945, she had been admitted to the Regent Polytechnic with a scholarship, but the Polish military had said that she was still a necessary employee, so she had to turn it down. Bruno and their many friends encouraged her now to apply to the School of Foreign Trade, so she took the entrance exam. After their honeymoon, Maria got a letter saying that she had been admitted with a scholarship, one of only three women admitted to a class of 110 out of 450 people who had taken the exam.

The School of Foreign Trade and Port Administration was a university-level program run by the British government for Polish students interested in international commerce. They took courses in business administration, shipping and marine insurance, math and accounting, economics, contracts, English, and commercial correspondence. The teachers were primarily drawn from British schools, but some of them were scholars displaced by the war in Europe. Others were professionals—a broker from Lloyds of London to teach insurance, for example, and a barrister for law courses.

Because she was married, Maria's scholarship was only 2/3 that of unmarried students. Bruno had also returned to school. He received 20 pounds a month and Maria about 15 pounds; their rent alone was over 17 pounds. Although students were not supposed to work if they were on scholarship, Maria continued to waitress at an exhibition hall when there were shows, looking around carefully to make sure she was not seen. Occasionally, when she needed to work for a week or ten days to make enough money that they could live well, she would go to the Polish medical center to get a certificate that she was sick and be excused from school.

Completing the one-year program was difficult, and not only because of the lack of money. Maria appears to have encountered a good deal of prejudice against women students from both the other students and the principal of the school, who was constantly trying to get rid of her. He was rather nasty to her during the oral admissions interview, then stood over her during an exam to make sure she wasn't cheating. Another professor warned Maria to watch her step because the principal had told the faculty he wanted to fail her. It was also hard to study in the tiny apartment, especially if Bruno brought someone home to study with him. "I would go with friends to study in Hyde Park. When we saw the old man coming to collect for use of the chairs, we would move. I studied there, but it rained a lot." Despite the difficulties, in September 1951, at the end of a year's course of study, Maria received the diploma, one of only 45 students to do so.

By that time, however, she and Bruno had already decided to emigrate to the United States. "I had always wanted to come here," she says. "I read about it, saw it in the movies. I met some Americans and they were very relaxed. Somehow America was a bright spot on the firmament. We knew one thing, that it was a country of opportunity for everybody. In America, I could work and get ahead. I wouldn't always be a foreigner. When I met Bruno, he was going all over the world and nowhere. Before meeting me, Bruno applied to go to the U.S., Canada, South Africa, Argentina. When he told me, I knew he would not go anywhere. So I thought 'We'll go where I want.'"

The decision to emigrate to the U.S. was heavily influenced by Maria's conviction that, as foreigners, they would never really be accepted in England or be able to make a success of life in the closed society there. "Although we were a privileged group of foreigners in the Air Force and could easily have had British citizenship, we would always be regarded as foreigners. I had great recommendations from the Air Force but still always felt not welcome. One English girlfriend told me about an open clerical position at the British Automobile Club. I filled out a long application [and was clearly over-qualified for the position]. They told me, 'That's outstanding, it's marvelous. But we have such a longstanding tradition; we can't afford to hire someone who is not English born.' I went to Lyons' costing headquarters and took a test, which I apparently passed. I got called for an interview and offered a job at 3½ pounds a week. I said 'That would be just enough for transportation and coffee; I have to live.' The interviewer said 'Why don't you go back home?'"

It was difficult to gain entry to the United States because the quotas for each national group were quite small. But the veterans bill for which the Polish American Congress had lobbied set extra quotas for a period of time which would end in April 1952. "You needed a sponsor in America to guarantee to cover your expenses if necessary, but it was not so difficult as the regular process. Many of our friends applied for it, but Bruno's friends said 'You shouldn't go; you'd be working all the time to maintain our easy way of life. Here we have tea every few hours; there you'll be running all the time.' So we didn't apply when the program was first announced."

When Maria was at school, other friends who were waiting for visas to the U.S. asked her why she didn't apply. "We don't know anyone there to sponsor us," she said. But then Bronek, a friend of Bruno's who was with him in Russia and in the air force but who had grown up in Chicago, found a woman who lived there to sponsor them. "I was disappointed; I wanted to go to California, for the climate," says Maria.

So in 1950 Maria and Bruno went to the United States Embassy in London to apply for a visa to emigrate. They had all but forgotten about it when, on January 18, 1951, Bruno's birthday, they received a letter with an American quota number assigned to them. So, tells Maria, "Bruno said, 'If we got it on my birthday, it means we've got to go.'"

The timing posed problems for Bruno's education. Maria's course of study was complete by the following September, but Bruno's finals at the Polish University College at the University of London would not take place until June 1952. The special visa program would expire in April of '52. He therefore quit school in 1951 and registered for transport to the United States. He found work in the accounting department of an export-import firm to replace his scholarship money.

——

Emigrés were given free passage by the British government. When Bruno went to register for transport, the couple was assigned to leave on a Greek boat right after Christmas. But Maria still wanted to attend the big New Year's Eve Ball at the Polish Air Force Club. She refused to leave on the boat assigned, saying that one of her maritime commerce professors had told her that Greek boats were not seaworthy. Bruno returned to the transport office and said that his wife did not want to go on this boat. When told that all the other ships were full, he said "Okay, I'll send my wife to you." The official said "Oh, no!" and assigned them to leave on the Liberté, a French ship, in mid-January. "And so we had delicious food and fantastic service," reports Maria.

Maria and Bruno went to the New Year's Eve Ball and stayed up all night dancing and saying good-bye to friends. "Most of our friends were now gone to heaven or hell or somewhere around the globe, though," Maria says. Those who were left all visited them in their last few days in England.

They packed very little to bring with them, one heavy trunk and two suitcases. "We mostly gave the kitchen stuff away; we had little anyway. We brought a couple of sheets, one change of bedding. I don't remember if we brought a blanket. I wanted to bring some duty-free stuff, to be delivered to the boat. We arranged to go shopping at Selfridges, but when we met at noon, Bruno (who had stayed home because the shipping company was coming to pick up their luggage) said, 'You know what happened? I forgot that my money was in my jacket. I packed my suit and other things, and they took the luggage.' So we had no money for shopping."

In the second week of January, they took the train from Victoria Station to Southhampton, where they were put on a ferry to the boat. "It was anchored near the Isle of Wight because the port duties were so high. It was dark by then, and the boat was huge and illuminated. Right away we met a nice American guy named Morris, who started briefing us about life in the United States. He looked at me and said, 'Bruno, you have to buy your wife nice nylons.' And 'You won't like the bread; it's like cotton wool.' And lots of little details like that."

"We got assigned for dinner at a table with Americans. Bruno spoke good English, and I could communicate. There were some missionaries, an artist named Jane from Iowa, and Morris, who was so full of life. The artist would tease Morris, who had said his wife was very jealous. Jane said, 'When we get to New York, I'll throw my arms around you and say "I hate to part from you!"'" He was so scared that he didn't even come to breakfast the last day; he disembarked before we did." Maria laughs heartily at this memory.

The Channel was very rough at that time of year. Before leaving London, Maria went to a doctor for seasickness medicine. "Bruno laughed," she says, "and said he wouldn't need it. 'I am a pilot; I'll never need it.' When we were asked what we wanted for breakfast the first morning, Bruno said 'Order everything.' I asked, 'Wouldn't you rather have water crackers and tea?' By the time the steward brought breakfast, Bruno couldn't eat anything. I went to lunch, and hardly anyone was there except for me and one other woman. Later a friend of Bruno's came and asked me for a seasickness pill, and then another one for 'a friend.' It was for Bruno, but he wouldn't admit he needed it!"

When the sea calmed down, Maria and Bruno settled down to have a good time. "We would dance and play games, like dancing with a piece of fruit on your forehead between the two of you and see who lasted longest. We played bingo, and even borrowed a kid to go to the puppet show. On Sunday there was a Mass, way up on the top deck; you could hardly see the sea." And thus passed, in a characteristic fashion, the interval between their extraordinary, adventurous, disrupted, and ultimately unsatisfactory lives in Europe and their unknown new life in the United States—with both Bruno and Maria having a good time.

On January 22, 1952, the Liberté steamed past the Statue of Liberty and into New York harbor.

Maria in Air Force uniform, RAF station, Melton Mowbray

Maria and Brunon riding bicycles near Dunholme Lodge

Maria and Brunon outside London

Maria and Brunon on their wedding day, Brompton Oratory, London

CHAPTER 14

England, July 2003

In the summer of 2003 I went to England to visit the places where Maria had lived and worked. Planning this trip was more difficult than the previous summer's visit to Poland. For Warsaw, I had Maria's notes and her sister as guides to a city that had largely been reconstructed along the lines of the one that existed prior to the war. In England, by contrast, most of the traces of the Royal Air Force during World War II and the years immediately thereafter are disappearing. Fortunately, I discovered an RAF website that detailed the location of the wartime stations, their use, and what had become of them in the years since. Only one still existed—Bentley Priory, from which the Battle of Britain was directed; I was even able to find a book with numerous photographs of it. So I packed my notes on Maria's life in England and set off in July 2003 with my partner Ben, who is English.

Wilmslow was the recruiting station to which Maria was sent upon her arrival in England from the Netherlands, soon after liberation from the Oberlangen POW camp. We visited the town of Wilmslow, now an upscale commuter community south of Manchester, at 7 on a summer evening. There was a Starbucks on the main street, but it was already closed for the day. Failing to find coffee, we stopped in a pub across the street. It was more like a modern bar. American music was playing, and none of the atmosphere one would expect in an English pub was evident. We drove to the train station. We couldn't find anywhere to park, but we could make out the old station, where the newly-arrived Maria was unable to read the signs, tucked away behind a new station building. We drove out of town on the highway where the RAF website said the recruiting station had been. It is now a housing estate, bisected by the highway bypassing Manchester. A rather discouraging start for our journey into the past.

We had better luck at Andover Amport, where Maria was transferred in the summer of 1945. It is near Salisbury. We drove there on winding roads in the light of a long English summer evening. Suddenly there was a vista across open fields to a very grand house, all that is left of the RAF station. Amport House, built in 1857, was the Headquarters of Maintenance Command during and for a while after the war. It is now a school for armed forces' chaplains. We drove into the small village and all around the estate. The community is filled with upscale housing; we passed women in jodhpurs astride expensive-looking horses. We returned to our first viewpoint and tramped into a peaceful field to take pictures of the mansion in the evening light. Here, it was easy to think of the homesick young Maria bicycling through the beautiful countryside in the summer of 1945, through villages with signs welcoming home the troops.

Stanmore, where Maria was stationed from the fall of 1945 until the winter of 1947, was easy to find. It's a bustling suburb of London. Indeed, it's hard to see where London leaves off and Stanmore begins. It was nonetheless difficult to find where the Stanmore RAF station had been. We resorted to the map I'd copied from the book about Stanmore and Bentley Priory, and traced a route around its location in our car. We then spied a sign marketing a housing estate called Stanmore Park, and realized that it was on the very spot where the RAF station once stood. The development was quite luxurious and looked as though it could be in a suburb of Chicago. Again, a total erasure of the past.

We stopped for lunch and asked at the restaurant where Bentley Priory was. The waiters were Indian and had no idea, but eventually someone told us that it was up the hill and pointed in the right direction. Just as Maria had said, the hill led up from the tube station, her route back from classes in the city on foggy nights. We drove up the hill and began to see some very large and impressive old buildings. We finally reached Bentley Priory and drove up to the guard post at the gate. It is still an active RAF station, still headquarters, and the sentry refused us entry. Indeed, he told us it was prohibited even to take pictures. So we were left to the book and the website, which recount:

> Opened in 1926 in what had been built as a country mansion, RAF Bentley Priory was expanded several-fold during the second world war when it was the Headquarters of Fighter Command. The ultimate responsibility for the defence of Great Britain rested on the high-ranking officers working there and on the personnel who backed them up so devotedly. With many modifications and updates, the task of this unique RAF Station remained similar during the 'Cold War' and since the easing of tension other units have taken up residence and are working on defence-related tasks. At RAF Stanmore Park demolition of another mansion took place to create space for the Headquarters of Balloon Command which controlled the thousands of barrage balloons flown as a deterrent to low-flying enemy aircraft, thus supporting Fighter Command in the overall strategy. After the war, when balloons

become redundant, the site at Stanmore Park was used for more mundane purposes until its official closure in April 1997.

So the housing estate now stands where the barrage balloons launched in the south of England to deter German planes were controlled. The book contained wonderful pictures of Bentley Priory, including a recent aerial photo of the mansion and surrounding buildings. Most interesting were photos of WAAFs plotting the position of aircraft during the Battle of Britain on a large table in the basement of the Priory building. Maria, of course, worked there after the war, when everyone, as she recalls, was expecting World War III.

We visited Torquay, to which Maria escaped on leave as soon as she was assigned to Melton Mowbray in February 1947 and found all the pipes frozen. Torquay, in south Devon, is a nice town apparently dedicated to hotels, which cover the rocky hills that plunge down to the sea. The harbor is lined with vulgar tourist shops much like what one would find at any seaside holiday center—fuzzy dogs and key rings proclaiming "Greetings from Torquay." Still, it was pleasant, and clearly would have been a welcome break from the conditions at an RAF station in the middle of winter. We spotted the park with a fountain and palm trees where Maria was photographed more than 55 years before.

The RAF station at Melton Mowbray stood, according to the RAF website, between the southern outskirts of Melton Mowbray and the village of Great Dalby and was used as a base for Thor IRBMs (Intermediate Range Ballistic Missiles) from 1958 through August of 1963 but was "gradually disappearing." The airfield was built in mid-1942 with "three standard 50-yard-wide concrete runways, the main being 5,400 ft and the two intersecting runways 4,350 and 4,020 ft long with an encircling perimeter track around which were . . . hangars." Spitfires, Mosquitos, Corsairs, Vengeances, Hellcats, and Halifax aircraft flew out of there.

Again, we arrived late in the evening. It must have been after 8 p.m., but the light had not yet faded. We stopped where the airfield and station must have been located, on flat fields outside the sprawl of town, with a mound in the center of the area. There were farms and cows all around. So little seemed left that I stayed in the car while Ben went to the side of the road to take a photo. He suddenly called, "Cynthia, come look!" When I got to his side, he pointed down. Stretching from the side of the road into the distance was what was left of an enormous concrete runway extending through fields of ripening grain; the circular perimeter of the airfield was still there too. We stood silently together on the deserted road in the fading light, tremendously moved. You could almost hear the Spitfires taking off.

Dunholme Lodge, where Maria met and dated Bruno, was not too far away, east of Manchester and north of Lincoln. When we arrived at the village of

Dunholme, we visited the tiny old church. It smelled musty, and there was a plaque on the wall commemorating the RAF pilots lost during the war. Dunholme is now a wealthy bedroom community of Lincoln—more properly-clad people on horses. There's still not much to do in the village, though.

The RAF website said that the station was one mile south of the village of Welton and 3.5 miles north of Lincoln, but noted that it "reverted to agriculture and by the 1990s most of its concrete and buildings had disappeared." We located where it must have been by the topography; that is, Ben spotted the only area of land that was flat enough to have been an airfield. It is simply English countryside once again and smelled of new-mown grass. It was peaceful except for an occasional car. You could hear the wind, and the birds singing.

On our route south we stopped in Lincoln, where Maria and Bruno went to the movies on dates. Unlike the airfield, the town appeared much as it must have been during the months Maria spent nearby, with its vast cathedral and medieval city center. On the High Street, we saw the Ritz Cinema, which looked as though it had been there since the war.

To complete the tale of Maria and Bruno's romance, we visited the sites of both their wedding and their honeymoon. We took the train to London and got off at Waterloo Station. It was such a beautiful day that we decided to walk to Kensington—past Buckingham Palace, which Maria thought looked "like a stable" on first impression, and through Hyde Park and Kensington Gardens. The Brompton Oratory, where Maria and Bruno were married, is off a busy street. It is very ornate inside, filled with Italianate paintings, marble, and gold. Sunlight streamed through a dome onto a large gold baldachino. Huge candles ringed the high altar. The enormous, high ceiling is cut by several domes, all decoratively painted. The Oratory reminded me in some ways of churches in Poland. It is certainly unlike Anglican churches in England.

There were many side chapels, one to the right of the altar dedicated to the Virgin Mary. The statues of both Mary and her child were garbed in brightly colored fabric, and in front of this chapel were many lighted candles and people praying. When I returned to Chicago, Maria identified this as the chapel in which they were married.

The guidebook stated that the Oratory, with a nave larger than St. Paul's, had been described as "a museum piece in a street of museums." Indeed, the church is just around the corner from the immense Victoria and Albert Museum. As we walked by the museum, I noticed that its outer walls had been left pockmarked by bombs from the Blitz, in remembrance. The bomb-pocked façade suddenly brought the past into this sunny, care-free day in modern London. So did a stop at the Sikorski Institute, a Polish museum at 20 Princes Gate, just across from Kensington Gardens.

The Institute is in an elegant white stone building. A charming older Polish woman insisted on showing me around and telling me about the artifacts inside. There was a great deal about Sikorski; there were pieces of Polish air force planes shot down; there was an Enigma code machine (the Nazi code was broken by Poles) and an exhibit about Monte Cassino, the abbey south of Rome captured by General Anders' Polish units on June 4, 1944, allowing the British and Americans to advance on Rome.

Most interesting to me, however, were the artifacts from the AK: ID cards, tiny messages, codes, and broadsides from the underground press. There were scrapbooks with pictures of women in the Polish Air Force, AK, and RAF; my guide showed me a photo of herself at age 19 in one of them. At the very end, with little time left (the museum is open very limited hours), we discovered a scrapbook of photos about the liberation of the camp at Oberlangen. I wondered which of the faces in the lines of girls was that of Maria. It was impossible to tell.

Our last visit was to the Isle of Wight, where Maria and Bruno spent their honeymoon; it was also their last glimpse of the Old World as they left for the New. We took the car ferry from the industrial port of Southhampton to Cowes, which is a famous center of yachting, beloved of Queen Victoria. It was Sunday, and we sat in the July sun on the shore and watched the sailboats dotting The Solent, as this piece of water is known. Then we drove across the surprisingly unpopulated island and checked into our B & B.

The night before my departure for England, Maria and I had gone to a drugstore to make a blow-up of the tiny photo in her scrapbook of the hotel where she and Bruno had spent their honeymoon. She couldn't remember its name, so this was all I had to go on. I asked the woman running the B & B whether she had ever seen the building in the photo. She took it to her husband and returned to report that it was Madeira Hall, which was close by, but now in private hands. I walked over to where they said it was, but with little hope of getting in. When I got there, I noticed a small plaque on the wall with the names of famous writers who had stayed there. The gate was open, so I boldly walked down the driveway to the back of the house, where I disturbed a sunbathing houseguest. But I had come so far that I was willing to tread upon polite sensibilities, and I could immediately see that this was the place. The lawn on which a smiling Maria and Bruno had posed for their photo was the same, though a swimming pool had been added lower down in the huge garden.

I explained my purpose to the houseguest, who immediately went to summon the couple who now own Madeira Hall. They initially appeared a bit affronted by my trespass, but when I explained my quest and showed them the old photo, they became interested. We chatted about the history of the house, and they let me take photos of it from all angles before departing. I then walked down to

Bonchurch, a charming village associated with the many famous writers who had stayed there, climbed down to the rocky beach and went for a swim, as Maria had described doing. I sat for a long while on the rocks deep in thought before slowly climbing back up the steep hill for dinner with Ben.

When I returned to Chicago and told Maria about our adventures, she was fascinated to hear this story in particular. "It is July 30th today, our anniversary," she said. "If Bruno were still alive, we would have been married 54 years."

CHAPTER 15

Chicago, 1952 and 2004

More than 150,000 Poles entered the United States between 1945 and 1953. When this postwar wave of immigrants reached Chicago, there was already a large Polish community in the city and suburbs, along with a network of institutions the previous immigrants had built. The earlier wave of immigrants consisted of those who had left Poland in the late 19th and early 20th centuries, causing the Polish population of the city to jump from 24,086 in 1890 to 401,316 in 1920.

Most of the earlier group of immigrants had been peasants escaping from dire economic circumstances in partitioned Poland. In Chicago they found jobs in rapidly developing industries, primarily steel and meatpacking, and recruited their relatives and friends in Poland to join them.

These first groups settled in a number of different areas of the city, including the ½ by ¾ square mile area around the intersection of Division Street with Ashland and Milwaukee Avenues known as "the Polish Triangle." Polish immigrants used their income to acquire homes rapidly and to fund the construction of the huge and magnificent Polish churches that mark the landscape of Chicago. Their children attended parish schools, where English was a second language.

The first Polish immigrants established self-help organizations. The Polish Roman Catholic Union (PRCU) was established in Chicago in 1873 as a social welfare organization, with a focus upon preserving Polish Catholicism, with its traditional rituals, mysticism, and veneration of the Virgin Mary. The Polish National Alliance (PNA) was founded in Chicago in 1880 as an association of nationalist clubs; its goals were to preserve the Polish identity of the immigrant groups and to work for the liberation of Poland. And in 1898 a group of middle-class nationalist women organized the Polish Women's Alliance. Membership of these Polish fraternal organizations was, and still is, based upon the purchase of insurance.

With their active parishes, schools, fraternal and mutual aid organizations, the Polish areas of Chicago made up complete, if somewhat insular, communities. Yet despite their high rate of home ownership and comparatively high median income, Poles in

Chicago remained largely working class prior to World War II. Moreover, with the slowing of immigration after passage of restrictive immigration laws by Congress in the early 1920s, and as interest in Polish culture waned among subsequent generations, the community became increasingly Americanized.

The occupation of Poland by Germany and the Soviet Union in 1939 led to a reawakening of interest in Poland in this community. Though still under restrictive quotas, in 1939 the first of a new generation of immigrants began to trickle into the United States and to organize on behalf of their homeland. In 1944 representatives of this group and of the PNA and PRCU formed the Polish American Congress (PAC), an umbrella organization to lobby the U.S. government against cooperation with Stalin and recognition of the territorial changes in eastern Poland, which the Soviet Union had annexed. Although unsuccessful in those goals, the PAC did effectively lobby against forced repatriation of Polish displaced persons, for expanded immigration quotas, and for passage of the Displaced Persons Act, under which more than 150,000 Poles arrived in the country.

This new wave of immigrants was substantially different from the first. Its members—40,000 of them ex-servicemen and survivors of the Warsaw Uprising and 25,000 members of their families—came primarily from the upper and middle classes in prewar Poland. Most had lived in cities and were well educated. One study estimates that 47% of these immigrants either had university degrees or some university education before leaving Poland. Most of them did not come directly from Poland but had spent time in other countries, many in England, and many knew at least some English. These traits assisted them in adjusting to life in the United States, where 39% soon completed additional education. These characteristics sharply contrasted with those of Polish-Americans of the first wave and led to tension with them. Although some of the new immigrants initially settled in or near Polish areas, most did not; and although 92% of them were Roman Catholic, only 39% joined a Polish parish.

Polish-Americans from the earlier generations, while assisting the new immigrants, were somewhat threatened by them. Fearful that the newer veterans, with their superior education and class backgrounds, would take over the Association of Veterans of the Polish Army, the organization passed rules requiring all officers to have been citizens for five years. So the postwar immigrants formed new organizations, such as the Association of Polish Combatants and the Polish Home Army Veterans Association. While many older immigrants resented them for their educational and economic advantages, the newcomers saw many of the older Polish-Americans as both uncultured and unfamiliar with the conditions of independent interwar Poland and wartime Europe, from which the new wave had emerged. The postwar immigrants also preferred institutions and events promoting Polish "high" culture, such as art, classical music and literature, to those preserving folk culture out of the rural past.

The new immigrants adjusted well economically, with many of them finding white-collar jobs quickly, but many suffered from what one scholar describes as "status inconsistency," occasioned by losing the social and occupational status they had enjoyed in Poland before they were forced to emigrate. Former military officers, in particular, experienced difficulties adjusting to occupational changes after their high levels of education and wartime experience. Many of the new immigrants, because of lack of facility with English, non-transferability of their occupational and educational credentials, or interruption of their education by the war, were forced to accept employment below the status they would have occupied in Poland. Many thus lived in two worlds—in Polonia and in mainstream America—treated "in one situation according to [their] pre-emigration status and in the other according to [their], most usually, degraded social standing in the adopted society."

Chicago was a center for Polish immigration. Its population of Poles and Polish-Americans had for a long time been the largest in the United States, and after the destruction of Warsaw it was for a while the largest Polish city in the world. There were numerous Polish language newspapers, several dailies, radio stations in Polish, churches where Mass was celebrated in Polish, and countless groceries, delis and other service industries where Polish food could be obtained and business transacted entirely in Polish. Like earlier generations of immigrants, the postwar arrivals also found former friends, relatives or neighbors who were at least partly established in the city and in the institutions of Polonia.

1952

"It was daytime when we passed the Statue of Liberty," Maria tells me, "and I felt very happy. Our boat anchored right next to the Queen Mary, and they gradually let us out, to go through immigration formalities. Someone from a Polish organization was there to help us. He gave us the name of a small hotel on 42nd Street. We wanted to stay a few days to see the city. Although it was very cold and windy, we walked all over—to Columbia University, to the Public Library, to St. Patrick's Cathedral."

"After three days, we went to Penn Station and got on a train called the Trailblazer, which left at 5 p.m. and arrived in Chicago in the morning. I was dressed elegantly, but when we went to the observation car, everyone was staring at me. Nobody wore hats here. And I was wearing long cowboy-style boots that I bought in London after seeing the American musical 'Annie Get Your Gun.' Even though my coat was lightweight, English-style, we were too warm in the coach because we were used to English under-heating."

Maria and Bruno's friend Bronek was waiting for them when the train arrived in Chicago on January 25, 1952. Born in Chicago before returning with his family to Poland, Bronek had arranged a sponsor for them there, and had arrived himself six weeks earlier. He had rented a furnished room for his friends near Sheridan and Lawrence, for $17.50 a week, an area at that time frequented by prostitutes and other down-and-outs. As soon as they had dropped off their things and, after years of rationing, eaten as many eggs as they could for breakfast, Bronek took them to a Social Security office to obtain cards. It was slushy, cold, and wet, and Maria's cowboy boots were not waterproof. Later he took them to his brother's house, where he and his wife were staying, for dinner, after which they visited another friend who had left London before them. "When we got there, we were so miserable, wet, and cold. Our friend said, 'Don't even dream of having babies. Everyone has to work here. It won't be enough for Bruno to work.' I felt so miserable after we left there and returned to the neighborhood of prostitutes, which I was comparing with the elegance of London. Bruno said to me 'You wanted the States; it was your idea. Now you've got it.'"

"The next day, Saturday, I called some friends, one named Irena who was in the POW camp with me. She said 'You must come to us and then to a dance of the Polish Home Army; you'll meet many people you know there.' I also called Professor Wagner, whom I'd known in Warsaw, who was then a teaching fellow at Northwestern Law School, and he invited us to a party on Sunday." So Maria and Bruno set off for Irena's house on Saturday evening, finding it with great difficulty, and then to a dance at the Polish Women's Alliance on Ashland Avenue near Division Street, the heart of the Polish area on the north side.

"Chicago was horrible at that time," Maria tells me. "In the Polish Triangle— Ashland, Division, and Milwaukee—the sidewalks were broken, and they were so high up you had to jump down to the street. There were tramcars, which were so noisy that you couldn't talk. It was so shabby; the Polish neighborhood was horrible." But Maria and Bruno met many friends from the past at the Home Army Veterans dance that first Saturday night, including Professor Wagner, and danced until very late.

After a weekend getting acquainted with the Polish community and re-acquainted with friends from Warsaw and London, Maria and Bruno set out on Monday morning to find work. "There was snow all over; it was melting. My boots were full of snow. We went from place to place on LaSalle Street, jumping from one building to the next because it was so cold. Bruno found a job at the City National Bank, but they wouldn't hire me. They said 'Our policy is not to employ two members of the same family.' I did have an interview for a position I saw in an ad, but the man seemed very mean, and I was glad when Bruno interrupted the interview and the man refused to hire me."

Maria rolled up her diplomas from England to take downtown to look for work, thinking they would help her find a job. But there was no international trade in Chicago at that time, so they were of little relevance. "Someone told me, 'It doesn't matter; frame your diplomas, put them on the wall. You will prove yourself if you are capable of doing whatever job you get.' One insurance company offered me a job, but it was a huge place like a factory with desks in cubicles. I didn't want to work there, but the pay was relatively good. About the same time, Professor Wagner told me about an opening in the law library at Northwestern. He said that a Miss Elaine Teigler was looking for an assistant but wanted someone with no more than a high school education so that she wouldn't leave for a better job after being trained. He warned me not to admit to any higher studies."

Here Maria entered territory I know. I too once was looking for work, the summer before I entered law school. I was offered a job working for Elaine Teigler, the martinet known as "Miss T." Though I had a Ph.D. and years of college teaching experience, Miss T intimidated me so much that I turned down the job and made do with whatever else I could find, though it involved having to hire a babysitter every evening.

Miss T was assistant to the director of the Northwestern Law Library, and Maria was offered the job as her assistant after lying about her background to conceal her post-secondary education. "She made me an offer that day, and I went home and debated what to do because the insurance company would pay more. But I felt more comfortable in a university surrounding. Bruno said 'Take the job where you will feel better. It's probably better to take the academic job because the academic world is happier than business.' So I took the job and started work on February 11, 1952."

"There were eight of us working in the library. I had to take care of mail—go get it from the general office, sort it, and circulate looseleafs to the faculty according to their fields. I had to go through the shelves, to find any mistakes in shelving, which was done by students. I wrote out overdue notices. I filed looseleafs."

"One of the first days Elaine took me around to introduce me to faculty. My English was very English and very polite. One day Professor Inbau said 'Hi!' to me, and I said 'Good morning, sir,' like the English do. He looked at me as though I came from the moon. After a while I got used to the American way."

As soon as Bruno found a job, Maria and Bruno moved out of the furnished room where prostitutes pounded on their door during the night. They found another furnished place on Damen Avenue near Fullerton, which consisted of one large room and one small room with gas rings to cook on and a place to keep groceries. They shared the bathroom with other residents. Polish friends who arrived from England after them commented, "What a gorgeous apartment you have!" After living there for a couple of months, they gave the apartment to the newcomers and moved to a tiny unfurnished one a few blocks south, which other friends were vacating. There was a big kitchen, another room so small that they had to custom order a sofa bed small enough to fit in it, and an unheated screened porch where a friend of Bruno's stayed when he arrived from England in May. They still had to share a bathroom, but with a real estate office, and it wasn't open in the early morning or evening when they were there. Maria and Bruno gradually began to acquire furnishings and stayed there for a year.

In 1953 a friend told them about an apartment that was going to be vacant in a nice building at 913 North Francisco Avenue, near Humboldt Park, and they rented it. The Office of Price Administration still controlled rents, as it had done during the war, so the rent was cheap, and it gave them a separate bedroom for the first time. ("When we had children, we gave them the bedroom and slept on a sofabed in the living room.")

The woman who owned the apartment building was a Pole from the earlier generation of immigrants. "She was a primitive woman. She hated us," Maria says. "She said, 'You came here but you don't work in a factory. You are just arrived but don't want blue collar jobs but to go into offices.' The earlier immigrants resented us in part because they felt inferior since we were so educated and middle class. We didn't make as much money as those in factories but we didn't want to go there. Some of our friends did start to work in blue collar jobs, though. They made more money and got settled earlier than we did."

Maria often refers to people like her landlady on Francisco as "primitive." When I asked her what she meant by this term, she indicated that it means that someone lacks culture and education. Often it is someone from a rural area of Poland. I realize that her use of the term denotes, at least in part, social class.

Maria and Bruno fixed up the place on Francisco, doing all the work themselves. They worked long hours, with Maria cooking, taking care of all the other housework, and going to the Polish Triangle to shop for groceries on the weekends. Bruno took on a second job at Marshall Fields department store. In their leisure time they enjoyed a very active social life with friends from their previous worlds, from Warsaw and the RAF. "Each weekend we went to a famous Polish restaurant, Leonard's, on Milwaukee Avenue. On the second floor there was a band and dancing. We would meet friends there and dance, staying out until early Sunday morning. On Sundays, we would often go to Leonard's Casino in Beverly Shores [Indiana], on the lake. We would go with friends who had a car; most of us didn't in those days. There was no highway then. We would just drive down Lake Shore Drive and then on regular streets. The radiator would boil over. We would go for the day and come back in the middle of the night, or sometimes stay overnight." As in London, Maria and Bruno both worked and played hard.

2004

On January 11, 2004, I pulled up to Maria's house to go on a drive. "Show me the places where you used to live," I had asked her, and she readily agreed to do so. It struck me as fitting to do so on a day in January, so I could experience the city in the same general weather as when she and Bruno first arrived in Chicago, though changed in every other way. We were both bundled up, and Maria was chatty as ever. I just hoped she would remember to stop and point out the places I wanted to see, and that I wouldn't get so absorbed in our conversation that I'd forget to look.

We drove first to the furnished apartment where they lived for several months soon after arriving, which is near the intersection of Damen and Fullerton Avenues, north and west of the Polish Triangle. The house has been renovated, but Maria pointed out the top floor where they made their home. Cars rushed by on the expressway just a block away. "Of course, there was no highway then," said Maria. Close by is the Polish parish church they attended, St. Hedwig's.

We proceeded down Damen to Armitage and the tiny first floor apartment next to a Seven-11 convenience store, where they had lived for the next year. This area, known as Bucktown, has become gentrified. Damen is lined with fancy restaurants, but the little brown building which they were required to enter from the alley is still unassuming. I predict that it will not be long before it is gone too, or renovated to the point of unrecognizability. Again Maria directed my attention to a nearby church, St. Mary of Angels, near the highway. "It's beautiful," she said. "You should go in and see it sometime. My son Mark was married there."

I was beginning to get disoriented as we approached the intersection Maria always calls the Polish Triangle. We were in fact in an area I know well. My son attended a private elementary school nearby for many years, and I drove north and south along Ashland Avenue to take him there and pick him up. In addition, Milwaukee Avenue between North Avenue and Division Street has become the site of an annual art exhibit, and I had helped my partner Ben set up his photographs in a gallery close to Division Street just a few months before. Yet everything began to look different as it took on the cast of years gone by.

"Where did you go to that dance the first Saturday you were here?," I asked. Maria pointed out a building that used to be the Polish Women's Alliance, and I noticed the still-elegant façade that unites the second floor of what has been chopped up into many smaller spaces on the street level. As I stared at it, I suddenly realized that one of those spaces is the area where Ben's photos had been displayed. Maria then directed me to the high school established by the Polish Resurrectionist Brothers, where she had a Mass said after learning of her father's death in Poland. Startled, I realized that the building *is* the Montessori school my son attended for eight years. I had been living in this history without knowing it. Leonard's Restaurant, and almost all the Polish restaurants, are gone, with the exception of one small one on Division near the point of the "Triangle." "The Poles don't live in this area anymore," said Maria. "They have moved further up Milwaukee. We'll go there later."

We drove then to Humboldt Park, a huge park I know as the center of Puerto Rican life in Chicago. I had attended Puerto Rican folk music concerts there in the 1970s. A huge steel sculpture of the Puerto Rican flag spans Division Street, and the local high school is named for Robert Clemente, the Puerto Rican baseball player. In short, Humboldt Park means Puerto Rico to me. Now in my imagination I began to re-people it with Poles.

The apartment on Francisco Avenue, where Maria lived for 13 years, is on the second floor in the back, so we parked, got out of the car, and braved the cold so that Maria could point out its features to me. There is a bay window, and another window behind it, which was her sons' bedroom. "Mark fell out of that window one day when he was not quite 3, and I had to rush him to the hospital. Bruno was so mad at me, but Mark was fine; he didn't have a scratch." Her boys went to St. Helen's, the local Polish parish school, though Maria didn't much like the nuns who taught them there. Maria spoke of walking to Humboldt Park and how beautiful it was then. The neighborhood is almost entirely Puerto Rican now. There are gangs; and the park is considered dangerous.

CHAPTER 16

Marriage, Work and Family

The arrival of new ethnic groups in the inner city transformed many of the old Polish neighborhoods in Chicago. The Polish northwest side began to be penetrated by Spanish-speaking populations by the mid-1960s. New Polish areas were formed as the Poles moved from their previous neighborhoods, following Milwaukee Avenue north from the Polish Triangle to Avondale, Belmont-Cragin, and the Jefferson Park area on the far northwest side of the city. Large numbers of Polish-Americans also joined the postwar rush to settle in the suburbs. Many did so in clusters, creating Polish suburban areas in Park Ridge, Niles, and other communities. The Poles who remained in the traditional areas tended to be older and poorer, and they were fearful of crime.

Polish-Americans voted consistently and overwhelmingly Democratic until 1972, even after feeling betrayed by FDR at Yalta. In 1972, however, 53% of Polish-Americans voted for Nixon; and in 1980, 50% responded to Ronald Reagan's direct appeals to Polish groups such as the Home Army veterans. This was a rate much lower than that of other white ethnic groups in the 1980 election, however.

In the 1960s and early 1970s, for reasons that are unclear, the Poles were the targets of a great deal of ethnic stereotyping and the butt of ethnic jokes—the "dumb Polack" and the Polish joke. Polish-Americans were stereotyped as unsophisticated manual laborers, lacking in intelligence. The Polish American Congress campaigned against these types of ethnic slurs, and Polish organizations redoubled their efforts to celebrate Polish high culture as an antidote to the demeaning stereotypes.

The Polish joke reflected more deep-seated discrimination against Poles in America at this time. Poles occupied lower occupational ranks than other groups and only began to break into the professions in the 1970s and thereafter. Although by 1970 72% of Polish families in the city owned their own homes, and 85.1% in the suburbs (compared to 35% of all Chicago households), and their median income was higher than other groups in both city and suburbs, they remained in low-status jobs. As members of the community entered higher education in larger numbers after World War II, "choice" became a less credible explanation for their absence from high-status positions.

———

134

Poles' own perception of discrimination against their community led many to change their names. Name-changing by Poles in America predated World War II, but in 1963 3,000 out of some 300,000 Polish-Americans in the Detroit area changed their names, either to Anglicized equivalents or to Anglicized spellings. At the same time, many Polish-Americans were disappearing into what was characterized as the American melting pot. Polish schools ceased to teach Polish language or history; 80% of third-generation Poles married non-Poles; and fewer than 1/3 spoke Polish in their homes by 1979.

The 1970s, however, also gave rise to a movement known as the "new ethnicity." Universities established departments of ethnic studies; federal grants funded ethnic heritage centers; and ethnic groups asserted a renewed pride in their origins. Polish-Americans began to self-identify as Polish-Americans again, and there was a wave of name-changing in reverse. Children restored names their parents had modified, and their children went to Polish school on Saturdays, to learn the language and study Polish history and culture. Polish organizations held festivals and numerous cultural events, many of which continue to this day.

As Maria and Bruno struggled to establish themselves and start a family in Chicago, Bruno worked several jobs—at the bank during the day and at Marshall Field's department store at night and on Saturday. He also went to night school at Northwestern, earning a B.A. in business. All of this activity spoke well of his intelligence and ambition, but it also meant that Maria was left alone a good deal of the time. She was required to undertake all the housework, which increased substantially, of course, after the children were born.

After five years of residence in the United States, Bruno and Maria were eligible for citizenship, but they waited an additional three years while deciding whether to use the event to Americanize their names. There were many Germans at City National Bank, where Bruno worked, and they were pressing him to change his name. "I had an uncle who had come to Chicago at the beginning of the 20th century," Maria tells me, "although I didn't know he was here until after I arrived. He had lived through that period when the Polish were ostracized, so he said I should change my name for the sake of the children. I didn't want to, so I suggested hyphenation, adding 'Chase' to 'Chudzinski.' The easiest way to change your name was at the acquisition of citizenship, so we did it then."

Maria and Bruno applied for citizenship and were called for an interview in January 1960. "I took the oath in a courtroom in the old Post Office building that was on Dearborn and Adams. I got my papers on April 1st; but they didn't call Bruno, and the FBI was asking about him all over. So he went straight to someone we knew who worked at the FBI. The guy said, 'Let's get down to business; we didn't call you because you are a Communist.' 'Me?', said Bruno, astonished. 'If I had been, I would've stopped after my time in Russia!' The agent said, 'You were seen going into the Polish consulate [which represented the Communist regime].' 'I've never been there!', Bruno said." Apparently the FBI had written down the license number of the couple's car when Maria had parked it in front of the consulate at the time she went to get the consular stamp on a power of attorney form in connection with legal matters in Poland; and the car was registered in Bruno's name. So Bruno had to swear out a statement to this effect and to deny that he was a Communist in order to revive his hopes of becoming a citizen. When he was eventually sworn in, he too became Chudzinski-Chase.

"But," continues Maria, "my sons were already born, so they have the old name. And Bruno went to court and dropped 'Chase' when he first went back to Poland. But I had an inheritance case pending, so it was hard to do. So I'm the only member of the family with the name of Chase, though I didn't want to do it in the first place!" Maria was known generally at work as Maria Chase, while in the Polish community she was Maria Chudzinska,* symbolizing the split worlds in which she existed.

Maria and Bruno's son Mark was born in October 1956. They barely made it to the hospital before he arrived. When she returned home a week later, having quit her job shortly before giving birth, Maria's life was totally transformed. "I was busy night and day. Mark had colic; one time I counted 35 times I got up during the night. I was worn out. I had no help. Bruno would leave at 8 a.m. and return at 10:30 p.m. I asked the pediatrician what I was going to do with the baby. He said, 'Just live your regular life, ignore the baby.' But my regular life was to be out all the time, working with organizations, having a big social life; how could I?"

Andrew was born three years later, in December of 1959; and Maria's life became even more complicated. "I did all my own cooking. I washed diapers in the basement and hung them down there while the kids napped. I had to take the boys with me wherever I went. If it was bad weather or they were sick, I couldn't even get to the store for bread. So I shopped on weekends when Bruno was home. It was a problem just to get to the doctor. I would take the kids to Humboldt Park for two or three hours a day for the fresh air; and when they were older, I would meet friends in the park—Bronek's wife and others. We never got a babysitter and went out. Bruno was too cheap, and I was too nervous to leave them. We used to have these staff lunches once a week when I worked at the library. Everyone hated those lunches, but when I was stuck at home I dreamed about going to them!"

By the 1960s there were increasing tensions in Maria's marriage to the dashing Bruno, attributable primarily to quarrels over money. Bruno was an inveterate gambler. His earliest adult experiences involved extreme risk—flying a small

---

* Chudzinska is the form properly used to refer to female members of the Chudzinski family.

fighter plane across Nazi-controlled areas of Europe, when the statistics of those coming back alive were grim. Perhaps this explains how he acquired, and could not shake, the taste for risk that drove him repeatedly to the racetrack and later in life to gamble on the stock market. Maria disapproved of Bruno's gambling and had repeated arguments with him about it.

Other tensions seem to have been generated by questions of control over money within the family. Bruno would keep his own earnings, those he did not lose at the track, and dole out money to Maria for the household. He also was clearly ambivalent about her working. This is not surprising, given both his background and the prevailing sentiment in the United States at that time, which disapproved of women who worked, seeing it both as a sign of the husband's inability to support his family and as detrimental to their children. When Maria went back to work after the children were nearing school age, Bruno concluded that she should pay for household needs with her earnings. "He wanted complete power over me, yet also wanted me to bring in money," she says. Bruno's conflicted attitude probably also stemmed from having been raised in a traditional family in rural Poland, where a patriarchal family structure was the norm. His life spanned several worlds and generations.

When Maria went back to work in 1962, she did so in part because she felt she needed her own money in order to be more independent. "In Poland after World War I, women worked. My stepmother was working at City Hall. Many women were at the university. When I started at Northwestern, I was shocked to see that there were only two women in the third-year class; one of them was Dawn Clark [future candidate for governor of Illinois]. I guess it was assumed that married women were supported by their husbands." So though Maria had found freedom in the U.S., she had also apparently stepped back a generation in terms of sexual equality (at least for middle-class women).

Maria also was clearly bored with being at home alone. She is so sociable that it is hard to imagine her doing so. "The Library called several times asking me to come back. I got tired of being home; I like to be with people and to use my brain. Bruno got mad because I wouldn't be wholly dependent on him. There is a Polish proverb that says 'You keep your wife pregnant in winter and barefoot in summer.' In other words, keep your wife dependent on you." The independent Maria was coming to the conclusion that she could not tolerate this much longer.

About the same time the law school library was trying to entice Maria back to work, a fellow refugee from Poland, a man Maria describes as "an attorney, an elegant man with old-world manners," called to tell her about a woman who used to be a journalist in Poland who was looking for a job. "I was already mad at Bruno; I couldn't take it any more. So I hired her as a babysitter. She was almost 70, very strict and old-fashioned, and looked like a witch. She did not speak English and didn't put up with nonsense. The boys had to eat whatever she served them and couldn't fool around. They were not allowed to watch TV; they had to do their homework. If they misbehaved, they had to kneel in the corner for a time. But she was very intelligent and well-educated. I felt confident that she would take proper care of them, so I wasn't worried about leaving the children."

The sitter also put up with no nonsense from Maria and Bruno. "The first day I went back to work, Bruno came back from the office while she was still there, and he told her off. 'I don't want you here!,' he said. *She* told *him* off. She said, 'I'm doing you a favor taking care of your kids. If you want to, you take care of them!' After that, she was the only person he respected; he was afraid of her. She treated me like a school kid too."

Returning to work, as Maria did on October 13, 1962 (for some reason, Maria always remembers precise dates), was not without its own problems. Now 39, she returned to the same job she had held before the children were born, because Miss T's assistant had just left. So Maria had to deal with all the stresses of working for this difficult boss again. "Elaine was mean. She wanted me back, but she was a jealous old maid. When I came back she wouldn't arrange a parking permit for me for weeks and weeks. I had to park far away and walk, though I had no extra time because I drove Mark to school and then to the office. Miss T never drove and hated women with a car; I couldn't function without one. I walked for eight weeks before I got mad and went to Adminstrative Services, and they got me a permit right away. Elaine was just playing tricks on me."

The 26 years Maria worked for Elaine Teigler were difficult indeed. "She treated me badly. She told me I couldn't do things well enough. She resented any vacation I ever took. She was also very anti-Catholic and anti-Polish. Once she told me about buying shoes in a shop in Minneapolis, and said the man who sold them to her said 'You are lucky; if you went into another shop, they wouldn't have your size. They cater to Poles and Italians; I cater to Anglo-Saxons.' When the pope got elected, she was mad that he was Polish."

On another occasion, a Northwestern alum came into the library and wanted to see the Polish Civil Code. Maria ordered it from the University of Chicago law library for him. When Miss T heard about this, she was angry. "She made a big scene in front of everybody. 'The Polish Code is not important,' she said. 'Don't bother the University of Chicago about it.' I told her off. 'What?,' I said. 'The French and German codes are important, but the Polish is not?' Then I walked out and bummed three cigarettes after having not smoked for a year."

"It was hell sometimes. She liked me in a way. I had been useful. I had to pretend to be dumb, but when she was away, I had to know everything and be able to replace her. Many law firms didn't want to deal with her, so they would call me instead. When she returned, I would have to play the dumb little girl again." It strikes me that Maria was very well suited to carry off this kind of dissembling after her forced training during the Nazi occupation of Poland. Anyone who could participate in the charade that university classes were in fact low-level clerical training sessions in front of an S.S. inspector, or convince the Gestapo that classes held in her home were really just a birthday party, under pain of deportation to a labor camp, could surely deal with Miss T—and stand up to Bruno.

"Shortly after I went back to work, Bruno and I had a big showdown about money, and I told him to move out. I had learned from some friends that he was going to Sportsman's Park [a race track], so I wanted to teach him a lesson, to scare him, not to divorce. What I was telling him just didn't reach him; he was a stubborn man and had a fantasy. So I got an attorney, and he was told that he had to move out. He looked for a place nearby and moved out a few days later."

Although Maria and Bruno were separated for four years, Bruno repeatedly urged her to reconcile. "He also was trying to break me. He was supposed to give me $200 a month but he would give me $150, and my attorney would say it wasn't worth fighting about $50. I asked the judge at a preliminary hearing for the car because I had to drive the boys to school, take the sitter home, and get to work. The judge said it was a luxury and gave it to Bruno, who sold it the same day. So I had to borrow money to get a used Chevy." In short, Bruno thought that Maria would not be able to make it on her own and would ask him to come back. But she did manage by herself, at least for a time. "I had no money; it was a really hard time," she says.

After three years of separation, in 1965 Bruno tried a carrot instead of a stick, offering to pay for Maria's first trip back to Poland if she would reconcile. They did, temporarily, and Maria went to Poland; but when she returned she discovered that he had cashed in some stock that he wasn't supposed to touch, and the reconciliation fell apart.

Ultimately Bruno's strategy did work. "In 1966, my babysitter quit. I got another but she was crazy. Everything was falling apart. I was getting nervous and sick. I had no money. It was September and school was starting. The world was burning under my feet, I had so many troubles. Bruno wanted to reconcile, and I decided it would be best for the kids. So I said 'Okay,' and we went to Acapulco for a week. It was difficult after that, up and down. But I knew I could not give the kids what I wanted to alone." There was clearly much more than this behind their reconciliation, though. For one thing, Maria is an observant Roman Catholic, though she says "I'm not like the old ladies with babushkas." She tells me that, "I dated some, but I did not want to marry someone else. I felt that if I divorced, I wouldn't be able to die peacefully."

After getting back together, Maria and Bruno moved to a larger apartment, on Palmer Square, to the north and west of the apartment on Francisco. Maria and I went there on our tour. Their apartment was on the first floor of a handsome large stone building and had seven rooms—a large living room, a formal dining room, three bedrooms ("one was a den," Maria says), and a kitchen. At last Maria had a home that resembled the one in which she grew up, though the neighborhood was decidedly less elegant. The building stands on the well-kept square, and the parochial school the boys attended is across the square, as is their parish church, St. Silvester's. Around the corner stand the huge mansions on Kedzie Avenue, now being renovated. The perennially Polish Milwaukee Avenue is not far away; and if you take it north a couple of miles, you enter the newer Polish neighborhoods, filled with Polish delis and restaurants. We ate at one on the day of our tour of Maria's Chicago past. The food was cheap, good and plentiful. The restaurant was full of smoke and the sound of Polish words.

Maria, Bruno and their sons lived in the Palmer Square apartment for ten years, until they at last bought a home of their own on the northwest side of the city, the two-story, three-bedroom house in the nice neighborhood where Maria still lives. "Unlike other Polish immigrants, we didn't buy a house right away and instead spent money on private schools for our boys."

And that is exactly what they did. Although Mark and Andrew did not know a word of English before entering school, they picked it up when they began at the local parish school, and both are bilingual today. "By the time they were older, they would complain that my English was not good enough," says Maria. After completing elementary school close to their home, both boys were admitted to the premier Jesuit school in Chicago, St. Ignatius College Prep, which is on the near south side, and commuted long distances to get there. Maria served on the board of the Mothers Club at St. Ignatius, and for several years as its treasurer.

Maria was absolutely determined that Mark and Andrew would have the best possible education, and the route to that was through the Northwestern University employee tuition discount. So although working for Elaine Teigler continued to be stressful, Maria persisted. "Twenty-six years with Elaine; I almost had nervous breakdowns. Mark would say I should leave this job, but I said 'No, I want you to be able to get a discount at the university.'"

After Miss T retired in 1983, things were better for a while; but after five years or so Maria had problems with her successor as well. "At first she was charming to me. Nothing was written down, so she needed details of how to do things, which I knew. But then one year I was running a ball at the Conrad Hilton for 1,000 people, and I invited her to come. After she saw me in that setting, she started to be nasty. She would always ask for memos, and then say 'If you can run a ball, you can write a better memo.'"

Maria stuck to it, though, and both her sons received undergraduate degrees from Northwestern. Mark went on to attend Northwestern's law school under the employee discount program as well, in the joint program with Kellogg Business School, so that he emerged with both a J.D. and an M.B.A. He went on to study foreign and comparative law at the Sorbonne. Andrew also has an undergraduate degree from Northwestern and an M.F.A. in film studies from the

University of Southern California. So both received the education Maria valued so much, although the cost to Maria in emotional distress was substantial. While acknowledging the sacrifice, she swears that it was absolutely worth it.

Maria and Bruno lived together for 34 years after their four-year separation, until his death at age 80, having celebrated their Golden Anniversary. They were both such strong-minded personalities that they scrapped repeatedly. Her stories of life with Bruno are filled with minor clashes. They continued to have conflicts over Bruno's gambling. This never changed. When he became unable to go to the track late in life, he gambled, and lost, on the stock market instead.

Bruno worked at City National Bank for about 15 years, then left it for Continental Bank, where he had a good job as an auditor. Later, he went into the travel business for a few years, but it did not pay well. "When we bought the house in 1976," Maria says, "we got the mortgage on my credit instead." Bruno then decided to go into real estate, taking the salesman's exam and then a year or two later the exam to become a broker. He opened an office on Milwaukee Avenue near Bryn Mawr and eventually employed several other people. Bruno called his real estate office "Pilot," in memory of his flying days. It was for this office that his son Mark bought the limited edition poster of the Spitfire that now hangs over Maria's couch.

After working in real estate for about ten years, Bruno wasn't feeling well and went to a doctor at the veterans' hospital. (Anyone from the active forces under the Allied Command in World War II could go there for free.) "He had a test related to his intestines, and the technician said, 'It looks bad, as though you have cancer.' Bruno came home shocked and upset. 'What am I going to do?,' he asked. 'I'm going to die. I can't keep my own business.' We met Mark in New York City, where he had been working for a law firm that was transferring him in London, for a weekend that would have been wonderful except that Bruno was so worried. When we came back, the doctor called and said the tests were wrong. But he took other tests, which were not conclusive, and it dragged out so long that Bruno got so worried that he listed his business for sale. When it was clear that he was okay, he wanted to withdraw it from the market, but it was too late, so he sold it. He was 60 or so. After that, he worked for a while for a friend who had a big real estate office, but then he retired when he got sick. He also did people's taxes. But the last years of his life, he was too sick to work."

When I have asked Maria to describe Bruno, she has told me, at various times: "Bruno had ambition; he was very clever; he had a great memory." "He was intelligent and able." "He was always so lucky. In the delivery room, I wanted a girl but I knew it would be a boy because that's what Bruno wanted. He left our car unlocked with all our luggage in Quebec City, and the car next to his was robbed but nothing was taken from his." "He was a strong personality, full of life, the heart of a party. He danced well, would joke and compliment the ladies. Everyone remembers him as a jolly good fellow. He was not colorless." And, "He loved me."

The conflicts between Maria and Bruno are clearly not the whole story of their relationship. I know that simply from having seen how long it took her to recover from his death. How much she cared for him became abundantly clear to me as she told me the story of his lengthy illness and death. "We used to go to Michigan in the summer." (Maria replicated her father's pattern of getting the children out of the city during the hot months.) "Bruno had hay fever, and once he had a bad attack there. He went to the V.A. Hospital to get shots. They examined him and found that he was a diabetic, though he had never known it." After testing and experimenting with his diet, Bruno was required to have insulin shots. "He put a diagram on the bathroom door, to mark where he should put the shot. When the kids had parties, they would joke about having someone with drugs in the house."

Bruno also had Parkinson's disease. He had it for a while without being aware of it, but then began to have fainting spells. "One day I had to call an ambulance. It turned out he also had a bleeding ulcer. I said 'Either you go see my doctor or I'll move out and not take care of you.' He weighed 112 pounds and was in pain. The doctor asked me, 'Why did you wait so long?' I said, 'Don't you know any stubborn men?'." This same doctor attributed the fact that Bruno lived for another five years to Maria's good care.

Bruno wanted Maria to continue to work because she maintained them both on her group health insurance, so she hired a recently arrived Polish woman named Sophie to look after him during the day. "He was in such poor shape, it was tragic. I made the TV room into a bedroom, and he had a special device so he could ring to wake me. He was in and out of the hospital about four times, and in a nursing home for three weeks once. One day after work I found him tied to the bed at the nursing home because he had messed the floor with a hemorrhage. He was skin and bones. When I was washing the blood out of his clothes, I would cry."

Maria took Bruno out of the nursing home as soon as possible, but was required to give him an intravenous at home for seven weeks. "Sophie was a nurse in Poland, so she knew how to do the IV during the day; and I learned how to do it in the evening. I would hope that it would just go in fast enough that I could go to bed by 1 a.m. Northwestern Hospital always had someone on duty all night, and they would wait on the phone while I tried to do what they said, in such a gentle voice. Sometimes this went on until 3 a.m., and I had to get up at 7. Finally the doctor told us, 'I have a Christmas gift for you; we are taking him off the IV.'"

During all this time Maria tried to make Bruno's life as comfortable and as interesting as possible. "When he was still walking fairly well, Sophie would walk him to the church nearby, where he would sit and rest before walking back. He would go to church on Sundays too. He was religious; country people were always very observant."

"I used to take him out a lot—to parties and to Polish shows, though he couldn't walk well. I would take him to Michigan in the summer and put the TV on the verandah of the place I had rented for the season, so he could watch the ball game while I went to the beach. We had friends with houses there, and would take drives around the countryside."

In April of 2000, Maria went to Poland for a reunion of the Home Army. "I went to the doctor with Bruno before I left. The doctor told me Bruno was okay, so I could go. I hired Sophie to be there 24 hours a day. I spoke to Bruno at length by phone on April 12th, and he said 'Stay as long as you want.' The next day he had a stroke. I used my connections from the Air Force to get out and back to Chicago the following day, but by the time I was back he was on life support. He looked at me, but I don't think he knew I was there." Bruno died two days later. "We held the funeral at the Basilica [the church near Maria's house], but with a Polish priest, not the parish priest. Lots of people came—all our friends, the boys' friends, friends from the Air Force and other organizations. It was raining—so much that it was hard even to lower the casket into the grave. I stayed there alone with Mark and Sophie while Andrew went on ahead with the others to the White Eagle for dinner. There were over 60 at dinner."

Bruno was buried at Mary Hill Cemetery on Milwaukee Avenue, in a special section for Polish veterans. Maria often visits his grave on holidays like Easter, and she took me to visit it as well. It is on a grassy swell, with a monument to the veterans standing over it. The grave is marked by a granite stone flush with the ground, which says "Capt. Pilot Brunon A. Chudzinski, 1920-2000." At the top left of the stone is the emblem of the Polish Air Force—a flying bird with a wreath in its beak, and to the right the emblem of Bruno's last squadron, Squadron 318.

Maria seated with General Bor Komorowski,
10th anniversary of Warsaw Uprising, Chicago

Maria with sons Mark and Andrew

Maria and Janina as adults, Warsaw

Maria and Brunon dancing the Polonaise at
the White and Red Ball, Chicago

CHAPTER 17

Poland and Polonia

After the death of Stalin in 1953, and of the Stalinist leader of Communist Poland in 1956, the repressive police state in Poland slowly began to thaw. Foreign travel and contact with the West became easier. The centrally run economy continued to stagnate, however, and living standards were low. In 1970-71 workers' protests spread across the country, beginning with strikes in the shipyards in Gdansk and Gdynia; the workers were supported by student activists and the Catholic church. The 1970s were marked by some liberalization, and some improvement in the standard of living, as well as further relaxation on foreign travel. Karol Wojtyła, the Archbishop of Krakow, was elected and installed as Pope John Paul II in 1978; he toured the country and made appeals for change to the immense throngs who turned out to hear him.

Strikes again swept the country in the summer of 1980 and led to the creation of a national (though illegal) trade union called Solidarity, under the leadership of an electrician from the Gdansk shipyard named Lech Wałęsa. Solidarity quickly attracted eight million members, about a third of the population of Poland, including many ex-Communist Party members. As historians have noted, "Solidarity was not an ordinary trade union; it was evolving into a mass social movement committed to the democratization of political life, the dismantling of the command economy, and the introduction of autonomous production units." In response, Moscow forced the Warsaw regime to crack down or potentially face invasion. Martial law was proclaimed in December 1981; 6,000 Solidarity activists were arrested and the organization banned. The political situation and continuing economic problems led some 500,000 Poles to emigrate in the mid-1980s.

The movement for democracy in Poland was saved by the ascendancy of Mikhail Gorbachev in the Soviet Union and his declaration that his country would no longer interfere in the political life of its former satellites. Solidarity was relegalized and entered into negotiations with the Polish government that resulted in constitutional changes and elections in 1989 and the establishment of the Third Polish Republic.

146

The Communist Party dissolved in 1990 and reorganized as a social democratic party. Poland is now a parliamentary democracy. In 1999 Poland joined NATO. Economic reforms led to an expansion of the economy, and Poland was admitted into the European Union in 2004.

By the time the situation in Poland began to improve, the post–World War II refugees were long settled in Chicago. They had adjusted well to life there. While retaining their identity as Poles, they are also an extremely patriotic group. But now their allegiance is owed to the country which made it possible for them to settle down, find work, and enjoy freedom.

The Polish-American community in Chicago was joined by yet another wave of refugees from Poland during the Communist era, especially after reform of the U.S. immigration law in 1965 made it easier for them to be admitted to the country. The more recent immigrants settled in the Polish neighborhoods around Avondale and Belmont-Cragin on the Northwest side. They, in turn, were joined by a wave of "Solidarity refugees" after martial law was declared in December 1981. Even after Poland regained the right to determine its own political path, immigrants continued to come, drawn by the dream of a better life in the United States. Unlike the earlier arrivals, however, the newcomers freely travel back and forth between Poland and the United States.

Poland:

After leaving Poland as a German POW in 1944, Maria was not able to return until 1965. Telephone connections were so inadequate that she couldn't even speak with her family by phone; they were forced to rely on letters. On February 25, 1953, a year after she arrived in Chicago, Maria's father died, without her ever having seen or talked to him again after the day she left the pierogi dinner before the last battle for Warsaw. Her stepmother sent a cable to inform her of the death. After long litigation, Maria eventually received some money from the sale of the farmhouse in Ozarow to its tenant, which helped with her children's education.

By the summer of 1965, the political situation had eased in Poland, and Bruno bought Maria a ticket to Warsaw as an enticement to end their separation. The children were old enough for her to leave them for a time, so she rented a cottage in Michigan and paid her long-time sitter to stay with them there. The ticket Bruno bought her allowed stop-overs. Not having traveled for over a decade, Maria took bountiful advantage of this fact. She stopped in London and was amazed to see how it had changed since she had left. She visited Switzerland, then flew to Vienna and retraced her steps to the places she had visited there as a child. "I remembered the Ring and how to get around. I went to the Rathaus because I remembered having dinner in the basement as a child.

147

When Sunday morning came, I went to Mass at the Karlskirche. It was the first time I attended a Mass in German, and my German was not good anymore." (Indeed, Maria seems entirely to have lost the ability to speak German, to have repressed the whole language, though her French is still fluent. One can understand why.)

Finally Maria flew to Warsaw, staying initially at the Europeski Hotel. "The city had been rebuilt but only partly. I could still see ruins. It didn't feel like home; I wasn't going to the building where I had lived." It was the first time Maria had seen her sister after more than 20 years. "I felt like a stranger. Nina wanted me to come to the convent with her right away, but I said I wanted to go to a hotel so they could handle registering me with the authorities. Nina was almost in tears. The driver of the taxi said 'Why don't you go with your sister? Why stay here?' Nina thought it might be because she was a nun, and was sensitive about that. But I told her I had nothing against the nuns. It was a little awkward at first, though, until we got to know one another again."

After three days, Maria moved to the convent to stay with Nina there. Her stepmother was still alive, but in a hospital and in poor shape, suffering both from the effects of a fall and from mental confusion. Maria visited, but found it hard to see her in such a condition. Maria then paid a friend with a car to drive Nina and herself to the north of the country, to meet some of Bruno's family for the first time. "We didn't go to the village but instead to see his favorite sister, who lived north of Malbork. Her name was Salomea; we called her Salka. She was very warm and friendly, and she loved me."

After three weeks, Maria left Poland but was still not ready to return to Chicago. She flew to Rome for a few days, then visited Capri and Nice, where she, quite literally, danced in the streets during an all-night celebration. She met another American woman, and they shared a room, went on tours, and visited Monaco together. Finally, Maria spent several days in Paris, where she stayed in a small hotel on the banks of the Seine, seeing the sights by day and going to the theater at night, reminiscent of her trip to Paris in 1946, when she was in the RAF. All of this traveling—and freedom—must have seemed a tremendous escape from her everyday life as Miss T's assistant and evenings spent cooking, shopping, and doing housework.

In 1968, Maria sent her sons Andrew and Mark to stay with her sister in Poland for the summer. They were 11 and 8, but Janina had not yet met them. When she and another nun picked them up at the airport, Andrew pulled out a photograph and compared it with their faces to make sure he had got the right aunt. The boys became very close to Nina over the years after that first meeting.

Bruno himself went to Poland for the first time since his departure in 1939 on a trip arranged by a society of Polish professionals in Chicago. It was at this time, in 1974, that he went to court and rid himself of the Americanized surname. By that time, Maria's sister had visited Chicago and met Bruno, so he stayed in Warsaw with her. She took him around the city, which he did not know, and then visited some of Maria's cousins before going to his home in Pomerania. When he returned to Chicago, he brought Maria the water color of the shepherd boy that hangs in her dining room, which had belonged to her father. Because it was an original by a painter of the Moda Polska school popular in Krakow at the end of the 19th century, it was illegal to remove the painting from the country without permission, but Bruno smuggled it out in a large suitcase Maria had bought him for this purpose.

Maria herself didn't return to Poland again until 1980, when her children were grown. She visited again in 1983, when the country was still under martial law, for the Pope's second visit to his homeland. And in 1985, the entire family went together. By that time Mark was working for a law firm in London and Andrew was in Los Angeles, but they all converged on Warsaw. This was the first and only time Maria and Bruno were together in Poland. "We went to Holy Cross Church, I remember. And we drove to Bruno's home. Everybody was waiting for us; the table was full of food. His nice sister took me around the village to see other people. But Bruno went only twice. He didn't feel like it; he didn't have much in common with his family, though he loved them."

Maria, by contrast, re-established her connections with Poland and with friends and relatives there from the 1980s on, returning at first every other year, then from 1989 at least once a year, and sometimes more than once if there were a special event. After the Communist regime fell and it became possible to commemorate the Warsaw Uprising in an official fashion, she has returned repeatedly for reunions and memorials, such as the one in 1994, when her photo with Vice-President Al Gore as part of the U.S. delegation to the 50th anniversary called her past to my attention. A ceremony was held at the Warsaw Uprising Monument, and representatives of ten nations laid wreaths at the eternal flame that burns in the middle of the bronze statues of AK fighters there. Vice President Gore spoke, among others, saying: "If you would see the true monument for these noble martyrs look around you . . . ."

Maria remembers that "It was incredibly hot on the day of the Uprising, but I took a group to visit Old Town and was photographed with a very famous American pilot. There was a garden party at the U.S. Ambassador's residence. Vice President Gore was so nice to me all the time. He said to me, '*You* were fighting? You must have been seven years old!' On the last day, we went out to a cemetery where a U.S. pilot who was shot down is buried, and I was standing right among the highest-ranking Polish generals!"

After her children were grown, Maria returned to London often as well. "I always enjoyed going to London. Once I even went as a DHL courier! I would go every year, or more often while Mark was there. I love British theater." While Mark was working in London, he would visit friends of his parents from the Air Force. In 1985, he heard that a 40-year reunion of the Polish women who had been imprisoned at Oberlangen was to be held, and he urged his mother to attend. "I was broke at the time, but I managed to get a charter flight from Detroit. One day, we went to see the exhibit about the liberation of Oberlangen at the Sikorski Institute. But the meeting, a dinner, was held on Sunday, in a blue-collar suburb of London. About 250 women attended, but I could only easily recognize one girl—in the queue to the washroom!" The "girls" must all have looked quite different from the days in the spring of 1945 when they had dispersed from captivity into their new lives.

Polonia:

By the time she attended the reunion in London, Maria's life as a Pole had long been focused on participation in the Polish-American community of Chicago. From her very first weekend, when she and some 800 persons attended the Home Army Veterans Association dance, she has been very involved, an activist. "The Polish Home Army Association was the first group I joined here. It was very large then; many combatants had come here and started to organize. I had a friend on the board when I arrived, who asked me to join the Board in 1953 or so; I was the treasurer. Bruno wasn't a member, of course [because he didn't participate in the Uprising]." It is clear that Maria was already quite active by the fall of 1954, as she shows me a photograph of herself at an event sitting next to General Bor-Komorowski, the commander of the forces in Warsaw during the Uprising, who visited Chicago for an event commemorating its 10th anniversary. Although the Uprising could not be commemorated in Warsaw itself at that time, Maria and others on the Board of the Home Army Veterans Association had organized an event in Chicago.

Asked about the activities of the Home Army organization, Maria says, "We sent aid to veterans here and in Poland. We also sent money, illegally, to an underground AK organization in Warsaw. We would organize meetings and other functions so people could meet veterans and we could tell about our war experiences. We would organize educational activities; I put together an exhibit about the AK to show at events like the Festival Polonaise we used to have on Navy Pier or in Grant Park. We would give talks on Pulaski Day and celebrations like that. We also dedicated a plaque in Dayton, Ohio to the American pilots who took part in the big raid during the Uprising."

"Right now [2004] we are supporting mostly children's institutions and a clinic for AK veterans in Poland; many are in financial difficulties. I was recording secretary of the national board for a while in the 1990s; but it was too much work, so I quit. I still attend meetings sometimes, and I go to their functions. Some of these groups will die out relatively soon."

In 1976 or thereabouts, Maria also became involved in the Legion of Young Polish Women, which she describes as a powerful organization in Polonia. The Legion was organized in September of 1939, just after the beginning of the war. The young women raised money to send ambulances to the front; they also sent letters and parcels to POWs and later to displaced persons. Maria served as President of the Legion from 1986-1988 and is still on the advisory board and committees, attending two meetings a month.

The Legion's main fundraiser is a debutante ball, called the red-and-white ball for the colors of the Polish flag, at which new debs dress in white and past debs in red. "One of the founders went to New York City to visit some Polish organization and attended a ball that had debutantes, so she brought back the custom. The debutantes collect ads for the ad book and raise money for the organization in this way. In recent years we sent surgical equipment to Poland when there was a shortage, things like syringes to be used by small clinics and private hospitals. We give a scholarship in Chicago to people of Polish descent for college or graduate school."

Maria chaired the ball for the first time in 1984; it was held in the largest ballroom at the Conrad Hilton and almost 1000 people attended. "It's a black-tie ball, with women in formal gowns, to show that we are not just polka party and sausage. The debs are chosen by word of mouth, some from Polish scouting, some from Polish schools. Successful newcomers like their daughters to be debs. We start to organize it in May, and there are teas for prospective debs once a month; I still go to the teas. From Christmas until the ball, which is at the end of February, there are rehearsals, with a special choreographer. The ball starts with the Polanaise, which is danced in a line, and around 1 a.m. past debs dance a mazurka. The mazurka is danced with a partner; it is rather wild and vivacious. It is usually so beautiful that people ask for an encore."

"The queen of the ball is the deb who brings in the most money; one father donated $30,000 because he wanted his daughter to be queen! We would make $20,000 when the economy was not good, but up to $90,000 when it was really good." Every year Maria, as a past president of the organization, serves as a hostess, standing in the receiving line along with the debutantes and their fathers. She has asked me several times if I would like to attend. I have attended other events of Chicago Polonia, but this is one I turn down without hesitation. No black-tie functions for me. But I nonetheless pour over Maria's scrapbook, perusing photos of her looking beautiful in long ball gowns and dancing with Bruno. Is this more what her life would have been like without Hitler? More balls and less library stacks? The photos certainly do point up the two very different lives Maria has lived in Chicago.

Maria's activities in Polonia have often intersected with events in Poland. In 1978 she attended the installation of Karol Wojtyła as pope, going as a representative of the Legion of Young Polish Women but mostly to see her sister again. "I called the Ursulines in Canada and found out that my sister would be there." So she decided to go on Wednesday, worked on Thursday, and then stayed up all night cooking to leave food for Bruno and the boys while she was away, rushing to catch the charter flight the next day. "I called Nina when I got to Rome and we went to a Polish Mass together, at which Cardinal Wyszyński was preaching. [Cardinal Wyszyński was at this time the symbol of resistance to the Communist Party in Poland]. We had great tickets for the installation, very close. The Italians were *so* mad because the pope was not Italian! I stayed and visited Rome with my sister and four other women from the Legion of Young Polish Women for the week after the installation. We went to basilicas during the day and shopping in the evening."

"One night I was shopping for shoes near the Trevi Fountain when suddenly shooting started. They pushed us upstairs in the store while the shooting was going on and people were rushing around. They told us to get away from the window. It was just like the wartime." Violent or not, it had been a long time since Maria and her sister had been able to travel together in Europe, apart from Maria's one visit to Poland in 1965.

When martial law was declared in Poland at the end of 1981, Poles in Chicago turned out in great numbers to support Solidarity. "There was a big march from Wacker Drive to the consulate, over 100,000 people. Andrew was up at the head in his scouting uniform, and Mark was acting as a liaison with the police. Our whole family was there. It was very cold." Daily demonstrations took place in front of the Polish consulate on Lake Shore Drive, and the building showed marks of the red paint and eggs hurled at it. When the neighbors began to object, a place for Solidarity was set up in the park that runs along the shores of Lake Michigan instead.

Along with groups and activities of the post-World War II immigrants, Maria participates in the older Polish-American organizations as well. She regularly attends community events such as the Pulaski Day celebration at the Polish American Museum and the subsequent banquet. She marches in the Polish Constitution Day parade on May 3 each year. She has been a member of the Friends of Warsaw Club for more than 30 years and goes to their functions. "They meet once a month, mostly as a social group, for tea. They also collect money for an orphanage in Warsaw."

Maria is very knowledgeable about, though less involved in, the 19th-century fraternal organizations, and she lives a couple of blocks from the PNA's new home. "First there were the PNA, PRCU, and Polish Women's Alliance," she tells me, "from the late 19th century. All have insurance businesses. The PNA got large very fast. All of them have to give a certain percent to the Polish cause because they are so-called fraternal organizations, but they are businesses. Other organizations are just charities, like the Legion of Young Polish Women [no relation to the Polish Women's Alliance], which is non-profit. The combatant organizations are apolitical. The Polish American Congress was created in 1945 or so with the idea of being a political organization, so it could lobby for Polonia and for Polish affairs. But the PAC has no means of finance, so it is customary that the President of the PNA is President of the PAC and the PNA backs him financially. Other groups belong as groups to the PAC, with delegates according to the size of their own organization. I go to meetings once a month as a representative of the Polish Air Force Veterans Association Chicago Wing."

Maria has been president of the Polish Air Force Veterans in Chicago since 1990. "Bruno was president for one year too. We used to go to all their affairs in the 1950s—a ball, teas, some meetings. There would be large balls at the Palmer House; 500 to 600 people would come. We had international reunions every two years in the U.S. and Canada as late as the 1990s, and there were several in Poland as well. Now everyone is getting old, so we are just keeping up the tradition. It's a social connection, but also to teach people about the Polish Air Force. There are 56 members right now, but only 22 or 25 active ones. We have an Easter party; we march in the May 3d parade."

On May 3, 2003, I attended the Constitution Day festivities with Maria. The event commemorates the Polish Constitution of 1791, the first, though short-lived, written constitution in Europe, and the second in the world (after the American Constitution). After days of cold and rain, May 3 was sunny, showing off the earth's recovery from the rigidity of winter. I was to meet Maria at the Congress Hotel at 9:30 a.m. Although Maria is always so well dressed, she was wearing her Polish Air Force uniform for the parade. When I arrived at the assigned spot, there she was—a tiny golden-haired woman in a dark blue suit with medals and decorations all over it and a navy blue air force tie.

We went into the hall where people were meeting and greeting before the brunch. Maria knew everyone. She quickly worked her connections to obtain a ticket to the reviewing stand for me during the parade. Many older people were there with their offspring dressed in Polish national dress, floral garlands in their hair. "The new immigrants don't come," says Maria. "They are economic refugees, many of them not patriotic."

The brunch itself was held in a large ballroom with mahogany walls and a vaulted ceiling. All the politicians were there or, if they could not be, had sent messages. The Consul General of Poland spoke. "We didn't invite him during the

Communists," Maria whispers. At the pre-parade brunch, I was given a program of events for the weekend; it began with an exhortation to "Display the Polish and American Flags! Show you are proud to be a Polish American!" Numerous events were announced in it, including a special celebration at the PNA after the parade, with entertainment for the children. A gala Constitution Day banquet was to be held in the evening, at the White Eagle, the restaurant and banquet hall on the northwest side where many Polish functions are held. The next day, Sunday, there was a wreath-laying at the Kosciuszko monument in the park, followed by Mass at a traditional Polish church, then a charity game between various Polish soccer clubs, and a concert at the Copernicus Foundation in the evening. Maria planned to attend most of these events.

Soon it was time for Maria to report to the location where she would muster with the other members of the Polish Air Force Veterans Association and for me to locate the reviewing stand. The parade began, flowing down Columbus Drive, which cuts through Grant Park in the center of the city. People lined both sides of the street, American flags in one hand and Polish flags in the other. There were bands and Polish music—brass, drums, cymbals—and traditional dance troupes. Polish schools from the suburbs came by, one after another, with the children all dressed up in traditional costumes. The Polish Youth Association and the scouts. The Polish American Police Association came by, and the Polish American Medical Association. Polish American engineers and lawyers followed later. Politicians marched, and Polish businesses mounted floats—a Polish travel agency, a Polish radio station. CBS, NBC, ABC came by on floats, with their announcers waving Polish flags. A Latino alderman who represents many Polish—Americans stumbled through a few sentences in Polish; the crowd looked skeptical but then cheered him for the effort. Men on horses came by looking like hussars, with banners and swords. The Polish Highlander Alliance with their flat hats. Band members wearing hats with feathers and playing Polish songs. I spotted Maria's son Mark in the crowd, and he introduced me to the commercial attaché from the Polish consulate, a charming man who bowed and doffed his hat in an Old World greeting.

The groups of veterans were interspersed with the other participants in the parade. Some of the first included survivors of Siberia. At long last, the group my eyes had been searching for came by—the Chicago Wing of the Polish Air Force Association, a small group of very old men, walking slowly, with little Maria in their midst. She looked both happy and proud.

I left soon after. As I walked to the subway, I was surrounded by Polish flags. I could hear no English spoken as I descended the stairs to the train. This was an aspect of Chicago I had never seen before.

"Why are you involved in all these things?" I asked Maria one day. "It's the tradition in me," she replied. "I am a primary American citizen, but I do not forget my roots. Because I was so involved in Poland in patriotic affairs, I keep up with this automatically. I am in a city with such a big impact by ethnic groups, and I want to show that we are such a group and not forgotten. If I had been in a small city in the south, probably I wouldn't have been so involved." So both Poland and Polonia have co-operated in maintaining Maria's continuing connection with her homeland since she left it at the age of 21, over 60 years ago.

Maria and the Chicago Wing of the Polish Air Force Veteran's Association before the annual Polish Constitution Day parade, Chicago

United States delegation to the 50th anniversary of the Warsaw Uprising with Vice President Al Gore, Warsaw

Maria at her eightieth birthday celebration with her family.
Sons Mark (left), Andrew (right).

Maria and her friend, Bogus

CHAPTER 18

Chicago, 2005

Chicago Tribune, April 24, 2002: "Mapping out ethnic, racial change"

> . . . *Chicago's Polish-American community, like old European immigrant communities in other U.S. cities, has been losing its cohesion during the very same decades that its members have begun to assimilate and scatter into America's cultural mainstream.*
>
> *In that sense, its new political problems are a sign of its continuing economic and social successes.*
>
> *For decades, Chicagoans boasted more Poles than any other city outside Warsaw. But in recent years, as younger members of the community have scattered deeper into the suburbs, it has become increasingly difficult for the city's Polish-American voters to pull a strong enough bloc together to elect their own anointed candidate.*
>
> *Community leaders watched in dismay while three candidates of Polish descent lost major races in March . . . .*

Chicago Tribune, September 14, 2003: "Polish-American pride reawakens"

> . . . *with about 1 million Poles, Chicago and Illinois register the biggest Polish community outside of their home country—exceeded only by Warsaw's 2.1 million.*
>
> *There are no precise numbers for the Polish in America. The Polish American Congress estimates that at least 30 percent of Poles living in [the] Chicago area are here illegally, some of them having lived here for decades. Also, within the "second generation" immigrants who came over after World War II, less than 50 percent speak English.*

*　　*　　*

> *Poles have become one of the three economically strongest ethnic groups in the U.S., according to a survey by the University of California.*
>
> *Cook County Treasurer Maria Pappas confirms that Polish-Americans have average assets of $100,000.*

ChicagoTribune, February 22, 2004: "Their hearts on their sleeves"

> *There are about 1,000 Polish Boy, Girl, Cub and Brownie Scouts in the Midwest....*

*   *   *

> *Almost all of the activities are in Polish, including all the commands that are given and any training issued....*

*   *   *

> *Polish scouting also has a place in history through its participation in the Warsaw Uprising against the Nazis in 1944. Boys helped destroy supply depots, trains and communication links and got supplies and equipment to resistance fighters. Girls aided the wounded in underground hospitals.*

Chicago Tribune, March 5, 2004: "Milwaukee Avenue"

> *It's 9:30 a.m. Saturday at Kurowski's Sausage Shop on Milwaukee Avenue, and the place is jammed.*

*   *   *

> *Like so many businesses in the Avondale neighborhood's "Polish Village" along Milwaukee Avenue, Kurowski's serves the dual purpose of delivering a taste of home to Eastern European immigrants while serving up a delicious glimpse of another culture to visitors....*

*   *   *

> *Avondale isn't the biggest Polish business district in the city either (that would be around Belmont and Central Avenues, according to the Polish American Chamber of Commerce). But it does represent the geographical middle of the journey up Milwaukee Avenue that the Polish community has taken. Starting at about 2900 North and ending around 3500 North,*

this strip presents a reflection of what is important to those in the Polish immigrant community.

Chicago Tribune, March 26, 2004: "Polish-school founder eased way for immigrants"

A native of Poland, Maria Zamora [who died March 22 at age 99] always found a way to create a little bit of her homeland wherever she lived.
   In Hungary, where she fled from the Germans during World War II, in a Nazi work camp in Germany and in Chicago after the war, Mrs. Zamora established schools to teach Polish language, culture and history.

*   *   *

In 1951 she established the Ted Kosciuszko Polish School and was its director, principal and teacher. She had six pupils.
   The school now has about 1,200 pupils and teaches Polish language, history, geography, culture, Spanish, French, art and music. The school operates on Friday and Saturday in three locations in the city.

Chicago Tribune, August 1, 2004: The heroes of Warsaw at last get their due"

This week, [the Warsaw Uprising] will be remembered with modest ceremonies in the rebuilt Polish capital. A new museum will be dedicated and . . . the U.S. will be represented by a high-level delegation headed by Secretary of State Colin Powell that includes Chicago Mayor Richard Daley and former congressman from Illinois and Secretary of Veterans Affairs Edward Derwinski. The recognition is a belated acknowledgement that Poland, too, has its "Greatest Generation."

*   *   *

The catastrophe that befell Warsaw in those weeks in hard to overstate. In terms of death and destruction, it was the equivalent of a Sept. 11 attack every day for 63 days in a row.

*   *   *

Stalin quickly set up his puppet regime and began rewriting history. Surviving members of the AK were labeled "Hitlerite fascist collaborators." They were hunted down and jailed by the thousands. Many were executed or shipped off to the gulag.

160

*   *   *

It was, however, a fearless Polish pope, returning to his homeland in June 1979 for the first time since ascending to the throne of St. Peter, who drew a direct line between the AK resistance and what was soon to become the Solidarity Movement, an unarmed army that would finally liberate Poland from the Soviet bloc.

But even after the collapse of communism in 1989, recognition has come slowly for the aging survivors of the AK. A large, somewhat garish monument was unveiled in 1989, and AK veterans now get a government pension—about $50 a month.

Chicago Tribune, August 2, 2004: "German chancellor bows at memorial to the '44 Warsaw Rising"

German Chancellor Gerhard Schroeder bowed on the steps of a memorial to the Warsaw Rising against the Nazi occupation, acknowledging Sunday the "immeasurable suffering" inflicted by Germans when they crushed the revolt 60 years ago.

*   *   *

Schroeder bowed on the steps of the Warsaw Rising Memorial as a lone trumpeter played taps. Just before, sirens sounded across Warsaw at 5 p.m., the hour the uprising began on Aug. 1, 1944.

*   *   *

Remembrance of the 63-day battle against Nazi troops by Poland's poorly armed and outmanned Home Army resistance movement and civilians— even children—has provoked an outpouring of patriotism in Poland.

Chicago Tribune, October 22, 2004: "2nd wave of Poles calls suburbs home"

Polish bakeries and delis have popped up on every block along a strip of Milwaukee Avenue in Niles. Polish-language schools catering to the children of second-generation Poles have begun Saturday afternoon sessions in Wauconda and other suburbs. And Bobak Sausage Co., a longtime fixture in Chicago's Polish enclaves, recently opened a store in Naperville.

All are signs of a Polish community that has been moving out of Chicago and into the suburbs in the last decade, according to a report being released Friday. Immigration has prompted a resurgence in the Chicago area's Polish population. The number of Polish immigrants in the region has reached nearly 138,000, a level that approaches the historic high of 165,000 in 1930.

*　　*　　*

Census data showed Polish immigrants as the second-largest immigrant group in the region behind Mexican immigrants, whose numbers reached 582,000 in 2000. In 2000, nearly half of the region's Polish immigrants had been in the United States less than a decade . . . .

"No other immigrant group came in such large numbers 100 years ago and continues to come in such large numbers today," said Rob Paral, research fellow at the American Immigration Law Foundation and co-author of the study.

I'm reading the newspaper differently now. I devour all the stories about the Polish community in Chicago—I've never noticed before how many there are. The ones set forth above are a sampling of those that appeared just during the time I've been working on this book. They chronicle the many things I've discovered in the last few years—the continuing attachment of Poles in Chicago to their homeland and its traditions, the very active life of the Polish-American community here, and the long-overdue recognition of the 1944 Uprising in Warsaw. Maria, of course, follows all this news in Polish, in Chicago's daily Polish press. "I get the Polish daily because I have to read the obituaries to see if one of my members is gone," she says.

As we've worked together, both Maria and I have aged. At one point we scheduled interviews around physical therapy appointments for both of us. Maria's walking has become more difficult, but she is still beautiful. I attended her 80th birthday party in July of 2003, a surprise party organized by her sons and held in an elegant tea shop in a suburb. I was one of three from Northwestern seated at the only English-speaking table in the room. A hush settled on the room as Maria approached, lured by the ruse of a dinner at a fancy restaurant with her sons. She was dressed in a beautiful long white dress with brightly-colored flowers on it and looked astonished when she saw us all there, enthusiastically singing Sto Lat! ("100 years!") to wish her long life.

Maria's schedule has not slowed down over this period. It often makes me tired to hear what she has done since the last time we met. She remains very active in her Polish-American organizations—the Air Force Veterans and the Legion of Young Polish Women in particular. She constantly attends events related to Poland, Polish culture, or Polish-American causes. I've started to do the same.

Without Maria in my life, I would have missed the spectacular exhibit of Polish art at the Milwaukee Art Museum in 2002.

In a sense Maria still lives in an almost entirely Polish environment, especially since she retired in 2003, after 45 years. When I inquired how many non-Polish people she had seen in the previous week except for me, she replied "Almost none. I'm just with my group, a bit ghettoized, I guess. But I've had no opportunity to meet nice American people of my generation. I was in an in-between category— not a professional, but that's what I came from." I asked how much of the time she speaks Polish since leaving Northwestern. "About 90% of the time," she replied. Interestingly, some of the time she speaks English is at meetings of groups such as the Legion of Young Polish Women, where most of the members are now second-generation Poles and English is their mother tongue. And at family gatherings, English is spoken because her granddaughter Ania does not speak Polish—yet. She is studying Polish at Saturday school. "But my group from the AK and Air Force mostly speak Polish together," Maria says. "I'm friendly with some people from the previous immigration, who were born here, but I entertain them separately because they usually speak English and some of my group have trouble speaking English."

Maria is very close to her children, both of whom live in the suburbs. Mark married a Polish-American woman—a daughter of someone from the AK. Andrew married a Pole who was working in Chicago. They were married in a civil ceremony in December 2000 to enable her to remain in the country, but waited to have an elaborate church wedding until Nina and the bride's mother could be there. It took place in the summer of 2002, and Ben and I were lucky enough to be invited. The wedding itself was in Maria's church, Queen of All Saints, the impressive-looking basilica on Devon Avenue. Part of the ceremony was conducted in English, and part in Polish. The bride in her elaborate dress made her way slowly around to the Marian altar behind the main altar after the marriage was complete, to lay flowers in thanksgiving at the feet of the statue of Mary.

The reception was held that evening in a banquet hall, which was jammed with guests. Dinner was served at tables of about 10 persons each. Ben and I were considerately seated with Polish-Americans whose English was good, one of them the director of the Polish-American museum we had recently visited. Maria, radiant in a long gown with a beaded top and skirt of chiffon, made her way from table to table, greeting the guests. Her appearance was a marked contrast from that of Nina, in her plain nun's gray. During dinner there were boisterous toasts and loud singing of traditional songs of congratulation in Polish, including the perennial Sto Lat! We had to leave before the evening was over, but the dance floor was full as we departed.

Maria herself remains a loyal member of the Catholic church, attending Queen of All Saints Basilica every Sunday. It is not a Polish parish. "They used to call it 'Queen of all Cadillacs,'" she tells me. Although the PNA headquarters is located three blocks away, Maria's neighborhood is not a Polish one. Because it is one of the most suburban areas that is part of the city, many police and firemen live there, to fulfill the requirement that they be residents of the city they serve. Many people of Irish and Italian descent live there. But several of the Polish women of Maria's generation—those she calls her "girlfriends"—live nearby, and they get together every weekend.

Maria's political views separate her from some of her friends in the Polish community. She remains a staunch Democrat, while some of her girlfriends are Republicans. And when the head of the PNA made statements that were perceived as anti-Semitic, Maria's judgment was simple: "He's an idiot. But I have to be careful about taking political stands because of my work in organizations that are apolitical."

Maria has continued to travel frequently. Each year she goes to Poland, and usually plans an interesting itinerary for her stay there. While we've been working together, she has traveled with her sister and friends to the Tatra Mountains in the south, to the lake district and Lithuania in the north, and once to a spa in Slovakia for three weeks. She sends me postcards depicting the places she visits, and I post them in my kitchen. Inspired by her, Ben and I plan to visit the Tatras and do some hiking. Like her father before her, Maria values vacations—in the mountains, at the sea, and at places of cultural interest throughout Europe and in the Americas.

In Chicago Maria has served in the past as a kind of travel agent for her girlfriends, organizing trips for them to warm places in the winter. But in 2003 she got frustrated with this role. After organizing a trip for them all to Punta Cana, in the Dominican Republic, her friends said they didn't want to go because they were afraid of SARS. So Maria met her sister in Rome instead and attended the canonization of the founder of Nina's order of Ursuline sisters. After six days in Rome, she traveled south with a group, to visit Assisi, Monte Cassino, and Pompeii, all for the second time.

Whenever she returns from a trip, Maria shows me photographs. The excursions often appear a bit daunting for someone of her age; Pompeii can be challenging for anyone. After her trip to Italy, Maria told me "Our tour guide would never use the word 'old'; instead he would say, for example, 'those who were born earlier may wait for us here.' So now the way to refer to old people is to say 'those who were born earlier'!" This struck us both as hilarious, sitting in her kitchen eating sausage and cheese, vegetables and fruit. As we dissolved into laughter, I noticed what blue eyes she has, and how they twinkle. As I took my leave, I referred to us as "those who were born earlier." "Not you," she says. "Yet," I retort.

Maria has recently retired as travel agent for her friends. In 2003, her life took a wonderful new turn: she has a boyfriend. Bogusław, called Boguś (pronounced

"Bo-goosh"), is an 88-year-old ex-Polish Air Force pilot. Indeed, he was a celebrated pilot, shot down during the war over the Netherlands. Previously a resident of Chicago, he and his then-wife were friends of Maria and Bruno when they first arrived. He now lives alone in a condominium on the east coast of Florida. Maria and a friend went to visit him for two weeks during the winter of 2003, and since then he has been smitten. Maria is very fond of him. They have great fun together, swimming every day and going to dances and events of the Polish community in Miami. During her first stay there, Maria had to call Sophie and have her send several ballgowns down to her.

But Maria is also determined to keep both her independence and her connection with Chicago, where her children and her Polish-American organizations are. So she now goes back and forth—six weeks in Florida, back to Chicago for a month or two, and then to Florida again. She and Boguś were together during the 60th anniversary commemoration of the Uprising in Warsaw last summer and plan to travel together again.

In July of 2004, Boguś visited Maria in Chicago for two weeks; and they invited Ben and me for dinner. It was a delight to meet him and to see them together. Boguś is charming, and the twinkle in his eye matches that in Maria's own. He is also a wonderful raconteur, telling us stories of his career as a pilot.

In 2004, at long last, the world began to take note of the valor of the AK combatants. During the 60th Anniversary celebrations in Warsaw, a new museum of the Uprising was opened. CNN made a documentary about the Uprising, which was shown amongst the D-Day specials on June 6, 2004; and a gala premiere was held at the Chicago Public Library Cultural Center. Ben and I attended and sat among the now-elderly AK members with their red-and-white armbands. Throughout October, Maria was in great demand as a speaker to accompany the film to schools and regional centers on behalf of the Warsaw Uprising Project of the Chicago Sister Cities Program.

On September 16, 2004, the City of Chicago officially paid tribute to the survivors of the Uprising to whom it had given refuge. The event was held in the old Chicago central library, now the Cultural Center—an 1895 building in classical style—in a beautiful room with a tiled dome. Commemorative proclamations by both the Mayor and the House of Representatives were printed in the program.

The AK veterans, many in uniforms and all wearing red-and-white arm bands, marched into the room to the sounds of the Polish national anthem—"Poland has not perished so long as we still live!" As they reached their seats of honor and all stood at attention, the Star-Spangled Banner was played as well. Mayor Daley spoke, then the Polish Consul-General read a message from the Mayor of Warsaw. A history professor gave a talk about the Uprising; I noted that one elderly man in uniform fell asleep during it. He woke up and began to tap his cane, though, when the speech was followed by the Paderewski Symphony Choir singing songs of the Uprising. Some were march-like; others were operatic hymns, preceded by dream-like piano introductions. The sounds of the concert swelled to fill the dome of the large hall, which was filled with people.

Three old men were sitting in the front row, one of them the one with the cane whom I had been watching. When the music stopped, they were called to the stage. They turned out to be Americans, former airmen, veterans of the squadron that attempted to relieve Warsaw on September 18, 1944. One of them made his way to the podium with some difficulty, but his voice was strong. He recalled the weather that turned them back when they first tried to make it to Warsaw on September 15th, their eagerness to relieve the AK fighters in the city, and their sadness when the Uprising failed. In response, an AK veteran who had been on the ground that day in 1944 spoke words of thanks for the American pilots' help sixty years ago. A priest offered a prayer for those who had died. Everyone in the room then stood in tribute to the small group of now-aged combatants, cheering their fight for freedom.

Epilogue

It is now the summer of 2005, more than three years after Maria and I first began to talk about her life. We are both rather sad that the project is coming to an end; we'll miss our meetings. But we are good friends now and speak often. She is often sad. So many of her old friends are dying. Krystyna, her girlhood friend, died earlier this year in Australia. A favorite cousin in Warsaw just died. Another good friend from London and Chicago suddenly is no more. Maria is constantly going to funerals for members of her Air Force Wing.

But together we have preserved Maria's past. What was only in her heart is now on paper. The experiences, the stories she has told herself for years and now to me, have constructed a life. I don't know how to end it. So Maria sends me an e-mail that goes like this:

> Cynthia,
>
> I got an idea for the epilog. If you like it, you can work with it. It goes like this: Maria is playing with Ania, her granddaughter. The phone rings. Ninka is on the line. She is calling from Warsaw. "My friends won an American Visa that entitles them to settle in the U.S. They plan to leave pretty soon. They are selling almost everything. They have a nice apartment in a new, modern building, in the centre of Warsaw, a very good location. You may like it. Once you said that you would like to buy an apartment and move to Warsaw. You have a good opportunity now, but you have to act right away." Maria thinks for a moment and answers. "I changed my mind. I have my family here. I have been living in Chicago for 53 years. I don't even have a Polish passport. I love to visit you for a month or two, but I cannot move over there for good. Chicago and Warsaw officially, legally, are "sister cities." I love both of them, but my place is here.
>
> What do you think about this idea?
>
> Maria

"Did that really happen?," I write back. "Well, almost," she replies. "I did think about moving back, but Nina said, 'You don't transplant old trees.' I think she was right."

REFERENCES

Chapter 1: Origins

My description of the history of Poland between the wars is drawn from the following sources: Norman Davies, God's Playground: A History of Poland, Vol. II: 1795 to the Present, pp. 369-434 (New York: Columbia University Press, 1982); Jerzy Lukowski and Hubert Zawadzki, A Concise History of Poland, pp. 172-224 (Cambridge: Cambridge University Press 2001); Adam Zamoyski, The Polish Way: A Thousand-year History of the Poles and their Culture, pp. 324-55 (New York: Hippocrene Books, 1987).

Figures from the 1921 Census are from Davies 1982: 410. For description and effects of proportional representation, see Maurice Duverger, Political Parties: Their Organization and Activity in the Modern State 245-55, ed., trans. Barbara and Robert North (2d Eng. ed., John Wiley & Sons, 1963). Statistics about the Jews in interwar Poland are from Zamoyski 1987:344-46. The description of Sanacja as "a secular authoritation government of a non-fascist type" is from Lukowski and Zawadzki 2001:216. The excerpt from the 1932 poem "Dawns" by Czeslaw Milosz is taken from Czeslaw Milosz, New and Collected Poems (1931-2001), trans. Czeslaw Milosz and Robert Hass, p. 16 (New York: Harper Collins, 2001).

Chapter 3: The Coming of the War

My description of the beginning of World War II in Poland is taken from Norman Davies, God's Playground: A History of Poland, Vol. II: 1795 to the Present, pp. 435-53 (New York: Columbia University Press, 1982); Jerzy Lukowski and Hubert Zawadzki, A Concise History of Poland, pp. 224-32 (Cambridge: Cambridge University Press 2001); Adam Zamoyski, The Polish Way: A Thousand-year History of the Poles and their Culture, pp. 356-62 (New York: Hippocrene Books, 1987). This chapter also relies heavily on a document called "Personal Reminiscences of World War II," set down by Maria herself and edited by her son Andrew in 1989, on the 50th anniversary of the invasion of Poland. Most quotations in this chapter are from that document.

169

Statistics about the numbers of tanks, airplanes and troops of the Poles and Germans are drawn from Zamoyski 1987: 356.

Chapter 4: Warsaw under Nazi Occupation

The description of the Nazi occupation of Poland and the organization of the underground state is derived from the following books: Norman Davies, Rising '44: The Battle for Warsaw, pp. 169-204 (New York: Viking 2003); Richard C. Lukas, The Forgotten Holocaust: The Poles under German Occupation: 1939-1944, pp. 1-181 (New York: Hippocrene Books rev'd ed. 2001); Stefan Korbonski, The Polish Underground State 1939-1945, pp. 1-139, trans. Marta Erdman (Boulder, CO: East European Quarterly 1978); Norman Davies, God's Playground: A History of Poland, Vol. II: 1795 to the Present, pp. 453-72 (New York: Columbia University Press, 1982); Jerzy Lukowski and Hubert Zawadzki, A Concise History of Poland, pp. 234-36 (Cambridge: Cambridge University Press 2001); Adam Zamoyski, The Polish Way: A Thousand-year History of the Poles and their Culture, pp. 356-62 (New York: Hippocrene Books, 1987).

The number of Polish intellectuals sent to camps or executed in 1940 is taken from Davies 1982: 447. Quotation about life in Warsaw for the Poles is by Maria Trzcinska, quoted and translated in Davies 2003: 94. Statistics about size of the underground in Poland are from Zamoyski 1987: 360. For assessment of AK as the primary resistance group, see Davies 1982: 464-66; Zamoyski 1987: 361; Davies 2003: 182. Reduction of the population of Poland between 1939 and 1945 is taken from Lukas 2001: 38-39. "There was no Polish Quisling": Davies1982: 464. Vidkun Quisling was a Norwegian fascist leader who helped the Germans conquer Norway in 1940 and served as premier from 1942 to the war's end, when he was arrested, convicted of treason, and shot. The word "quisling" has become a synonym for traitor.

Chapter 5: The Home Army

About the Katyn Forest massacre, see Davies 1982: 452. On the assassination of General Franz Kutschera and subsequent reprisals, see Davies 2003: 197-98.

Chapter 7: The Uprising

The history of the Uprising is drawn from a variety of sources, including both scholarly histories and accounts of participants. Historical accounts used include: Norman Davies, Rising '44: The Battle for Warsaw, pp. 243-428 (New York: Viking 2003); Norman Davies, God's Playground: A History of Poland, Vol. II: 1795 to the Present, pp. 472-88 (New York: Columbia University Press,

1982); Jerzy Lukowski and Hubert Zawadzki, A Concise History of Poland, pp. 239-49 (Cambridge: Cambridge University Press 2001); Adam Zamoyski, The Polish Way: A Thousand-year History of the Poles and their Culture, pp. 364-69 (New York: Hippocrene Books, 1987); Richard C. Lukas, The Forgotten Holocaust: The Poles under German Occupation 1939-1944, pp. 182-217 (NY: Hippocrene Books, rev'd ed. 1997) (orig. pub. 1986); George Bruce, The Warsaw Uprising 1 August—2 October 1944 (London: Rupert Hart-Davis, 1972).

Participant accounts consulted include: Wacław Zagorski, Seventy Days: A Diary of the Warsaw Insurrection 1944, trans. John Welsh, with introduction by Gen. Bor-Komorowsky (London: Frederick Muller Ltd, 1957); J.K. Zawodny, Nothing But Honour: The Story of the Warsaw Uprising, 1944 (Stanford, CA: Hoover Institution Press: 1978); Leokadia Rowinski, That the Nightingale Return: Memoir of the Polish Resistance, the Warsaw Uprising and German P.O.W. Camps (Jefferson, N.C.: McFarland & Co., 1999); Irena Orska, Silent is the Vistula: The Story of the Warsaw Uprising, trans. Marta Erdman (New York: Longmans, Green and Co. 1946); Miron Białoszewski, A Memoir of the Warsaw Uprising, ed., trans. Madeline Levine (Evanston, IL: Northwestern University Press, 1977); Stefan Korbonski, Fighting Warsaw: The Story of the Polish Underground State 1939-1945, trans. F.B. Czarnomski (London: Allen & Unwin, 1956); Stefan Korbonski, The Polish Underground State: A Guide to the Underground, 1939-1945, trans. Marta Erdman (Boulder, CO: East European Quarterly, 1978); Jerzy Lando, Saved By My Face: A True Story of Courage and Escape in War-Torn Poland (Edinburgh and London: Mainstream Publishing 2002).

Figures on the losses of civilians in Wola and Ochota in early August are taken from Davies 1982: 470 and Davies 2003: 279. The numbers of soldiers and civilians evacuated from Old Town on August 31-September 1 are from Lukas 1997: 211. Description of action at 5 p.m. on August 1 is quoted from Davies 2003: 245. "After the first week . . ." is from Davies 2003: 254, 256. Description of religious observance during the Uprising is taken from Davies 2003: 402. Quotation about the evacuation of Old Town is from Davies 2003: 354.

Chapter 8: The Surrender

The same general sources cited for Chapter 7 were used for the history of the surrender of Warsaw. The numbers of AK soldiers who surrendered is from Davies 2003: 435. The total number of Warsaw residents killed during the Uprising is from Lukas 1997: 219. The Homeland Council's final appeal is from Winston S. Churchill, Vol. 6 of The Second World War: Triumph and Tragedy, pp.144-45 (Boston: Houghton Mifflin Co. 1953). "The streets had become no-go areas" is from Jerzy Lando, Saved By My Face: A True Story of Courage and Escape in

War-Torn Poland, pp. 201-02 (Edinburgh and London: Mainstream Publishing 2002), also quoted in Davies 2003: 339. "Few historians have cared to describe . . ." is from Davies 2003: 384. The description of the September 18 Allied air drop is from Davies 2003: 377. The losses in the battle for the Cherniakov Bridgehead are taken from Davies 2003: 396. "The desperate scenes on the Vistula beaches on 23 September" is from id., p. 397. The October 29, 1944 speech is quoted in Davies 2003: 423. The description of the surrender of the insurgents to the Germans is taken from Stefan Korbonski, Fighting Warsaw: The Story of the Polish Underground State 1939-1945, trans. F.B. Czarnomski, pp. 399-400 (London: Allen & Unwin, 1956).

Chapter 9: Prisoner of War

The description of Oberlangen is taken from Leokadia Rowinski, That the Nightingale Return: Memoir of the Polish Resistance, the Warsaw Uprising and German P.O.W. Camps, p. 121 (Jefferson, N.C.: McFarland & Co., 1999). The description of the ceremony upon liberation of the camp is from the same book, pp. 133-34.

Chapter 10: Warsaw, Summer 2002

An excerpt from German President Herzog's speech in which he both paid tribute to the Polish fighters in the Warsaw Uprising and begged forgiveness is set forth in Davies 2003: 609.

Chapter 11: The Air Force

Information about the establishment of the People's Republic in Poland is derived from Davies 2003: 509-77; Davies 1982: 556-86; Lukowski and Zawadzki 2001: 250-60. Specifics about treatment of the AK by the Communists can be found in Davies 2003: 464-68, 486-99; Zamoyski 1987: 369-71.

Chapter 12: Resettlement

The history of the Polish and their resettlement in England is drawn from Keith Sword, with Norman Davies and Jan Ciechanowski, The Formation of the Polish Community in Great Britain 1939-1950, pp. 200-457 (London: School of Slavonic and East European Studies, University of London 1989).

Results of Gallup poll in June 1946 are in Sword, Davies and Ciechanowski, p. 349. Number of AK veterans ineligible for the Polish Resettlement Corps is at id., p. 333. Information about the bill enacted to allow 20,000 Poles into the

U.S. is at id., p. 311. Quotation about being "saddled" with "burden" of Poles is at id., p. 305.

Chapter 13: Bruno

For history about the Anders Army, see Davies 2003: 42-46; Zamoyski 1987: 361-63; Lukowski and Zawadzki 2001: 237-39. Two very good books about the Polish Air Force in World War II are available in English: Adam Zamoyski, The Forgotten Few: The Polish Air Force in the Second World War (New York: Hippocrene Books 1995); Lynne Olson and Stanley Cloud, A Question of Honor: The Kosciuszko Squadron: Forgotten Heroes of World War II (New York: Knopf 2003).

Chapter 14: England, July 2003

Sources consulted about the R.A.F. stations include: John F. Hamlin, The History of Royal Air Force Bentley Priory and Stanmore Park (London: Borough of Harrow 1997). Websites helpful in locating old RAF stations are available at: http://www.raf.mod.uk/bombercommand/stations/. Quotation about the Brompton Oratory taken from Michael Napier, The London Oratory (available for purchase at the church).

Chapter 15: Chicago, 1952 and 2004

Sources from which the history of Polish Americans in Chicago is drawn include: Edward R. Kantowicz, Polish-American Politics in Chicago 1888-1940 (Chicago: University of Chicago Press 1975); Dominic A. Pacyga, Polish Immigrants and Industrial Chicago: Workers on the South Side, 1880-1922 (Columbus: Ohio State University Press 1991); Melvin G. Holli and Peter d'A. Jones, eds., The Ethnic Frontier: Essays in the History of Group Survival in Chicago and the Midwest (Grand Rapids, MI: William B. Eerdmans Publishing Company, 1977); Melvin G. Holli and Peter d'A. Jones, eds, Ethnic Chicago: A Multicultural Portrait (Grand Rapids, MI: William B. Eerdmans Publishing Company 4th ed. 1995) (orig. pub. 1977); John J. Bukowczyk, And My Children Did Not Know Me: A History of the Polish-Americans (Bloomington and Indianapolis: Indiana University Press 1987); Djro J. Vrga, Adjustment vs. Assimilation: Immigrant Minority Groups and Intra-Ethnic Conflicts, in Ethnic Groups in the City: Culture, Institutions, and Power, ed. Otto Feinstein (Lexington, MA: D.C. Heath & Co. 1971), pp. 39-56; Joseph A. Wytrwal, The Changing Role of the Polish-American Congress, in id., pp. 165-72; Stanislaus A. Blejwas, Old and New Polonias: Tensions within an Ethnic Community, 38

Polish-American Studies 55-83 (Autumn 1981); Victor Greene, Poles, in Harvard Encyclopedia of American Ethnic Groups 787-803 (1980); Danuta Mostwin, Post-World War II Polish Immigrants in the United States, 26 Polish American Studies 5-14 (Autumn 1969).

The number of Polish immigrants to the U.S. between 1945 and 1953 is derived from Bukowczyk 1987: 93. The census figures for 1890 and 1920 are taken from Chicago Department of Development and Planning, The People of Chicago: Census Data on Foreign Born, Foreign Stock and Race: 1837-1970, pp. 21, 30 (1976). They include both Polish foreign-born and their children. Information about the postwar generation of immigrants, including statistics about their education and parish membership, is from Mostwin 1969: 8-9, 11. The discussion of tensions between the first and second waves of Polish immigrants draws upon Blejwas 1981; information about the veterans groups is on Blejwas 1981: 71. "Status inconsistency" among the postwar immigrants is discussed in Vrga 1971: 49-50; "in one situation . . ." appears on p. 50.

Chapter 16: Marriage, Work and Family

The history of the postwar Polish immigrants to Chicago is drawn from John J. Bukowczyk, And My Children Did Not Know Me: A History of the Polish-Americans (Bloomington and Indianapolis: Indiana University Press 1987); Dominic A. Pacyga, Polish America in Transition: Social Change and the Chicago Polonia, 1945-1980, 54 Polish-American Studies 38 (Spring 1987); Helena Znaniecka Lopata, Polish American Families, in Ethnic Families in America: Patterns and Variations, ed. Charles H. Mindel and Robert W. Habenstein (NY and Oxford: Elsevier 2d ed. 1981), pp. 17-42; Paul Wrobel, Becoming a Polish American: A Personal Point of View, in White Ethnics: Their Life in Working Class America, ed. Joseph Ryan (Englewood Cliffs, NJ: Prentice Hall 1973), pp. 52-58; Eugene Obindinski, Polish American Social Standing: Status and Stereotypes, 21 Polish Review 79-100 (1976); Konstantin Symmons-Symonolewicz, The Polish-American Community—Half a Century after "The Polish Peasant," 11 Polish Review 67-73 (Summer 1966).

Statistics about Polish voting patterns are taken from Bukowczyk 1987: 130-39. Information about the "Polish joke" is found in Obindinski 1976: 79-81; Pacyga 1987: 51. Statistics about Polish home ownership in 1970 are taken from Pacyga 1987: 45. A 1974 study showed that very few Polish-Americans were executives of banks, corporations, public utilities or other influential groups in the Chicago area. Obindinski 1976: 99. Discussion of Polish name-changing can be found at Symmons-Symonolewicz 1966: 69-70, n.10; Lopata 1981: 35-36; the statistics are from Lopata 1981: 36. Statistics about Polish exogamy and the percent speaking Polish at home in 1979 are from Bukowczyk 1987: 123. Information about the "new ethnicity" appears in Pacyga 1987: 50-51.

Chapter 17: Poland and Polonia

The history of the liberalization of Communist Poland, the growth of Solidarity, and post-Communist Poland is taken from Jerzy Lukowski and Hubert Zawadzki, A Concise History of Poland, pp. 260-89 (Cambridge: Cambridge University Press 2001); Adam Zamoyski, The Polish Way: A Thousand-year History of the Poles and their Culture, pp. 373-97 (New York: Hippocrene Books, 1987). The number of members in Solidarity is from Lukowski and Zawadzki 2001: 273. "Solidarity was not an ordinary trade union . . ." appears in id., p. 274. The number of arrests and emigrants resulting from the declaration of martial law in December 1981 is from id., pp. 276-77.

Information about recent events in Polonia is taken from Danuta Mostwin, Post-World War II Polish Immigrants in the United States, 26 Polish American Studies 5-14 (Autumn 1969); Edward R. Kantowicz, Polish Chicago: Survival Through Solidarity, in Melvin G. Holli and Peter d'A. Jones, eds, Ethnic Chicago: A Multicultural Portrait, pp. 196-98 (Grand Rapids, MI: William B. Eerdmans Publishing Company 4th ed. 1995) (orig. pub. 1977); John J. Bukowczyk, And My Children Did Not Know Me: A History of the Polish-Americans, pp. 85-146 (Bloomington and Indianapolis: Indiana University Press 1987).

Quotation from Vice President Gore's speech in 1994 is from Thomas R. Wolanin, With the American Delegation at the 50th Anniversary of the Warsaw Uprising, Polish Heritage, Winter 1994, p. 4.

BIBLIOGRAPHY

Białoszewski, Miron. *A Memoir of the Warsaw Uprising*. Ed. Madeline Levine. Trans. Madeline Levine. Evanston, IL: Northwestern University Press, 1977.

Blejwas, Stanislaus A. "Old and New Polonias: Tensions within an Ethnic Community." *Polish-American Studies* 38 (Autumn 1981): 55-83.

Bruce, George. *The Warsaw Uprising 1 August—2 October 1944*. London: Rupert Hart-Davis, 1972.

Bukowczyk, John J. *And My Children Did Not Know Me: A History of the Polish-Americans*. Indianapolis: Indiana University Press, 1987.

Chicago. Dept. of Development and Planning. *The People of Chicago: Census Data on Foreign Born, Foreign Stock and Race: 1837-1970*. Chicago: Dept. of Development and Planning, 1976.

Churchill, Winston S. *The Second World War: Triumph and Tragedy*. Vol. 6. Boston: Houghton Mifflin Co., 1953. 6 vols.

Davies, Norman. *God's Playground: A History of Poland, Vol. II: 1795 to the Present*. New York: Columbia University Press, 1982.

—————. *Rising '44: The Battle for Warsaw*. New York: Viking, 2003.

Duverger, Maurice. *Political Parties: Their Organization and Activity in the Modern State*. Trans. Barbara and Robert North. 2nd ed. New York: John Wiley & Sons, 1963.

Greene, Victor. "Poles." *Harvard Encyclopedia of American Ethnic Groups*. 1980.

Hamlin, John F. *The History of Royal Air Force Bentley Priory and Stanmore Park*. London: Borough of Harrow, 1997.

Holli, Melvin G. and Peter d'A. Jones, eds. *Ethnic Chicago: A Multicultural Portrait*. 4th ed. Grand Rapids, MI: William B. Eerdmans Publishing Company, 1995.

_____. *The Ethnic Frontier: Essays in the History of Group Survival in Chicago and the Midwest*. Grand Rapids, MI: William B. Eerdmans Publishing Company, 1977.

Kantowicz, Edward R. *Polish-American Politics in Chicago 1888-1940*. Chicago: University of Chicago Press, 1975.

_____. "Polish Chicago: Survival Through Solidarity." *Ethnic Chicago: A Multicultural Portrait*. Eds. Melvin G. Holli and Peter d'A. Jones. 4th ed. Grand Rapids, MI: William B. Eerdmans Publishing Company, 1995.

Korbonski, Stefan. *Fighting Warsaw: The Story of the Polish Underground State 1939-1945*. Trans. F.B. Czarnomski. London: Allen & Unwin, 1956.

_____. *The Polish Underground State: A Guide to the Underground, 1939-1945*. Trans. Marta Erdman. Boulder, CO: East European Quarterly, 1978.

Lando, Jerzy. *Saved By My Face: A True Story of Courage and Escape in War-Torn Poland*. London: Mainstream Publishing, 2002.

Lopata, Helena Znaniecka. "Polish American Families." *Ethnic Families in America: Patterns and Variations*. Eds. Charles H. Mindel and Robert W. Habenstein. 2nd ed. New York: Elsevier, 1981. 17-42.

Lukas, Richard C. *The Forgotten Holocaust: The Poles under German Occupation: 1939-1944*. New York: Hippocrene Books, 2001.

Lukowski, Jerzy and Hubert Zawadzki. *A Concise History of Poland*. Cambridge: Cambridge University Press, 2001.

Milosz, Czeslaw. *New and Collected Poems (1931-2001)*. Trans. Czeslaw Milosz and Robert Hass. New York: Harper Collins, 2001.

Mostwin, Danuta. "Post-World War II Polish Immigrants in the United States." *Polish American Studies* 26 (Autumn 1969): 5-14.

Obindinski, Eugene. "Polish American Social Standing: Status and Stereotypes." *Polish Review* 21 (1976): 79.

Olson, Lynne and Stanley Cloud. *A Question of Honor: The Kosciuszko Squadron: Forgotten Heroes of World War II.* New York: Knopf, 2003.

Orska, Irena. *Silent is the Vistula: The Story of the Warsaw Uprising.* Trans. Marta Erdman. New York: Longmans, Green and Co., 1946.

Pacyga, Dominic A. "Polish America in Transition: Social Change and the Chicago Polonia, 1945-1980." *Polish-American Studies* 54 (Spring 1987): 38.

_____. *Polish Immigrants and Industrial Chicago: Workers on the South Side, 1880-1922.* Columbus: Ohio State University Press, 1991.

Rowinski, Leokadia. *That the Nightingale Return: Memoir of the Polish Resistance, the Warsaw Uprising and German P.O.W. Camps.* Jefferson, N.C.: McFarland & Co., 1999.

Sword, Keith, with Norman Davies, and Jan Ciechanowski. *The Formation of the Polish Community in Great Britain 1939-1950.* London: School of Slavonic and East European Studies, University of London, 1989.

Symmons-Symonolewicz, Konstantin. "The Polish-American Community— Half a Century after *The Polish Peasant.*" *Polish Review* 11 (Summer 1966): 67-73.

Vrga, Djro J. "Adjustment vs. Assimilation: Immigrant Minority Groups and Intra-Ethnic Conflicts." *Ethnic Groups in the City: Culture, Institutions, and Power.* Ed. Otto Feinstein. Lexington, MA: D.C. Heath & Co., 1971. 39-56.

Wolanin. Thomas R. "With the American Delegation at the 50th Anniversary of the Warsaw Uprising." *Polish Heritage* (Winter 1994): 4.

Wrobel, Paul. "Becoming a Polish American: A Personal Point of View." *White Ethnics: Their Life in Working Class America.* Ed. Joseph Ryan. Englewood Cliffs, NJ: Prentice Hall, 1973. 52-58.

Wytrwal, Joseph A. "The Changing Role of the Polish-American Congress." *Ethnic Groups in the City: Culture, Institutions, and Power.* Ed. Otto Feinstein. Lexington, MA: D.C. Heath & Co., 1971. 165-72.

Zagorski, Waclaw. *Seventy Days: A Diary of the Warsaw Insurrection 1944.* Trans. John Welsh. London: Frederick Muller Ltd, 1957.

Zamoyski, Adam. *The Forgotten Few: The Polish Air Force in the Second World War.* New York: Hippocrene Books, 1995.

_____. *The Polish Way: A Thousand-year History of the Poles and their Culture.* New York: Hippocrene Books, 1987.

Zawodny, J.K. *Nothing But Honour: The Story of the Warsaw Uprising, 1944.* Stanford, CA: Hoover Institution Press, 1978.

Cynthia Grant Bowman is a professor of law at Cornell Law School in Ithaca, New York. She met the subject of this biography, Maria Chudzinski, while teaching at Northwestern University School of Law in Chicago, where Maria worked in the international section of the law library. Maria was born in Poland before the German invasion and the Second World War and joined the underground resistance, or Home Army, as a teenager. She fought during the 1944 Warsaw Uprising and was taken prisoner by the Germans when the city fell. In 1945 Maria moved to England, where she was a member of the Polish Air Force, ultimately settling in Chicago in 1952. She has been very active in the Polish-American community in Chicago since that time. Intrigued by Maria's past, Professor Bowman asked her to tell her story. This book is the result.

Made in the USA
Lexington, KY
18 May 2010